PHILIP MIRONOV
AND THE
RUSSIAN CIVIL WAR

PHILIP MIRONOV AND THE RUSSIAN CIVIL WAR

SERGEI STARIKOV
& ROY MEDVEDEV

TRANSLATED BY GUY DANIELS

Alfred A. Knopf, New York, 1978

Library of Congress Cataloging in Publication Data
Starikov, Sergei.
Philip Mironov and the Russian Civil War.
Includes bibliographical references and index.
1. Mironov, Filipp Kuz'mich, 1872–1921.
2. Revolutionists—Russia—Biography. 3. Russia
(1917– R.S.F.S.R.). Armiîa—Biography. 4. Soldiers
—Russia—Biography. I. Medvedev, Roĭ Aleksandrovich,
joint author. II. Title.
DK254.M56S7213 1978 947.084'1'0924 [B] 77–20353
ISBN 0–394–40681–8

Manufactured in the United States of America

First Edition

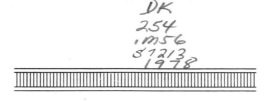

CONTENTS

v

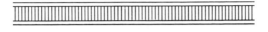

TRANSLATOR'S NOTE

Both in the authors' text and in the numerous documents quoted, this book contains a good many abbreviations and acronyms. Except on occasion, these have not been expanded. The reason for this is threefold. First, Russians themselves use copious abbreviations for the multitudinous Soviet agencies, etc., that mushroomed after the October Revolution and that were characteristic of the new bureaucratic mentality. (The bureaucrats of the Russian Empire had tended to employ tediously long and florid appellations for the somewhat less numerous agencies of that government.) Second, specialists in Sovietology are likely to be more disconcerted than grateful when one, say, expands "Sovnarkom" to read "Council of the People's Commissars." Finally, when a single sentence may contain as many as three or four acronyms or abbreviations, to expand all of them would be to make the sentence totally unreadable in English. For the benefit of the nonspecialist reader, a list of these terms with explanations has been provided at the end of the book.

No such clearly indicated solution was available for the second problem which arises with a text of this kind; viz., whether to keep certain key words in Russian or translate them. The former course is generally favored today: as Russian affairs become increasingly important in our lives, we absorb more Russian words into English; e.g., "sputnik" and "samizdat." (For that matter, I see no reason at all why we should go on translating *ulitsa* as "street" in Russian addresses—after all, the actual address is what one wants to know—while being so terribly scrupulous to preserve *rue* in French addresses.) Accordingly, I have added to this stock by leaving in Russian such words as *stanitsa* (see Glossary). True, it is translatable, if only in a clumsy fashion. Thus, one could refer to "the large Cossack village of Ust-Medveditsa, near the large Cossack village of Khoper." But this sort of thing ultimately becomes intolerable to the reader—and it is especially so to the *Cossack* reader, for whom the word *stanitsa* is sacred.

Another class of words which ideally should be left in Russian comprises the names of "administrative-territorial units." Consider, for instance, *raion*, for which Russian-English dictionaries give at least a half-dozen equivalents: region, district, area, sector, etc. But in Russian administrative usage it has a very precise meaning (see Glossary), which, properly, is only preserved by leaving it in Russian. This I have done, both for the above reason and for others too arcane to elucidate.

I should have liked to be consistent and do the same with certain other words of this class—e.g., *okrug* ("district"—again) and *oblast* ("region"—again). But here a compromise imposed itself, because such consistency would have resulted in such monstrous (to our ears) phrases as "the Ivanovskii Raion of the Ust-Medveditskii Okrug of the Donskaya Oblast." Even excising the adjectival endings doesn't help matters much. By way of compromise, then, I have elected to translate *okrug*, a high-frequency word in our text, as "district" (see Glossary), leaving all other Russian words usually so translated (e.g., *volost*) in the original, with an explanatory note in parentheses. For the same reasons, *oblast* has been rendered "region" (see Glossary). I am not especially enamored of this solution; but for a text crammed with place names, I could find no better one.

Finally, the matter of transliteration. There are several systems of Russian-English transliteration in common use, each one about as good as the next. For the most part, they differ only with respect to a few letters. I have dealt with those letters as follows. For Russian E: *ye* after vowels and soft signs; otherwise *e*. For й: *i*. For X: *kh*. For Ю: *yu*. And for Я: *ya*. Soft signs (transliterated ') and hard signs (transliterated ") have not been used in the actual text, only in bibliographic material (Notes section). Likewise, except for the names of raions (*raiony*), in the text I have used the traditional English "sky" ending for proper names, rather than "skii" or "skiy"—e.g., Stravinsky rather than Stravinskii or Stravinskiy.

*   *   *

The reader should note that this translation represents an abridgment of the original Russian text.

GUY DANIELS

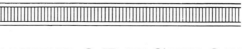

INTRODUCTION

Thousands of scholarly and fictional volumes, articles, sketches, and narratives have been devoted to the turbulence of the Great October Revolution of 1917 and the ensuing civil war which ravaged the territory of Russia between 1918 and 1920. It might seem that not a single page remains unwritten in the history of this pivotal era. But this is far from true. An increasing number of documents from archives, unpublished reminiscences, and the oral testimony of those still-living participants of the Revolution and the civil war are bringing to light previously ignored events and vivid life stories. One such story not yet accurately elucidated by either Soviet or foreign historians is the amazing and tragic fate of the Don Cossack, Philip Kuzmich Mironov. By studying his life it becomes possible to understand many of the complex social processes of revolutionary Russia.

Philip Mironov is a central figure in the civil war as a whole and in the civil war on the Don in particular. The acknowledged leader of the revolutionary working-class Cossacks and a talented

military commander, he led large units of the Red Army in 1918–
19. He reached the summit of his military career in 1920 as commanding general of the 2nd Cavalry Army, a unit that played an
especially important role in defeating General Wrangel's best
troops. Mironov was appointed Chief Inspector of Cavalry in the
Red Army early in 1921. But en route to Moscow to take up his
new duties, he was arrested by the Don Cheka on the basis of a
slanderous denunciation and transferred to Moscow's Butyrskaya
Prison. And there, on April 2, 1921, while exercising alone in the
prison yard, he was shot from behind. It was only after this murder,
many details of which remain unclear, that the VChK decreed
Mironov's death by shooting "for preparing a counter-revolutionary uprising on the Don."

From that time on, Mironov's name and deeds were doomed to
oblivion and defamation. His photograph in the Museum of the
Soviet (Red) Army was captioned: *Bandit and former commander
who betrayed the Soviet regime.* In many published accounts of
the civil war there is no mention of the actions of the military
units commanded by Mironov. As for Mironov himself, the
authors of these accounts either said nothing at all or wrote merely
of "rebellion" and "treason." In 1937–38, many soldiers and
officers who had served under Mironov were arrested simply for
seeking to restore their commander's good name.

After the Twentieth Congress of the CPSU, Mironov's relatives,
along with dozens of his comrades-in-arms and people from the
Don, repeatedly petitioned the CC CPSU to rehabilitate Mironov.
As a result of these persistent demands the Military Collegium of
the USSR Supreme Court was instructed to investigate carefully
all circumstances of the so-called Mironov case. As it turned out,
there was absolutely no evidence to support the Don Cheka's
version of Mironov's treason.

On November 15, 1960, the Military Collegium of the USSR
Supreme Court revoked the decree of the Presidium of the VChK
on the Mironov case and fully rehabilitated him "owing to the
lack of a corpus delicti." On December 9, 1960, the Party Col-

legium under the Political Administration of the Soviet Army rehabilitated Mironov, posthumously restoring him to the ranks of the CPSU.

Six months later an article by V. Goltsov, "Army Commander Mironov," which briefly set forth the military career of this hero of the civil war, was published in the weekly supplement to *Izvestiya*, "The Week" (1961, No. 22), in the section headed "Pages of History." Since then the name of Mironov has often appeared in the Soviet press.[1]

Nevertheless, even after the civil and Party rehabilitation of Mironov, writings discrediting him and distorting his image are still being published in the USSR. Thus in all editions of Konstantin Fedin's novel *An Unusual Summer*, Mironov figures as an adventurist and rebel. A particularly large number of untruths about Mironov are contained in Marshal S. M. Budenny's memoirs, *The Path Traveled*. Most typical is Budenny's first chapter of his third part, published in 1969 in the journal *Don*. Budenny also wrote a tendentious letter to the editors of *Problems of History*, published in No. 2 of that journal for 1970. This letter, in complete contradiction of its heading—"Against Distortions of Historical Truth"—in fact seriously distorts the historical truth both about Mironov and about Budenny's former superior, corps commander B. M. Dumenko, unjustly shot in 1920 by a military tribunal and now fully rehabilitated. Budenny's writings have held up the publication of many interesting materials on the life and military career of Mironov and obstructed the proper birthday centennial celebration of this outstanding man in 1972. (The only thing published in October 1972 was P. Dmitriyev's brief note in the *Journal of Military History*, "P. K. Mironov, Commander of the 2nd Cavalry Army," which is inaccurate and unreliable.)

But it is more than these quarrels that attracts us to Mironov. A considerable number of his letters, proclamations, orders, and appeals in which he set forth his understanding of the socialist revolution and popular power have come down to us. And from these documents Mironov emerges as an eloquent exponent of the ideas and aspirations of the middle peasantry, particularly the working Cossacks. His fate typifies the ups and downs of that most numerous class in Russia and reveals the mistakes of local and central organs of the Soviet regime in dealing with the middle peasantry and the working Cossacks—mistakes which were often criticized by Lenin.

Philip Mironov was twice sentenced to be shot, the first time on October 7, 1919, six weeks after his willful departure for the southern front with the as-yet-incomplete Don Cossack Corps to engage the advancing forces of Denikin. After his arrest, Leon Trotsky, chairman of the Revolutionary Military Council, published several articles on Mironov and the "Mironov affair" without waiting for a decision from the Revolutionary Military Tribunal. He declared him a traitor and careerist who wanted "to climb upward on the backs of the toiling masses." But Trotsky was clearly premature in his evaluation. On October 8, 1919, the Presidium of the VTsIK had already pardoned Mironov and his comrades-in-arms. At a session of the Politburo of the TsK RKP(b) on October 23, Mironov was not only exempted from any punishment but political trust in him was expressed. The Politburo included him in the new leadership (then being formed) of the Don Region, and the question of his admission into the RKP(b) was settled in advance. In the autumn of 1920 he was named commanding officer of the 2nd Cavalry Army.

As early as October 19, 1919, after being taken to Moscow, where his fate was to be decided, Mironov had begun to write his memoirs, "dedicated to my faithful, charming, and unforgettable friend and wife, Nadezhda Vasilevna Mironova-Suyetenkova."

And so [wrote Mironov] twelve days of life . . . twelve days since I left behind me an already-prepared pit, later filled in again. . . . For me that pit is a symbol of death, in whose face people do not lie. Constantly glancing back at it, I want to be sincere in these notes— in these reminiscences of those forty-seven years of life left on the other side of that filled-in pit. In short, this is a confessional account of a life full of suffering—a life not understood by my contemporaries but one that is instructive. . . . But what especially prompts me to work on these notes now is the necessity for refuting the attacks of my political enemies, both revolutionaries and counter-revolutionaries.

Yesterday, October 18, the Cossack Section of the VTsIK delivered to me (I am still in custody at the Alhambra Hotel) a copy of Trotsky's article "Colonel Mironov" and a copy of an article by a White Guardsman, A. Chernomortsev, titled "Red Cossacks." Both of these articles are biased for reasons of a personal and political nature. It is important to note the end of Trotsky's article: "At the head of Mironov's grave, History will drive in an aspen stake as a fitting monument to a detested adventurist and miserable traitor."

Although I had only had "twelve days," human weakness had already succeeded in overcoming me: it flattered my self-esteem that the aspen stake would be driven in, not by the hands of a human, always prejudiced, but by History. And with respect to that little old lady, it is criminal to avoid sincerity and purity in one's confession. . . .

And so, as though by some miracle resurrected for a new life, I want to begin it by again fulfilling that purpose for which a man is put on this earth; and that, in our terrible times, is to ease the sufferings of one's neighbor. And how I conceived my own purpose among mankind will be told by these notes of mine and not by the articles of Trotsky, Chernomortsev, and others charging me with careerism, adventurism, etc.—traits that have been foreign to me all my life. My life's motto has been the truth.*

. . . All the misfortune of my life consists in the fact that for me, when it is necessary to speak the plain truth, there is no such thing as a general of the Tsarist Army or a general of the Red Army. As we all know, truth is a social necessity. Without it, life is inconceivable. Since it is the motive force for the best and loftiest aspects of the human soul, the truth must be protected against its seizure by dirty hands. The naked truth is burdensome, and whoever befriends it is not to be envied. For it, there are neither personal nor political considerations. It is impartial, but to live without it is unthinkable. As our people say, "The truth does not burn in fire or sink in water." And all my life I have been striving after that ideal. I fall, I get up again, and I fall again, sorely bruised, but I keep striving. . . . There is no perfection on this earth, but we are obliged to seek it if we are not living for the sake of selfishness. . . .

---

* *Pravda*, also translatable as "justice."—Translator's note.

The whirl of life has sucked me into the arena of social life and political struggle; and I take part in all this to the extent that my physical, moral, and mental strength is demanded by the moment being lived through. Even under Nikolai Romanov I did not like the feeling that someone was lording it over me. This too is one of the causes of my misfortune—if the struggle for the triumph of truth and social justice may be considered a misfortune.

Even when I knew nothing of the Bolshevik program, I had no thoughts of "personal ambition, careerism, and a striving to climb upward on the backs of the toiling masses," as Trotsky claims in his article, "Colonel Mironov." When I joined in the struggle for the Soviet regime, the struggle for putting the means of production into the possession of the laboring masses, for their socialization, I sincerely desired one thing: to prevent the generals, landlords, and capitalists from enlisting the uneducated and politically ignorant Cossacks on the counter-revolutionary side, since the former controlled many means of doing that. I strove to enlist the Cossacks in the struggle for the Soviet regime, in the struggle for an alliance with the laboring masses of Russia. . . .[2]

Unfortunately, Mironov was able to write only a few dozen pages of his memoirs. Yet even without those memoirs, there are still extant sufficient documents, eyewitness accounts, and other materials to paint an accurate picture of his heroic and tragic life.

The basic sources used in the writing of this book are authentic documents kept in the Central State Archives of the Red (Soviet) Army, the Central State Archives of the October Revolution, the Central Party Archives, the State Archives of the Rostov and Volgograd regions, and certain other archives. Almost all these documents are previously unpublished. We have also used certain personal archives and the reminiscences of Mironov's comrades-in-arms and members of his family.

*   *   *   *

I. P. Gavrilov, member of the CPSU since 1919 and former political worker with the 2nd Cavalry Army, has rendered the authors great assistance.

PHILIP MIRONOV
AND THE
RUSSIAN CIVIL WAR

THE DON COSSACKS
BEFORE THE
FEBRUARY
REVOLUTION OF 1917

Philip Mironov was a Cossack—a fact which largely determined his fate during the years of the Revolution and the civil war. It is therefore natural to begin this book with a brief account of the Cossacks as a special social category in Tsarist Russia, emphasizing the Don Cossacks, with whom Mironov's life and struggle were chiefly associated.

The word *kazak* (Cossack), probably of Tatar or Central Asian origin, is variously translated as "free," "to wander," "to roam," "horseman," or "landless peasant." Originally, in the fourteenth and fifteenth centuries, the Cossackry was formed of fugitive peasants, serfs, and townspeople who had fled from serfdom and oppression and sought refuge in the sparsely populated and "free" steppes in the southwest and southeast of the Russian plain. Their chief occupations were hunting, fishing, and beekeeping in the forest. Cossack bands frequently raided Turkish and Tatar lands and attacked merchant caravans. Later, they turned to farming and livestock raising as livelihoods.

Their special frontier position and their need to defend themselves against claims by the Muscovite Tsar and neighboring states caused the Cossacks to develop a specific military organization which radically affected their entire way of life. Uprisings (those, notably, of Ivan Bolotnikov, Stepan Razin, Kondraty Bulavin, and Emelyan Pugachev) against the power of the Tsar and the landlords frequently broke out in the Cossack regions. The Ukrainian (Zaporogian) Cossacks often rose up against the Polish landlords holding sway in the Ukraine. In the fifteenth and sixteenth centuries, however, Cossack leaders frequently allied themselves with Tsarist authorities and helped carry out military undertakings of the Russian State.

As the Russian Empire expanded, Moscow gradually subordinated the Cossack regions to its own authority. It was a struggle, at times bloody, that inevitably ended in victory for the centralized Russian State. Peter the Great was instrumental in dealing a decisive blow to the independence of the Don Cossacks by breaking their resistance and destroying many of their villages and settlements. But in subordinating the Cossacks the Tsarist authorities refrained from enserfing them or distributing their lands to the Russian nobility. The government understood the importance of having special Cossack military communes (*obshchiny*) on the frontiers of the empire. And although in time the Cossack regions became an integral part of the Russian Empire, the Tsarist government always extended various privileges to the Cossackry. This policy favored a special military caste with its own traditions and distinctive agrarian system. The few urban Cossacks became soldiers, but the free rural Cossacks were formed into Cossack *voiska*.

At the beginning of the twentieth century there were eleven Cossack voiska in Russia: those of the Don, the Kuban, the Terek, Astrakhan, the Urals, Orenburg, Siberia, the Semirechiyek, the Trans-Baikal, the Amur, and the Ussuri. All in all, the Cossack regions comprised about six hundred thousand square kilometers with a population of more than six million. The Cossack voiska had their own lands, capital, industrial enterprises, and government. Each voisko was headed by an appointed ataman subordinate to the main administration of Cossack Voiska of the War Ministry. For purposes of internal government a Cossack voisko was divided into *okrugi* (districts), each headed by an ataman, and *stanitsy* headed by a stanitsa ataman. For handling economic affairs, each voisko had an economic and voisko administration with the same rights as provincial authorities. The military activity of the voisko was handled by a special military staff. All Cossacks were subject to military service and all males served from the age of eighteen to thirty-eight. A Cossack was obliged to furnish, at his own expense, both a service horse and all personal military equipment. Besides military service, the Cossacks' chief occupation was agriculture, and all of a Cossack's military equipment was purchased with income "from the land." Agriculture encouraged the establishment of large Cossack families.

The Cossacks were not the only inhabitants of the Cossack regions. This is evident in the Don Region, for example, which had the largest Cossack population in Russia. As far back as the eighteenth century, rich Cossack atamans, generals, and deserving Cossack officers (Cossack officers automatically received titles of nobility), who had been granted huge tracts of land for services "to the Tsar and the fatherland," began to buy serfs and bring them to the Don Region. Thus, in time, a large native peasant population was formed in the Don Region. As a rule, these peasants lived not in the Cossack stanitsy and villages but in separate settlements. The majority of peasant villages were located in the Taganrog, Rostov, and (partially) Donets districts. After 1861 Don peasants were given their own strips of land averaging 2.5 to 3.73 desyatinas per capita and 800 square sazhens on the former manorial farmstead. Out of the fifteen million desyatinas of land in the Don Region, twelve million belonged to the Don Cossack Voisko. This glaring inequality in land distribution underlay the class enmity between Cossacks and peasants that showed itself during the civil war on the Don.

After the reform of 1861, poor people from other parts of

Russia were attracted to the relatively rich Cossack regions. These newcomers hired themselves out as laborers on the big Cossack farms or rented small tracts of land. They also worked on the "economies" (self-sufficient estates) of wealthy capitalists and on horse-breeding farms, or served as handicraftsmen or small traders. Thus a social stratum of "aliens" (*inogorodniye*) emerged in the Don Region that in general did not own plots of land and had the lowest standard of living in the area.

The economic development of Russia in the late nineteenth and early twentieth centuries—the sudden increase of industry, the building of railroads, the expansion of domestic and foreign trade —brought about in the Don Region the rapid growth of many cities, including Rostov-on-Don, Taganrog, Novocherkassk (capital of the Don Voisko), Aleksandrovsk, among others, as well as a number of workers' settlements (*slobody*) and railroad stations. Naturally, this increased the number of blue-collar workers, white-collar workers, Cossack and non-Cossack intelligentsia, etc.

On the eve of the February Revolution the total population of the Don Region was about 3.5 to 4 million. Cossacks and their families numbered more than 1.5 million, the native peasants approximately 900,000, and the "aliens" about 700,000. Though the Cossacks constituted only about 43 percent of the population, they were in the majority in rural areas.[1] Moreover, their special military organization and their land use and other privileges made the Cossacks unquestionably the dominant group.

The bulk of the Don Cossacks lived in some 120 stanitsy and the numerous villages adjacent to them. The *yurt*, the land assigned to the stanitsa, was considered the property of the entire voisko. From it, each adult male Cossack received a strip of land, or *pai*, for his own use.

In 1835 the size of the individual allotment was fixed at thirty desyatinas. But by 1915, in many stanitsy, the actual per-capita allotment had been reduced to a half or even one-third that figure. As the regional agronomist Kushnarenko-Kushnarev wrote: "In certain districts [okrugs] the land allotment had been so much reduced that the head of a household comprising only a wife and children felt that for all his industriousness he could by no means earn a living merely from his own strip of land. Unless he rented one or two other pais he had a very hard time of it."[2] At the same time, individual Cossacks spent an increasing proportion of their income on military service. Late in the nineteenth century a special commission headed by Major General Maslakovets wrote in its conclusion:

At the present time only 21 percent of the Cossack population are still enjoying economic conditions favorable enough so that they can bear the burden of military service. For 45 percent of the population this involves a severe dislocation of their economic life. Finally, the remaining 34 percent of the Cossack population belongs to that poor category which is almost always insolvent, so that the Cossacks' military equipment must be paid for out of the social funds of the stanitsa. This evident discrepancy between the burden of military service and the resources of the Don Cossack population would unavoidably lead . . . to an economic crisis which could have only one result: the transformation of the Don Cossacks into a category of the general rural poll-tax-paying population of the Empire and their subordination, as regards military service, to the conditions and regulations generally obtaining in the state.[3]

Thus only at first glance did the Cossackry constitute a kind of single organism. Actually, deep multifaceted changes had long since taken place within the Don Cossack society.

For example, there were substantial differences between the relatively wealthy stanitsy of the southern districts of the Don region and the poorer stanitsy of the northern districts. Not only that, but within each district (okrug) and each stanitsa Cossack households were divided into wealthy kulak households, middle households, and poor households. On this score, different sources give different figures.

By comparing these figures we can conclude that before World War I, in the Don stanitsy and villages, 20 to 25 percent of the households were wealthy, about 30 to 40 percent middle, and 40 to 50 percent poor.

The war deepened and accelerated this social differentiation among the Cossacks. According to the 1917 census in the Don Region (within the territorial limits of 1922[4]), the percentages were as follows:

	Without Agricultural Implements	Without Working Livestock	Without Cows	No Livestock	No Grain Crops
Cossacks	25.4	18.6	19.6	10.8	18.1
Peasants in Volosts*	30.7	30.8	28.8	13.1	18
Aliens	61.3	56.4	57.5	38.1	49.6
All Households	32.4	26.8	29.4	16.1	23

* A volost, particularly in the Don Region, was a subdivision of a stanitsa. —Translator's note.

The extreme hardship of the poorest Cossacks is evident from these figures. But the same figures show that the economic position of the peasants and the alien population was even worse.

At the same time there were a number of Cossack families in the Don Region, chiefly the families of colonels and generals, whose wealth rivaled that of the richest and most prominent landlord families in Tsarist Russia. One hundred forty-three families of the Don Cossack aristocracy owned 750,000 desyatinas of land.[5]

S. Syrtsov thus erred when, in summarizing the results of the civil war in the early twenties, he wrote: "The Cossack ideology (the Cossack traditions and love of the Don) was a perfect means of welding the Cossacks into *one solid mass* [emphasis ours] ready to slit the throat of anyone who had any notion of violating the Cossack privileges." Syrtsov goes on to say that "the Cossacks were the *janissaries of the imperial family* [emphasis ours]."[6] This erroneous viewpoint greatly damaged the young Soviet state.

The peasant situation in Russia, and the question of the peasantry as an ally of the proletariat in a socialist revolution, was thoroughly studied in prerevolutionary Marxist literature, especially in the works of Lenin. Yet the Cossacks received virtually no attention. Among several local Bolshevik leaders, this omission promoted incorrect notions about the Cossacks as a single, solid, counter-revolutionary mass.

Actually, as recently noted by F. G. Biryukov, a close contemporary investigator of the Cossackry, the Cossack question in Russia

> . . . is the peasant question all over again, but in a complex variant. The idea of friendship and collaboration between the proletariat and the working peasantry was fully applicable to the working Don Cossacks. True, this frontier region of Russia was under a more marked influence of the ideas of monarchy, class distinctions, autonomy, and artificial isolation, and preserved the vestiges of the past to a greater extent. But the laws of class division operated in the Cossack milieu as they did everywhere else. In the Don Region, before the Revolution, one-fifth of the households were prosperous, while the others were middle and poor.[7]

Despite their internal heterogencity, the Cossacks served the interests of the Russian Empire. Because of their privileges and military organization the majority of Cossacks strongly supported the Tsarist autocracy. Cossack forces took an active part in all the wars fought by Russia in the nineteenth century, providing most of the cavalry and reconnaissance units. In 1904–05, dozens of Cossack regiments were sent to the Far East to fight in the Russo-Japanese War.

When the first bourgeois-democratic revolution broke out in 1905, the Tsarist regime, relying on the Cossacks' fidelity to the throne, decided to throw Cossack regiments against revolutionary uprisings. This use of Cossack troops for police and punitive functions provoked resentment and protest among some of the democratically inclined Cossacks in the Don Region, especially among the intelligentsia. In meetings at many of their stanitsy, the Don Cossacks passed resolutions against using their units as police.

A number of Don stanitsy simply refused to mobilize. The Cossacks' mood did not escape Lenin's attention. In September 1906 he wrote in *Proletarian*: "The military dictatorship and the military situation have necessitated the mobilization of new masses of troops. But now the repeated mobilizations of the most 'reliable' troops, the Cossacks, have caused a great increase in fermentation in the ruined Cossack stanitsy and intensified the 'unreliability' of those troops."[8]

In the Don Region, the First Russian Revolution witnessed the formation of bourgeois-democratic organizations and groups. Individual Cossacks joined social-democratic organizations, which were active at that time in the largest industrial centers of the Don.

It should also be noted that in St. Petersburg, Moscow, Yuzovka, Lodz, and many other industrial centers of Russia there were numerous instances of individual Cossacks and entire units refusing to break up demonstrations and fire on the workers. Some Cossack squadrons (*sotnias*) refused to defend landlord estates against seizure by peasants. And Lenin wrote:

In the December days, the Moscow proletariat gave us splendid lessons in the ideological "processing" of troops. For example, on December 8, on Strastnaya Square, when a crowd surrounded the Cossacks, mixed with them, made friends with them, and persuaded them to go back. Or on the tenth on the Presnya, when two girl workers carrying a red banner in a crowd of ten thousand rushed to meet the Cossacks, shouting, "Kill us! While we're alive we won't yield up the banner!" The Cossacks were discountenanced and galloped away to the shouts of the crowd: "Long live the Cossacks!" These examples of courage and heroism should be forever imprinted in the consciousness of the proletariat.[9]

And in those same industrial centers of Russia, individual Cossacks of revolutionary inclination made contact with social-democratic organizations, and in a number of cases even joined the Social Democratic Party, adhering to its most revolutionary, Bolshevik wing. For example, the Cossack V. S. Kovalev, former chairman of the Central Executive Committee of the Don Soviet Republic, was one of the first to join the Bolshevik Party. For carrying on social-democratic agitation in the ataman's Cossack regiment in St. Petersburg, Kovalev was arrested, deprived of his Cossack title, and given a death sentence—subsequently commuted to hard labor.

Nevertheless, during the First Russian Revolution such instances of revolutionary activity were isolated. The great majority of Cossacks and Cossack units willingly carried out orders of the Tsarist authorities, and took part in breaking up demonstrations and putting down revolutionary actions by the working class and the peasantry. The gratitude of Nicholas II to the Cossacks for their "loyal service" was, of course, not unmerited. The Cossacks' whips, and sometimes their bullets, were long remembered by those who witnessed the revolution of 1905–07. It was precisely the events of those revolutionary years which engendered the notion of the Cossacks as "janissaries of the imperial family" in the minds of many Bolsheviks.

That notion proved to be erroneous. The revolution of 1905–07 made a deep mark in the consciousness of many Cossacks. This is the only explanation for those large-scale disturbances, unexpected by the Cossack leaders and Tsarist authorities, which took place in the Don Region during the spring and summer camp assemblies in the Khoper, Ust-Medveditsa, First Don, and Second Don districts in 1909–10. At that time the Cossacks demanded not only an increase in the land allotments of the small Cossack farms, the introduction of rural self-government, and the alleviation of military service, but also exemption from their employment for police functions. In 1909–10 more than eight hundred Cossacks were brought to trial and convicted for participating in the disturbances in those four districts. Hundreds of Cossacks were sent to Siberia. Nonetheless, the disturbances were repeated at the camp assemblies on the Don in 1911, and they were interrupted only by the World War.

In the summer of 1914 the outbreak of World War I evoked a surge of patriotic and nationalistic feeling among the greater part of Russian society, including the Cossacks. When the news of

Germany's declaration of war against Russia reached the Don Region, the stanitsy joined in the wave of patriotic enthusiasm. One after another, in a swift and systematic manner, mobilizations were effected in all Cossack districts; hundreds of thousands of Cossacks went off to the fronts which had been established in the south and west of Russia to fight "for the faith, the Tsar, and the fatherland." However, the World War soon had a great sobering effect on the consciousness of the working Don Cossackry.

During the war years more than four hundred thousand men— or more than 10 percent of the region's population and more than 20 percent of its male population—were called up for the army. As a rule, these men were the best Cossack farmworkers. Thus in the Don Region crop planting declined. When the Cossacks went off to war they took their horses with them; many Cossack horses were also requisitioned for military haulage. All this meant a lack of tractional power and a decline in livestock breeding in the Don Region. Cossack households were greatly hurt by the drop in exchange rate of the ruble, by speculation, and by the deteriorating economy.

These developments seriously disturbed Cossacks serving at the front. Moreover, the Cossack units were suffering great combat losses, as they were invariably deployed in the main battles and in the decisive phases of military actions. At the front—both in attacks and in the more frequent retreats—even the rank-and-file Cossacks became convinced of the ineptness of most Tsarist generals and the stupidity of the top military command, for which the Cossacks were paying with their heads. Also, there was a deterioration in relations between the rank-and-file Cossacks and many Cossack officers, whose chief attributes were caste spirit, arrogance, conceit, and rudeness. There were frequent cases of striking "the other ranks." In 1916 all this produced grumbling and dissatisfaction among Cossack soldiers.

THE LIFE
AND CAREER
OF PHILIP MIRONOV
BEFORE 1917

Philip Mironov was prepared for his part in the revolutions of 1917 by many events in his difficult life.

He was born on October 27, 1872,* into a poor Cossack family in the village of Buyerak-Senyutkin in the Ust-Medveditsa District. He went through parochial school and completed two grades at the gymnasium in Ust-Medveditsa. This would have been considerable schooling for most sons of ordinary Cossacks, but the young Mironov showed a strong desire to continue his education and completed the remaining course of gymnasium study on his own. He also showed zeal and achieved great success in the military games and training which were routine for all young Cossacks. This helped him to matriculate at the Cossack Cadet School at Novocherkassk, from which he was graduated in 1898. Four years later, at the age of thirty, Mironov had the rank of cornet (*khorunzhii*), no small achievement for some-

* Dates up to February 1917 are Old Style.—Translator's note.

one from a poor Cossack family. Mironov's election in 1903 as stanitsa ataman at the Raspolinskaya Stanitsa testifies to the prestige he enjoyed among the Cossacks in his district.

Even in the days when he first became a Cossack officer, Mironov was distinguished for his independent character, his self-reliance, his loathing for injustice, and his genuinely democratic outlook.

In 1904–05, during the Russo-Japanese War, as an officer of the 26th Don Cossack Regiment, Mironov fought in Manchuria. For bravery and the skillful command of his unit, he was awarded four orders and promoted to the rank of junior captain (*podesaul*).

The revolution of 1905 shook all Russia, including the Don Region—especially its northern sections. In the Khoper and Ust-Medveditsa districts there were riots by alien peasants, and the estates of several landlords were destroyed. In the Don Region cities, democratic groups proclaimed slogans of freedom of the press and assembly and demanded rights for aliens equal to those of the Cossacks.

While returning from Manchuria, the Cossacks heard news of the uprisings in Russia and on the Don. Many of them were hostile toward the beginning revolution, fearing the loss of their lands and privileges. Yet among the poor Cossacks and the Don intelligentsia there were others who listened carefully to the slogans of the revolution. Among these Cossacks Philip Mironov soon occupied a prominent place.

Mironov's first revolutionary speech, which to a considerable extent determined his subsequent career, was made on June 18, 1906, at a stanitsa assembly in Ust-Medveditsa that had been called to approve the mobilization of Cossacks for police service. A good number of those present, including the old men, were opposed to the mobilization. As a result, the stanitsa assembly passed a resolution not to effect the new mobilization of Cossacks. Mironov made an impassioned and well-received speech supporting the decision of the majority.

He was appointed to convey the decision of the Cossack assembly to the national Duma in St. Petersburg. On his way back, he was arrested and put in a guardhouse, and proceedings were instituted against him. Whereupon a new assembly of Cossacks arrested the district ataman and held him hostage. They compelled him to telegraph the appointed ataman demanding Mironov's release and that of his comrade-in-arms, Deacon Burykin. The authorities yielded. The mobilization order was canceled, and the arrested persons were released. The Cossacks picked them up and carried them on their hands to the stanitsa headquarters while singing revolutionary songs. More than two thousand Cossacks took part in this demonstration.

In his memoirs, Marshal Budenny sought to discredit Mironov and, without proof, to deny his revolutionary past. He wrote scornfully:

One journalist has claimed that as early as 1906 Mironov was doing revolutionary work; that he carried a revolutionary mandate from stanitsy to the Duma, and was imprisoned for so doing. . . . But there is not a single document to confirm all this revolutionary activity of Mironov's. There is no evidence as to his trip to St. Petersburg with a revolutionary mandate, or as to his imprisonment.*

This statement by Budenny is a deliberate falsehood. Actually, there are many documents in various archives confirming Mironov's revolutionary activity.[1]

Mironov was not brought to trial immediately: he was too popular in the northern stanitsy, and there were fears of new disturbances in the Ust-Medveditsa. He was even assigned to duty with one of the active regiments. But after his first run-in with the

---

* The journal *Don*, 1969, No. 11, p. 8. We hasten to note that Budenny's collaborators are two military historians, A. M. Zolotrubov and A. A. Tonkov, who together with a group of assistants selected and processed archival materials and then published them—with, of course, the approval of the aged marshal. Budenny's memoirs, compiled in this way, contain a great many distortions of historical truth of all possible types, tendentious and biased evaluations, and out-and-out conjectures, which do no honor either to the author or to his collaborators.

regimental commander, he was brought back and placed at the disposal of General Samsonov, the appointed ataman of the Don Voisko. An order deprived him of his officer's rank, dismissing him from the voisko "for actions discrediting the rank of officer."

Mironov returned to his own stanitsa and family, busying himself with farming. Later he began to transport water from the Don, as his father had done many years before.

In May 1910, during the disturbances in camps in the Khoper, Ust-Medveditsa, and Upper Don districts, the authorities of the voisko, fearing Mironov's influence, summoned him to Novocherkassk, where he was named chief of the agricultural section of the regional administration. While working there, Mironov not only became familiar with all the agricultural problems of the Don Region but worked out a project for the redistribution of land. This project provided for equalizing the land allotments of the Cossacks in the northern and southern stanitsy, chiefly at the expense of the landlords, nobility, and horse-breeders. Mironov also proposed assigning land to alien peasants, who in the Don Region were farming tracts rented from the voisko.

In late 1912 Mironov was transferred from his post and named deputy inspector of fisheries in the tributaries of the Don. This was a kind of exile.

When World War I broke out, even the democratically inclined Cossack intelligentsia were caught up in the fervor of patriotism. Nor was Mironov unaffected. He submitted a request to Novocherkassk that he be sent to the front, even if only as a private. (By virtue of his education he had the right to serve as a *volnoopredelyayushchiisya*—a volunteer with certain privileges.) His request remained under consideration until October 1914, when he was notified that his rank of junior captain was restored to him. Mironov selected a squadron (*sotnia*) of hunter Cossacks from the Khoper District and led them to the front as a part of the 30th Don Cossack Regiment.

Within a month Mironov and his squadron distinguished themselves in a battle, and he was awarded the highest officer's decoration, the Order of St. George, with rifle. In subsequent battles Mironov displayed bravery and military skill. He was awarded four more orders, climbing the ranks to captain, then to lieutenant colonel, and finally to deputy commander for operations of the 32nd Don Cossack Regiment. As the war dragged on, Mironov became increasingly perturbed by high-level command incompetence and by the scarcity of supplies, and the resulting costly defeats on the front. The dead included his oldest son, Nikodim, and his wife's brother. In December 1916 Mironov himself was wounded, and after a brief hospital stay he returned home to recover.

PHILIP MIRONOV
AND THE
DON COSSACKS
IN 1917

By the end of 1916, the Tsarist government had become aware of the instability of its position in Petrograd and Moscow. Under various pretexts, it began recalling from the front some of the Cossack regiments that were most loyal to the monarchy (or seemed so to the Tsarist ministers), restationing them in Petrograd, in Moscow, in cities near the capital, and in several other industrial centers of the country.

But the Cossacks did not save Nicholas II and the Russian autocracy. When in February 1917 the proletariat of Petrograd rose up against Tsarism and one Petrograd military unit after another went over to the side of the rebels, the Cossack units joined in the revolutionary struggle. The Don Cossack regiments stationed in the capital quickly aligned themselves with the Petrograd proletariat; and to a considerable extent this accounted for the relatively easy victory of the February Revolution.

The news of the revolution in the capital, the abdication of Nicholas II, the overthrow of autocracy, and the formation of the

Provisional Government was greeted with enthusiasm and joy, not only among the ordinary Russian soldiers at the front but also by the majority of the Cossack combat troops. The famous "Order No. 1 to the Garrison of the Petrograd Military District," approved by the Petrograd Soviet of Workers' and Soldiers' Deputies and published in *Izvestiya* on March 2, 1917, was supported by almost all the Cossack units. This "order" called for the creation of electoral committees, consisting of soldiers' representatives, in all military units, and required the political subordination of all soldiers to the soviets. It declared the equalization of soldiers and officers as regarded civil rights, and committee control over unit weapons.

Not surprisingly, most Cossack officers, imbued with rigidly monarchist convictions, were frightened and angered by news of the revolution. In certain outlying Cossack units commanding officers even tried to conceal Nicholas II's abdication from their troops. At the same time, however, officers were afraid to condemn the revolution openly. Finding themselves politically isolated, these officers were obliged to swear allegiance to the Provisional Government and agree to the formation of electoral committees (or "regimental circles") in the Cossack units. By the spring of 1917, many of the regimental and squadron commanders most hated by rank-and-file Cossacks were removed from their posts by the Cossack committees and re-assigned to the reserves.

The February Revolution also came as a surprise to the Don Region. Political development in this region lagged well behind that among Cossacks on the front, and even farther behind that in Petrograd and Moscow. The upper crust of the Don Cossackry —the atamans, high officials of the Don Voisko, landowners, officers, and clergy—were bewildered, frightened, and confused by the fall of autocracy and in a number of cases tried to conceal the news from the populace.

The northern stanitsy of the Don Region were better prepared to accept the revolutionary changes in the country, among them Ust-Medveditsa, where Philip Mironov was recovering from his wounds. When he learned of the revolution, Mironov welcomed its first results unequivocally. With a group of like-minded people he organized a big demonstration in support of the revolution and the new Provisional Government at his own stanitsa. Several thousand persons took part, most of them blue-collar workers, low-level white-collar workers, salesclerks, and combat soldiers. On the following day—not without the intervention of the district ataman—Mironov was summoned for medical recertification and ordered to return to combat duty.

Mironov wrote later in his unfinished memoirs:

On March 7, 1917, I left the stanitsa of Ust-Medveditsa. At the stanitsa of Sebryakovo I managed to find out more about what had happened, and decided to go to Petrograd. In Petrograd the members of the Duma were in complete confusion; and I could not get a positive answer to the pertinent questions about the war and army discipline in connection with Order No. 1. I decided to return to the 32nd Regiment, where I was assigned as senior deputy commander for operations. The regiment was encamped at the town of Reni. The regimental commander was Colonel Ruzheinikov, former district ataman of the Ust-Medveditsa District, with whom I had had disagreements about the revolutionary demonstrations of 1905–06. Colonel Ruzheinikov was a violent monarchist. He was completely unqualified for combat duty, but nonetheless concurred completely in the views of the autocratic government.

Immediately upon reporting for duty with the regiment, I brought up the political aspect of things, since I saw that with the promulgation of Order No. 1 there would be no army, and that it would be madness to think of fighting "to a triumphant conclusion." It was essential to take every care to see that the Cossacks were not drawn into a struggle against the revolution by their military superiors. One could sense that the majority of the officers were displeased by the revolution. The first talk with the officers and the Cossacks' representatives, numbering six men per squadron, was held in the open air in the town of Reni. On this occasion I explained to the Cossacks the different kinds of government systems in various countries, with their advantages and shortcomings. The ideal was the Swiss Republic, with its system, its memorandum [sic] and popular initiative. After three hours of discussion it was time to vote, by ballot, on the question: "What kind of governmental system is desirable for Russia?" It should be noted that by this time the Cossacks had learned of the Tsar's abdication . . . and the existence of the Provisional Government, to which allegiance had been sworn. On their fifty-five or sixty ballots, the rank-and-file Cossacks voted unanimously for a democratic republic. Of the sixteen officer ballots, more than half read: "a constitutional monarchy." Thus it was clear that the political paths of the officers and the rank-and-file Cossacks had begun to diverge. . . .

Having become a member of the Revolutionary Committee of the town of Reni, I took a very active part in the sessions of the committee and in meetings. One day in late March I suggested to Colonel Ruzheinikov that, as a member of the Black Hundreds,* he should leave the regiment. He protested. He was then told that if he did not leave voluntarily, he would be removed by the Military Revolutionary Committee. Two days later Ruzheinikov was summoned to division headquarters for testimony, and I was asked to explain my actions vis-à-vis the regimental commander. As a result Ruzheinikov had to leave the regiment, while I was compelled to undergo medical certification and went on sick leave. . . .[1]

When he returned home in April 1917, Mironov encountered the extremely complex and variegated social awakening of the Don Region. All kinds of trade unions, women's committees, student youth alliances, sports groups, etc., were forming throughout the Cossack districts, where in the past there had been no mass social organizations. Many new newspapers were being published, such as *The Free Don*, a newspaper for the whole Don Region, and many district papers. The *Ust-Medveditskaya Newspaper* was published twice a week in the Ust-Medveditsa District, and small newspapers like *Freedom*, the *Voice of the People*, and *Union* were appearing in the settlement of Mikhailovka in that same district.

The foundations of the former regime had not undergone any substantial changes: the power of the stanitsa, district, and other atamans, including the appointed ataman of the Don Voisko, was everywhere preserved. However, in several stanitsy, worker settlements, and peasant settlements soviets had been elected. And

* Extra-legal groups of monarchist extremists.—Translator's note.

in several peasant settlements the soviets had replaced the volost elders and the former volost administrations, and taken power into their own hands. But for the most part, nondescript "executive committees" were set up in the stanitsy and districts whose chief members—in Ust-Medveditsa as elsewhere—consisted of district civil servants, officers from the nobility, petty bourgeois, and teachers. The Ust-Medveditsa committee included only two craftsmen. Individual atamans and police officers were removed in not more than a few districts and stanitsy. In most cases the real power of the atamans in the area remained intact. A Don Executive Committee (DIK) with very limited functions was formed in Novocherkassk to handle the civil affairs of non-Cossack inhabitants. This executive committee, too, consisted chiefly of representatives of the bourgeoisie and the officer aristocracy.

Social change was clearly more vigorous in the towns, worker settlements, and peasant volosts than in the Cossack stanitsy. In some volosts the peasants began to cultivate the landowner's tract, and to pasture their livestock on it, while refusing to pay exorbitant rents. The Provisional Government issued a special appeal on April 3, called "To the Population of the Don Region," which stated that "the Cossacks' rights to land, as they have developed historically, will remain inviolate. The demands of the alien population of the region will be satisfied, insofar as possible, under a procedure to be worked out by the Constituent Assembly."[2]

All major parties in Russia created their own organizations and groups in the Don Region to recruit as many adherents as possible. Although the upper stratum of the Cossackry, including most of the "old"* Cossacks, was plainly in favor of a monarchy, overt activity by monarchist elements was virtually impossible in those months, even in the Don Region. Hence in the spring of 1917 the right-wing Cossacks began to seek an alliance with the Cadets (Constitutional Democrats), who occupied the most conservative

---

* *Stariki.* As applied to Cossacks, "starik" had not so much its usual meaning of "old man" as the sense of "a veteran."—Translator's note.

position in the Provisional Government. Through this bloc the upper stratum of the Cossackry hoped to maintain its power over the Don Region and thereby exert a powerful influence on the course of events throughout Russia.

It is not surprising, therefore, that in the spring of 1917 organizations of the Cadet Party were quickly formed and grew in all districts of the Don Region. Members in the Cadet organizations included primarily the owners of industrial enterprises, big merchants, kulaks, the upper stratum of the intelligentsia, employees of judicial organs, etc. For example, the Cadet organization formed in the stanitsa of Ust-Medveditsa was headed by an examining magistrate, a school superintendent, and an assistant professor from Petrograd University. There were no rank-and-file Cossacks or peasants in the Cadet organizations. As for the Cossack atamans, they did not formally join the Cadet Party but they supported it.

SR (Social Revolutionary) organizations soon appeared and expanded in the Don Region. Two factors contributed to this: the mood of revolutionary "defensism"* which swept over a considerable part of Russia in the spring of 1917; and the SR Party's lack of discrimination in creating its groups and recruiting new members. As a rule, the SR organizations were joined by students, traders, peasants, and some of the Cossacks. Only a few weeks after its formation, the SR organization in the worker settlement of Mikhailovka in the Ust-Medveditsa District had more than three hundred members. I. Lezhnev, a Social Revolutionary student, founded a "Workers' Alliance" in the district composed of representatives of the various political views in the stanitsa. At the Kletskaya stanitsa, a political group headed by P. M. Ageyev, director of the Kletskaya gymnasium whose ideology paralleled the SR's, exerted considerable influence.

---

* The belief that the interests of the Revolution could best be served by actively prosecuting the war against Germany; opposed by Lenin in his "April Theses."—Translator's note.

Alexander Kerensky was idolized by most SR groups, which fully supported the Provisional Government and demanded "war until victory is ours." Like Ageyev, the SR Cossacks supported an alliance between the Cossacks and the peasants in the Don Region, but only with the condition that further "distinctive existence of the Cossackry as a special organization in a free revolutionary Russia be insured." Ageyev went so far as to favor giving the Don peasants land at the expense of Cossack officers and Cossack landowners, but only by consent of the Constituent Assembly. As he wrote:

> To have a Constituent Assembly as the only lawful organ authoritatively expressing the will of the people is the goal of our time. . . . For the time being we must not pose any concrete problems of a more particular character; i.e., the autonomy of provinces, the agrarian question, the question of the workers, etc. . . . Only through a victory over the Germans can we accomplish this chief aim.[3]

There were relatively few Menshevik organizations in the Don Region. And outside such large cities as Rostov-on-Don and Taganrog, even Bolshevik groups were still weak. The peasants of the Don had as yet heard only rumors of the Bolsheviks. The Cossack upper stratum and the so-called democratic parties frightened the rank-and-file Cossacks and peasants with distorted accounts of the Bolshevik program.

Here and there, however—even as early as the spring of 1917—the first Bolshevik cells were formed. In Ust-Medveditsa, Cossack V. S. Kovalev initiated Bolshevik agitation among the workers in the settlement of Frolovo. (Kovalev, apparently the only Cossack who joined the Bolshevik Party in the years of the First Russian Revolution, was sentenced in 1906 to eight years of hard labor.) In the settlement of Danilovka, Vasily Fedortsev, a sailor, headed a group of Bolsheviks; and in the stanitsa of Malodelskaya and its environs a cavalry sergeant major, Semen Ruzanov, carried on Bolshevik agitation. Apparently the only exception among the Cossack stanitsy was Uryupinsk, the chief stanitsa of the

Khoper District, where early in 1917 a large group of Bolsheviks formed under the leadership of A. G. Selivanov. The Soviet of Workers' and Soldiers' (Cossacks') Deputies formed in March 1917 in Uryupinsk was very much under the influence of that group. Of course, at the front and in the Petrograd garrison pro-Bolshevik feeling among the Cossacks ran much higher.

In speaking of the various political alignments in the Don Region we must not neglect to mention pro-federalist sentiment. The tendency toward federalism and separatism of course varied within the Cossackry, in some cases manifesting itself chiefly in hopes of a revival of Cossack traditions and freedoms of the days before Peter the Great. The Cossacks were less interested in democratically structuring the political life of the Don or in aligning themselves with other segments of the population (peasants, workers, alien craftsmen, etc.) than in expanding their own privileges. At the very least, they hoped to strengthen their position as a separate, autonomous caste; at the most, they hoped for an entire separation of the Don Region from the rest of Russia—for establishment of a "Finland" on the Don, as one Cossack patriot expressed it. One of the most influential groups of Don separatists was headed by M. Bogayevsky, director of the gymnasium in Kamenskaya, an experienced speaker and skillful demagogue who was able to enlist the support of a considerable portion of the Cossack intelligentsia and officer class, especially in the southern districts of the Don Region.

When Philip Mironov came back to the Don Region in April 1917, he was faced with deciding which political faction he should align himself with.

At that time, according to Mironov's own admission, he knew little about the Bolsheviks and even less about the Social Democrats. As early as 1906, when he went to St. Petersburg with the mandate of the Cossack assembly, Mironov had favored the embryonic Trudoviks, the Popular Socialists, and the Popular Socialist Labor Party—or rather, the Cossack branches of those groups. And it is known that while in St. Petersburg he met with a representative of the Trudoviks—the Cossack writer and publicist F. Kryukov, who was a member of the Duma.

The political platforms of the Trudoviks and Popular Socialists were close to the SR's. Lenin lumped all these factions into one party of revolutionary petty-bourgeois democrats and mercilessly criticized them as a gang of opportunistic petty-bourgeois romantics who "falsified socialism in the interests of the economic muzhik."[4]

At the same time, however, Lenin repeatedly pointed out the progressive aspect of the struggle waged by revolutionary democracy against the landlords and autocracy. He wrote that the proletariat should support the petty-bourgeois parties "in their struggle against the landlords and autocracy because of the revolutionary bourgeois-democratic character of that struggle."[5] Lenin emphasized the tremendous importance of an alliance between the proletariat and the revolutionary petty bourgeoisie, gradually educating the latter and its political representatives, and bringing it into the main current of the democratic struggle headed by the proletariat. He prophetically wrote that the outcome of the Russian Revolution would depend upon the behavior of petty-bourgeois democrats:

> In a country like Russia the outcome of the bourgeois revolution depends first of all upon the behavior of the small producers. That the upper bourgeoisie will be treasonous is beyond doubt. . . . There is likewise no need to prove that, with respect to the Russian workers, the proletariat will be the most reliable fighter. . . . But the petty bourgeoisie is precisely that variable which determines the outcome. We must therefore keep an especially close eye on its current political vacillation between the loyal infirmity of the Cadets and the bold, pitiless revolutionary struggle of the Social Democrats. And of course we must not only watch that process closely but must also, insofar as we are able, influence it in a proletarian spirit.[6]

The February Revolution created widespread SR groups and groups of Popular Socialists of varying hue. In Ust-Medveditsa Philip Mironov was a founder of the local branch of the Popular

Socialist Labor Party with a membership of about sixty persons in the stanitsa. The group, headed by a committee consisting of Mironov, F. Popov, N. Kadynov, I. Chernikov, and I. Mordvinets, named Mironov its candidate for membership in the Constituent Assembly.

Federalist sentiments in the Don led to the creation of a supreme body to administer all Cossack affairs, a "Voisko Cossack Circle" —a congress which had been elected, over two hundred years before, by the Don Cossacks as a nation. The Circle was to convene in May 1917. All of the main political groups of the Don Cossackry decided to participate.

At the election assembly for representatives to the Voisko Circle in Ust-Medveditsa, Mironov made a major revolutionary speech. He dealt with the question of merging the Don Cossackry with the Don peasantry and the necessity of removing misunderstandings between these two elements, which had lived side by side in less-than-peaceful coexistence for centuries. "Today, on the Don, there are neither Cossacks nor muzhiks but only citizens equal in all respects. Down with this discord, which the generals are no doubt utilizing to assault the Revolution!" With these words Mironov closed his speech, which was loudly applauded by the members of the stanitsa. And yet in the election of delegates to the Voisko Circle, Mironov was blackballed. Emelyannikov, the stanitsa ataman, and other rich Cossacks were chosen.

The Voisko Circle of the Don Voisko met on May 26, 1917, in Novocherkassk for twenty-three days.* About seven hundred representatives attended from all stanitsy on the Don and from Cossack regiments. Though they included proponents of every political persuasion, right-wing sentiments dominated the scene. About half of the delegates were reactionary officers and among the others were several dozen big merchants and Cossack in-

---

* Here and subsequently all dates are given New Style.—Translator's note.

dustrialists. There were also quite a few old Cossacks of monarchistic leanings. The Cossack troops from the front lines tended to favor the Bolsheviks and rallied around two delegates: the Social Democrat V. S. Kovalev and a Bolshevik sympathizer, F. Podtelkov. There were also extreme separatists at the congress, headed by M. Bogayevsky, who presided over the sessions.

Most of the many speeches heard at the session called for the glorification of the Cossacks and their age-old traditions, for the preservation and expansion of freedoms and privileges, and for unlimited political power in the region. The majority of the delegates favored the slogan: "The Cossack is master of the Don." The Circle resolutely opposed the claims of the Don Executive Committee (DIK) to intervene in certain Cossack affairs. The Circle viewed itself as the only body fully empowered to administer, at the top level, the Don Cossack Voisko: "The problems of Cossack life do not come within the competence of the Regional Executive Committee, and no agency handling economic and administrative affairs of the Voisko has the right to enter into relations with the Regional Executive Committee."[7]

The Circle issued instructions for the liquidation in Cossack settlements of executive committees and all temporary social organizations of a revolutionary character. It was decided to recall the Cossacks from all soviets of workers' and soldiers' deputies.

As mentioned, Mironov was not chosen as a delegate to the Circle from his own district. Neither was he selected to represent the 32nd Don Cossack Regiment, of which he was deputy commander. Nonetheless, he attended the gathering as the head of a regimental delegation welcoming the Circle. But instead of a brief welcoming speech he made a long programmatic one, proposing many democratic reforms in Cossack life. In particular, he declared that the big tracts of land held by officers and officials should be redistributed to the rank-and-file Cossacks. This proposal was not well received by either the rightist element of the Circle or the more democratically inclined leftist element. The left-wing delegates felt that the land tracts of the officers and officials should be put into a fund to provide land allotments for the Don peasants so that their holdings would reach the level of the average Cossack allotment.

The Voisko Circle chose a government which included two representatives from each Don district. District atamans were elected at meetings of the district representatives, and the Circle elected the chief of the Voisko staff and the commander of the Voisko artillery. On June 18, 1917, the Circle elected General A. M. Kaledin as Don Ataman.*

As head of the Don Voisko, General Kaledin tried to convert the Don Cossackry into an instrument of reaction and generals' counterrevolution. He called upon the Cossacks to bring the war with Germany "to a victorious conclusion" and demanded that they use force to put down antiwar demonstrations by soldiers. In an order published in *The Free Don*, he stated:

> It may now be necessary for you, carrying out the will of the Supreme Command, to engage in open, mortal struggle against . . . mutinous soldiers who have forgotten their Motherland, duty, and honor. We expect of you, and we demand, that in this struggle you unswervingly take the path of the salvation of Russia—the path of pitiless struggle against the traitors to the Fatherland.[8]

In late July, Kaledin called an assembly of the Small Voisko Circle (the regular Circle comprised five representatives from each stanitsa, the small Circle only one) to discuss procedures for elections to the Constituent Assembly. The Cossack upper stratum decided to form a bloc with the Cadets for these elections. F. Radichev, a member of the Central Committee of the Cadet Party, made a long speech at the Circle, and other prominent members of the Cadet Party also came to the Don. But the northern Don districts

---

* Kaledin was born into an officer's family in 1861. After becoming an officer, he served on the General Staff and the Voisko staff. In 1914, with the rank of major general, he commanded a division, then took over the command of the 12th Corps of the 8th Army under General Brusilov. Several big, successful operations earned a reputation and glory for Kaledin, and he received many high military decorations. In 1917 he was commanding the 8th Army. Kaledin did not conceal his conservative, monarchistic views and his hostility toward democracy and socialism.

came out firmly against a bloc with the Cadets, opposing Kaledin and his deputy, M. Bogayevsky. Speaking at the Circle, a delegate from the stanitsa of Berezovskaya stated:

Yesterday, representatives of the People's Freedom Party said there was no firm authority in Russia. They were seeking a force on which their firm authority might be based. . . . As a Cossack, I would say: We, the representatives of Cossack democracy, can help the Motherland in these trying times; but we are repelled by the idea of police duties. In any case, at heart the Cossacks have been, and have remained, profoundly democratic; and they will go along with the laboring strata and not with the capitalists.[9]

The representatives of the northern districts announced that their stanitsy would put up their own electoral lists. Also, the bloc with the Cadets was opposed by many combat units, including the 32nd Don Cossack Regiment in which Mironov was serving. A declaration published in the name of this regiment stated:

The Voisko Circle, rejecting Russian democracy, is preparing to join forces with the landlords and capitalists, with the People's Freedom Party, in the elections to the Constituent Assembly. We, the Cossacks from the front lines—in particular those of the 32nd Don Cossack Regiment—protest the actions of the Voisko Circle. The working Cossackry will remain true to the behests of the Revolution.[10]

In the summer of 1917 the right-wing Russian parties and the upper stratum of the military were preparing a *coup d'état*. It was planned not only to destroy the soviets but to overthrow the Provisional Government, which, in the opinion of the bourgeoisie, was not in a position to stop the development of the revolutionary movement in the country. In their plans, the leaders of the counterrevolution especially counted on the Cossacks. To some extent the events of July 3–5, 1917—when Cossack units broke up a worker demonstration in Petrograd—reinforced these hopes.

Using his authority as Voisko ataman, Kaledin began gradually to recall certain Cossack regiments from the front to use them in combatting the revolution on the Don and throughout Russia.

In August 1917, speaking at a governmental conference in Moscow, General Kaledin demanded that the army be placed outside of politics; that meetings and assemblies in the army be prohibited; that soviets and committees, both in the army and in the rear of army units, be dissolved; and that decisive disciplinary measures be taken in the army. "The disciplinary authority of commanders must be restored," he declared, "so as to restore to the regiments their previous strength."[11] But at that same meeting the Cossack combat soldier Nagayev opposed Kaledin's demands. Nagayev stated that the demand for the dissolution of the soviets was being put forward only by the generals, and that the rank-and-file Cossacks would not go along with Kaledin against the people. These speeches were published and heatedly discussed among the Cossacks.

While preparing his military coup, General Lavr Kornilov, Supreme Commander of the Russian Army, kept in constant touch with Kaledin, counting on his help. When Kornilov launched his adventure and moved some of the units he had deceived toward Petrograd, he placed his chief hopes in General Krymov's 3rd Cossack Cavalry Corps. As early as August 26—i.e., at the very outset of the revolt—Kornilov sent Kaledin the following telegram:

Have been removed as Supreme Commander. Klembovsky named to replace me. Have refused to give up my duties as Supreme Commander. Denikin and Valuyev going along with me and have sent protest to Provisional Government. If you are supporting me with your Cossacks, telegraph same to Provisional Government. General Kornilov.[12]

Kaledin immediately informed Kornilov that he was supporting his claims and sent the following ultimatum to the Provisional Government:

General Kaledin warns the Provisional Government that if it refuses to make terms with General Kornilov, he, Kaledin, using the Cossacks under his command, will take steps to cut off Moscow from the south of Russia.[13]*

* The source for this quotation, although it has been numbered, is unfortunately missing from the Russian original.—Translator's note.

Both of these telegrams, along with Kornilov's ultimatum to the Provisional Government, were published in *The Free Don*. It is hardly surprising that at this time the Provisional Government issued an order for the arrest of both Kornilov and Kaledin.

Still uninformed of this, Kaledin was feverishly rushing from one Don stanitsa to another, trying to win over to his side all the Cossacks of the Don Region. On August 30 he reached the stanitsa of Ust-Medveditsa, where an assembly was to be held on the following day. The *Ust-Medveditsa Newspaper*, which was under the control of people opposed to Kaledin, described that assembly as follows:

Having begun his junket through the Don Region, Kaledin arrived at the stanitsa of Ust-Medveditsa on the night of August 30. The stanitsa ataman called a stanitsa assembly on the occasion of his arrival. The meetinghouse was overflowing, and the windows were open. A crowd of several thousand—Cossacks and aliens—gathered in the square. Speaking before the "elderly elected gentlemen," Kaledin said: "You know the viewpoint of the Voisko government as regards disorders in the country. Our program is known to everyone, both from the decision of the Circle and from the declaration I made at the governmental conference in Moscow. I declare once again that it is not for us Cossacks to go along with the socialists: we must support the People's Freedom Party." Touching upon events at the front, the ataman asked his audience not to become dispirited but to believe that with God's help everything would be straightened out. And he called for unity and peace of mind. He asked us to spare the quiet Don from anarchy, to dry our ration biscuits, to keep the powder dry in the powder flasks, and to combat the degenerate youth who had been infected with Bolshevism at the front and had lost the fighting spirit of the Cossacks. . . .

The old campaigners applauded Kaledin, shouted "Hurrah!" and expressed their readiness to support his measures. The combat soldiers at the assembly, grouped around Mironov, were alarmed by Kaledin's speech and kicked up a row: whistling, shouting, and other noise. Mironov asked for the floor. He was refused, since he was not an elected member of the assembly. But the combat soldiers pushed him up to the speaker's platform. Mironov sharply rebuked Kaledin, and exposed his counter-revolutionary designs. There were shouts of "Down with the counter-revolutionary generals!" and "To jail with

Kornilov and the Kaledinites!" The elected old men and the nonelected Kaledinites rushed to the speaker's platform and pulled Mironov down, hitting him on the sides and back. The combat soldiers defended Mironov. There was hand-to-hand fighting around the speaker's platform. Squadron Commander Stepan Igumnov appeared from somewhere in the crowd and rushed at Mironov with drawn sword, demanding he apologize to Kaledin and threatening to cut off his head. Mironov put his pistol to Igumnov's forehead and demanded he drop his sword. One of the combat soldiers picked up the sword, broke it, and threw it through a window. Kaledin and his entire retinue left via the rear exit. Coming out to the square, where a crowd of thousands was making an uproar in its turn, protesting the shady enterprise of Kaledin and Kornilov, Mironov made a long speech. He called upon the Cossacks not to yield to any provocations. With respect to the regime, he stated openly that the power must belong to the people as represented by soviets of worker, peasant, and Cossack deputies.[14]

At the very time the assembly was being held, a telegram reached the stanitsa from War Minister Verkhovsky, ordering the arrest of Kaledin as a co-conspirator in the Kornilov revolt. Military clerks from the headquarters rushed to the meeting with the telegram. Mironov and a group of combat soldiers tried to arrest Kaledin, but the latter had managed to gallop out of the stanitsa. Changing horses and avoiding the northern stanitsy, he was able to get back to Novocherkassk.

There Kaledin was under the protection of Cossack units, and it was difficult to arrest him. Several days later the Voisko government sent a telegram to Petrograd demanding that the order to arrest Kaledin be revoked. A similar telegram was sent to the capital by Kaledin himself, who threatened "complications in the region." Fearing a conflict with the Cossacks and anxious to reach a compromise with the Cadets and the Kornilovites, the Provisional Government complied and revoked the order for Kaledin's arrest, and he remained Voisko ataman.

Writing in September 1917, Lenin summed up as follows the first results of the Kornilov-Kaledin revolt and the Cossack participation in it:

All the power of wealth was behind Kornilov, but what a rapid and pathetic collapse! Apart from the wealthy, only two kinds of social forces could be detected among the Kornilovites: the "Savage Division" and the Cossacks. In the first case this was only the power of ignorance and deceit. . . . As for the Cossacks, they represented social strata from a frontier region of Russia consisting of wealthy, small, and middle landowners (the average holding was about fifty desyatinas of land) who had preserved a great many medieval traits in their style of life, economy, and everyday existence. Here we can detect the socio-economic foundation for a Russian Vendée. But what was shown by the facts of the Kornilov-Kaledin movement? Even Kaledin, the "beloved leader," supported by Guchkov, Milyukov, Ryabushinsky, & Co., did not stir up a mass movement! Kaledin was moving toward civil war far more "directly" and unswervingly than the Bolsheviks. Making no bones about it, Kaledin "went off on a junket to stir up the Don." Yet he could not even stir up a mass movement in his "own" region— in a Cossack region cut off from all-Russian democracy! . . .

There are no objective data as to which of the various strata and various economic groups adhered to democracy and which adhered to the Kornilov revolt. There are only indications that the majority of the poor and middle Cossacks were inclined toward democracy, while only the officer caste and the upper stratum of the wealthy Cossacks were completely committed to Kornilov. In any case, the extreme weakness of a massive Cossack movement in support of bourgeois counter-revolution has been historically proven since the events of August 26–31.[15]

In this same article, Lenin pointed out that the leftist SR's and Mensheviks moved closer to Bolshevism and internationalism after the Kornilov-Kaledin revolt.

Lenin's conclusions were confirmed by Mironov and his group of adherents. In September 1917, Mironov still regarded himself as a member of the Popular Socialist Labor Party. On September 12 he delivered a report on the position of the Cossacks at a meeting of that party in the stanitsa of Ust-Medveditsa. This meeting, in the hall of a Cossack club, was also attended by hundreds of non-Party Cossacks. In his report, Mironov condemned the Kornilov-Kaledin adventure and called for equality between the Cossacks and the rest of the inhabitants of the region. True, in these days Mironov still had a negative attitude toward the Bolsheviks. In an article published on September 8, 1917, in the *Ust-Medveditsa Newspaper,* he wrote:

> In their attack on the gains made by the people, on the gains of the revolution, they—the Cadets—are now acting through Bolshevism, which is again rearing its dreadful head—dreadful for the safety of Russia. Yes! The Bolsheviks and the reactionary forces are allies. Unnatural and unwilling allies, but frightening allies. This alliance is more frightening and dangerous than generals Kornilov, Kaledin, Krymov, Lukomsky, Denikin, Valuyev, Markov, Alekseyev, and others.

But Mironov did not entertain this view of the Bolsheviks for long. He tried to keep close track of everything that was happening in Russia. He read the newspapers of various parties, and increasingly favored a political platform similar to that of the Bolshevik Party. For example, he resolutely supported an end to the war, an immediate peace "without annexations and indemnities," and the "socialization" of factories and plants. In speaking to the Cossacks, Mironov said:

> It should be clear to us Cossacks that if we go along with the generals —and Kaledin yearns for this—we must first strangle the Bolsheviks, and then strangle the democratic republic, and will come close to a bourgeois republic and even . . . a constitutional monarchy. But behind the back of that monarchy stands Purishkevich, and he will favor an autocracy, which in its turn is the dream of the landlords, the nobility, and the generals. But if we go along with the Bolsheviks we shall not have to regret it, since their platform is clear. It may be that much of what they stand for is utopian and involves many extremes, that their goal is ideas of the distant future; but we should not break off relations with them because of this. We shall always make verbal agreements with them, but the basic gains of the revolution will be retained by the toilers.[16]

When his furlough expired in late September, Mironov returned to the 32nd Regiment at the front. He was eager to get back to his unit and for this reason was detached from the bureau of the Ust-

Medveditsa organization of the Trudoviks.* Actually, the Voisko staff had at first tried to prevent Mironov's return to the front. But he declared he would go back to his regiment without documents and ask the regiment to enroll him. After making that declaration, Mironov was provided with the documents needed. Early in October he reached Akkerman, where the regimental headquarters and some of the squadrons were located. He was warmly greeted by the Cossacks and many of the regiment, which was commanded by Colonel Morgunov.

The armed uprising in Petrograd led by the Bolsheviks, which overthrew the Provisional Government and laid the groundwork for the October Revolution, provoked varying reactions in the Don Region, among the Cossack units at the front, and in Petrograd and its environs.

General Kaledin and the Voisko government refused to recognize the new Soviet government or to comply with its orders. Kaledin sent a telegram to all district and stanitsa atamans demanding that they take "all steps, up to and including the introduction of martial law where required, and the use of armed force, to put down the slightest attempts on the part of anyone to take action, in the Don Region, against the Provisional Government."[17] It was proclaimed that all power in the region was transferred to the Voisko government, "pending restoration of the regime and order in Russia."

At that time the situation in the Don Region was fragmented. In Rostov-on-Don, a session of the Rostov-Nakhichevan Soviet had elected a Military Revolutionary Committee (VRK) headed by the Bolshevik S. I. Syrtsov, chairman of the soviet. The Soviet regime had been proclaimed in Rostov, Taganrog, and in most of the coal-mining regions of the Don. Of the Cossack stanitsy, however, only Uryupinsk and Morozovsk and a number of peasant volosts in the Don Region refused to recognize the authority of Gen-

---

* The Trudoviks had merged with the Popular Socialist Party in 1917.— Translator's note.

eral Kaledin. In the first weeks after October the armed forces at the disposal of Kaledin were still negligible, while Red Guard detachments had been formed in the industrial centers of the region. And peasant disturbances were growing in strength everywhere.

But the counterrevolution on the Don began to rally its forces. As early as November 2, General Kaledin had declared martial law in the coal-mining areas and in the districts of Rostov, Taganrog, and Cherkassk. The Soviet regime was overthrown in the stanitsy of Uryupinsk and Morozovsk. Selivanov, Seliverstov, and other Cossacks who headed up local soviets were sent to prison. The soviets at the mines were also destroyed. Detachments of Kaledinites carried out mass arrests, floggings, and in some cases shootings of Bolsheviks and workers who sympathized with them. General Kaledin issued an order recalling more Cossack regiments from the front to defend the Don Region. Leaders of the Cadet Party showed up in the Don Region with reactionary officers from all over Russia. With this officer caste as a base, General Alekseyev and General Kornilov began to organize a so-called volunteer army on the Don. On November 22 Kaledin declared martial law throughout the Don Region. The Voisko government received moral and financial support from the Western Allies to combat the Bolsheviks. That month the Kaledinite detachments of the volunteer army began an attack on Rostov, and by December, after capturing Rostov and Taganrog, the Kaledinites launched an attack on the Donets Basin. Bolshevik organizations went underground as the Don Region fell temporarily under the power of the counterrevolution, unleashing a fratricidal civil war on the Don and in many other regions of Russia.

Among the Cossack units at the front and in Petrograd, the situation at the end of 1917 was complex. Several hours before the overthrow of the Provisional Government, its prime minister, Alexander Kerensky, fled from the Winter Palace. He had counted on rallying the troops of the northern front for a campaign against revolutionary Petrograd. But the front-line soldiers refused to go along with Kerensky. His only support came from General P. N.

Krasnov, commanding officer of the 3rd Cavalry Corps, who ordered his units to Petrograd.

The SNK and Lenin personally had mobilized all Party organizations of the city to defend Petrograd. Red Guard detachments of workers, sailors, and soldiers, plus Finnish and Lettish regiments, were sent to the front against Krasnov and Kerensky. On October 30, near Polkovo, the revolutionary forces won their first decisive victory over the Cossack units. Tsarskoye Selo, previously held by the Cossacks, was retaken. After this the rank-and-file Cossacks refused to continue fighting and lay down their arms. Kerensky again fled, and Krasnov was arrested together with a number of Cossack officers. The Cossacks were allowed to keep their weapons, and they were promised they would soon be sent back to the Don. Moreover, the Soviet regime soon released the arrested Cossack commanders, including General Krasnov, who gave his word that he would not again oppose the new government. The Petrograd VRK even allowed Krasnov to resume command of the 3rd Cavalry Corps. But Krasnov did not keep his word. Taking command of the 3rd Cavalry Corps, he tried unsuccessfully once again to engage the Cossacks of the corps in the struggle against the Soviet regime.[18] Many Cossacks, propagandized by Bolshevik agitators, went back to their homeland in whole squadrons, giving up their weapons. In late November and early December the 3rd Cavalry Corps was disbanded. General Krasnov, declared a traitor by the Soviet government, escaped to the Don and soon turned up in the stanitsa of Konstantinovskaya.

Likewise unsuccessful, in most cases, were the attempts of the counterrevolution to stir up Cossack troops on the other fronts against the Soviet regime. The Third All-Cossack Congress of Front-Line Units, dominated by officers, which was held in Kiev in October, called upon the Cossacks not to recognize the Council of People's Commissars and to support the already overthrown, nonexistent Provisional Government. The Don Ataman Kaledin, along with the atamans of many other Cossack regions, demanded the same of combat Cossacks. Another Cossack organization which refused to recognize the Soviet government was the Council of Cossack Voiska, founded in Petrograd in the spring of 1917, which, according to its leaders, was to act as the coordinating body for all Cossack actions in Russia under conditions of revolution.

But these actions by the anti-Soviet Cossack upper strata were unsuccessful. The Cossack regiments at the front were under the influence of the Bolsheviks and the great majority of them wanted an immediate end to the war—peace "without annexations or indemnities." The Cossacks could clearly see the incipient breakdown of the old Tsarist Army. And they did not want to carry on a war that everyone was disgusted with or perform punitive functions against individual soldiers or whole units fleeing east. Few Cossacks wanted to take part in a civil war unleashed by the generals.

In Petrograd, most members of the counterrevolutionary Council of Cossack Voiska were arrested by the Soviet authorities. Representatives of the working Cossacks left the Congress of Cossack Voiska and reorganized into the Cossack Committee or Cossack Section of the VTsIK, which included among its membership such revolutionary Cossacks as A. G. Nagayev, M. Ya. Makarov, and I. A. Lagutin.

The situation in the 32nd Don Cossack Regiment, where Philip Mironov was serving, typified the mood among the front-line Cossacks.

Elections to the Constituent Assembly were held throughout Russia immediately after the October Revolution. In the Don Region, and among the Cossack units, these elections involved nine electoral lists: 1. The "Plekhanovite" Social Democrats. 2. The SR's. 3. The Old Believers. 4. The Cossack List. 5. The Bolsheviks. 6. The Cadets. 7. The Cooperators. 8. The Mensheviks. 9. The Property Party (*Sobstvenniki*). The basic contest involved lists 2, 4, and 5. In the Don Region the Bolsheviks received about 15 percent of the votes, the SR's 3 percent, and the Mensheviks 1 percent. The great majority voted the Cossack list. The Bolshevik votes were cast chiefly by the workers of Rostov, Taganrog, and the coal-mining regions, where power was in the hands of the soviets at election time. As for the Cossack stanitsy, it was only in Uryupinsk and Kotovo, and in the workers' settlement of Mikhailovka, that the Bolshevik slate garnered a few hundred votes. The other stanitsy voted en masse for the Cossack list. But in many Cossack combat units the results were different. Thus in the 32nd Don Cossack Regiment, two-thirds of the votes were cast for the Bolsheviks and the Left SR's, and only one-third for all the others combined.

True, the 32nd Cossack Regiment was the most revolutionary Cossack unit on the Rumanian Front. Here, there was less pro-Bolshevik sentiment and Bolshevik agitation. Although the command of the front, and most of the officers commanding divisions, regiments, and armies, had learned of the revolution in Petrograd by October 25 or 26, in many units the commanders completely concealed this news from rank-and-file soldiers and Cossacks, and until the end of November many orders were issued in the name of the Provisional Government and the commander-in-chief, Alexander Kerensky. As everyone at the front learned of the victory of the Soviet regime in Petrograd, and lines began to be drawn in combat units between opponents and proponents of the Soviet regime, conflicting sentiments arose among the soldiers and the Cossacks. Vigorous propaganda was carried on by the Kaledinites, who advocated the armed overthrow of the Bolshevik regime.

Four months after the October Revolution, Mironov wrote in a letter:

I came to the ideas of the Bolsheviks cautiously and gradually, over a long period of time. But I came to them in confidence, and I would yield up my convictions only with my head. . . . Frankly, when the Bolsheviks seized power on October 25, I was not sympathetic. I began to study intensively the program of the Social Democratic Party in general, since I saw that in one way or another the struggle in which I had taken part since 1906 would demand [more of] my efforts. In order to devote those efforts to the cause in which I had exerted myself for about twelve years, it was necessary to take a position that would end in the complete victory of the cause of the people without a great number of victims. And by December 15, after a long period of consideration, I had arrived at the following view of the Bolsheviks: they—i.e., the Bolsheviks—could be used to frighten only little children, and on that basis to build the secret plans hatched in the heads of the generals, landowners, capitalists, noblemen, and priests.[19]

Immediately upon hearing the news of the October Revolution, Mironov organized—in his own regiment and in several other regiments of the division—meetings on the subject: "Cossacks should not be put into the service of the generals and landowners. Let us not repeat the mistakes of 1905–06." The success of these meetings exceeded all expectations. Mironov resolutely opposed the intention of General Kaledin and the Don Voisko government to use the Cossack regiments to "defend" the Don and take up arms against the Soviet regime, which had triumphed over a great part of Russia. In an open letter to P. M. Ageyev, who had been his comrade-in-arms in the revolutionary struggle of 1906 and who was now a member of the revived Don Voisko government, Mironov wrote:

> It must not be forgotten that the regime was established by bayonets, and must be maintained by bayonets, and since you and the other members of the Voisko government have turned over those bayonets to the Don Cossacks, tell me for God's sake how many years more the Cossacks must be mobilized to defend that regime, since Russian democracy will try to take that power away from the People's Freedom Party?
> . . . So that I won't be labeled a Bolshevik, and a scarecrow in the eyes of the Cossacks, I herewith set forth my political platform: a democratic republic on federal principles; the right of popular referendum; the right of popular initiative; etc. This is the banner of the entire 32nd Don Cossack Regiment![20]

On December 1, a front-wide Cossack congress of the Rumanian Front was convened. Mironov and Sergeant Kharlamov, a Bolshevik, were elected as delegates to this congress from the 32nd Regiment. But they were unexpectedly summoned to divisional headquarters and detained, while the divisional commander himself, with a group of officers, attended the congress. Thus the congress was held without representation from the 32nd Regiment, the most revolutionary on the Rumanian Front. It is not surprising that this first congress of front-line Cossacks voted to support not the Soviet government but Kaledin.[21]

But the 32nd Regiment did not join in appeals to fight. When, on orders from Kaledin, Cossack regiments began to be withdrawn from the front to combat the Soviet regime, the Cossacks of the 32nd Regiment refused to carry out the order. They forced the removal of Colonel Morgunov, the commanding officer, and elected Mironov in his place. In his reminiscences, Mironov wrote:

On December 23, 1917, Colonel Morgunov returned from divisional headquarters. On the twenty-fourth, at 11:00, there was a meeting of the regimental committee attended by the commanding officers of the regiment and the attached squadrons—the 2nd, 3rd, and 6th. At this meeting Colonel Morgunov read an excerpt from some order, from which it was clear that by January 6 the 32nd Regiment was to reach Odessa for embarkation. Sergeant Kharlamov suddenly interrupted the discussion to say, "Colonel, you haven't told us everything. Let me read the orders to the Division."

Thunder from the heavens on a clear day would not have been so unexpected as was the content of the orders for many of those present. The regiment had been given a combat mission: on a certain day, to capture the town of Aleksandrovsk in Ekaterinoslav Province, to disarm the Bolsheviks and seize their weapons and all reserves of ammunition. A funereal silence ensued. The thing the regiment had been fearing— a counter-revolutionary action against the social revolution—had become a fact.

"Colonel," I asked, "how do you feel about that order?"

"I . . . it comes from higher authority, and we must carry it out."

"Then I will be the first to refuse, even though this order is supposed to be regarded as strictly operational."

The majority of those at the meeting supported my declaration, although no definite decision had been reached when the meeting broke up.[22]

On the evening of that same day, delegates from the Cossacks came to Morgunov and proposed that he leave the regiment and turn its command over to Lieutenant Colonel Mironov. The next day the Cossacks repeated their demand, warning that they would not hesitate to use force if it were not met. Morgunov had to comply, and on December 25 Mironov was named regimental commander by the regimental committee.

Mironov immediately ordered that the regiment prepare to return to the Don (a truce agreement was in effect on the front at that time).

On January 10, 1918, en route to the Don, the 32nd Regiment went to Aleksandrovsk (now Zaporozhe), not to disarm the Bolsheviks but to help the local revkom (revolutionary committee) beat off an attack on the town by Cossack units. After the commanding officer of the attacking Cossack division was taken prisoner along with his adjutant, the 32nd Regiment was provided with twenty railroad cars by the revkom, and on January 17 it reached the Don at the stanitsa of Sebryakovo in the Ust-Medveditsa District.

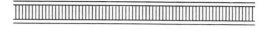

THE VICTORY
AND DEFEAT OF
THE SOVIET REGIME
ON THE DON

[January · May 1918]

By early January 1918 almost all the Don Cossack regiments had returned to their home region. Potentially, the Don Cossacks constituted a huge armed force. According to data for autumn 1917, the following units stationed in all districts were under arms: sixty cavalry regiments and seventy-two squadrons; dozens of artillery units and Cossack infantry battalions; two Cossack guards regiments and several dozen local units. It was therefore not without reason that the domestic counter-revolution placed its chief hopes in the Don Region. That region was chosen by generals Kornilov, Alekseyev, Denikin, and Lukomsky as a main base for forming a volunteer army. By mid-January 1918 this army comprised about five thousand men, chiefly officers and cadets (*yunkers*) who had fled to the Don from other parts of Russia.

Together with the volunteer army, General Kaledin planned to form a separate Don army. However, as General Alexander Lukomsky wrote later:

The formation of the Don units made poor headway. The units that had returned from the front did not want to fight: they made haste to disperse among the stanitsy. And the young Cossacks openly opposed the old men.

In many stanitsy this struggle was a bitter one, and the reprisals on both sides were harsh. But the Cossacks who had returned from the front outnumbered the old men, and they were better armed. In most cases the victory was won by the young men, who advocated Bolshevik ideas. It became clear that in the Don Voisko strong units could be formed only when the principle of voluntarism was used as a basis.[1]

And as a matter of fact, contrary to Kaledin's calculations, the return of Cossack combat units to the Don did not strengthen the Voisko ataman and the Voisko government he headed. Most rank-and-file Cossacks, upon returning to the Don Region after a long and hard war, left their units and went home to their stanitsy and villages. And most of those who remained with their units did not want to wage war against the Soviet government, favoring agreement with the Council of People's Commissars, the rapid conclusion of peace with Germany, and a return to a normal life. On January 27, 1918, General Alekseyev, one of the commanders of the volunteer army being formed in the Don Region, wrote to the chief of the French military mission in Kiev:

I had assumed that with the help of the Cossacks we could without trouble form the new, strong units required for restoring order in Russia and strengthening the front. I counted on the Don Region as a base for action against the Bolsheviks, although I knew that the Cossacks themselves did not want to move ahead in order to accomplish the broad governmental task of restoring order in Russia. But I believed that the Cossacks would defend their own property and territory, and would thereby provide security for forming—and the time for providing—new Voisko units. But I was mistaken. The morale of the Cossack regiments returning from the front is completely shattered. The ideas of Bolshevism have found adherents among the broad masses of the Cossacks. They do not want to fight—even to defend their own territory or to save their own property. They are deeply convinced that Bolshevism is aimed only against the wealthy classes—the bourgeoisie and the intelligentsia—and not against regions where order has been preserved, where there is grain, coal, iron, and petroleum.[2]

Therefore Alekseyev asked the chief of the French mission for help in transferring to the Don Region at least one division of the Czechoslovak Corps, if not the whole corps.*

Trying to compensate for the lack of support from the Cossackry, Kaledin suggested to the Circle the possibilities of expanding the political base of the Don government by bringing into it representatives of the non-Cossack population. In a speech to the Circle he said:

> The entire populace must have a part in the supreme authority in the region. And this must be brought about in a hurry. . . . In a very short time the government will exert a tremendous influence not only over the peasants but over the workers in the towns. Under present-day conditions we cannot ignore the workers. . . . I cannot now conceive of an administration without the immediate representation of the entire populace. . . . But of course we shall not tolerate Bolsheviks in our government. . . . Primary emphasis must be given to the unity of all Cossacks and their merger with the other inhabitants of the region. Then there will be firm support for the struggle against Bolshevism. We are standing on firm ground: to be the master in one's own house. And we shall throw out the uninvited guest.[3]

This proposal encountered some strong opposition from part of the Cossack upper stratum, who demanded full political hegemony over the Cossacks in the region, but the majority of the Circle supported Kaledin. A "united" Voisko government of the Don Region, which included representatives of the non-Cossack population, was formed in January 1918. Basically, it defended the interests of the well-to-do element of the Don peasantry and of the trading and industrial circles of the region.

In its first declaration the new government, headed by Bogayevsky, promised to protect freedom of speech, of press and assem-

---

* This was a force of some 40,000 troops who had been conscripted into the Austrian Army and were later captured by the Russians. Having conceived the hope of establishing an independent Czech state, they switched allegiance and, as a part of the Russian Army, fought against the Central Powers in the summer offensive of 1917.—Translator's note.

bly, and of association in the Don Region, and to effect the "restructuring of life on democratic principles." The government formally revoked martial law in the region, at the same time declaring it would combat "interference by outside forces" and "forcible attempts by the Council of People's Commissars to impose its will upon the population of the Don Region."[4]

Simultaneously with formal declarations on democratization and full amnesty for those imprisoned in connection with political and land disputes, the Kaledinite authorities stepped up military terrorism in the region, especially in towns and at the mines, where the influence of underground Bolshevik organizations was considerable. Unable to count on the units from the front, Kaledin organized "partisan" flying squads of officers. Among these, the detachment under Captain Chernetsov concentrated on reprisals against miners of revolutionary leanings.

But the days of the Kaledinites were numbered. The Council of People's Commissars, headed by Lenin, attributing great significance to a rapid victory for the Soviet regime on the Don, was already taking vigorous steps to put down Kaledin's revolt.

An "Appeal of the Council of People's Commissars to All Toiling Cossacks, with an Explanation of the Policy Pursued by the Soviet Regime," published on November 26, 1917, stated:

Brother Cossacks! You are being deceived. . . . You are being told that the soviets of workers', soldiers', and peasants' deputies want to take away your Cossack freedom. . . . Don't believe it, Cossacks! . . . Your own generals and landowners are deceiving you in order to keep you in ignorance and servitude. . . . The life of a Cossack has always been servitude and hard labor. At the first call from his superiors the Cossack was obliged to get on his horse and go on campaign. He had to spend his own funds, earned by his own sweat and blood, to assemble his military "gear." While he was on campaign, his farm was thrown into disorder and deteriorated. Is this state of affairs just? No, it must be abolished forever. The Cossack must be freed from servitude. The new people's Soviet regime is ready to help the toiling Cossacks. Only one thing is needed: that the Cossacks themselves decide to abolish the old ways, to cast off subservience to the serfholding officers, the landlords, the rich men; to throw off from their necks the accursed yoke. . . . We call upon you Cossacks to set up your own soviets of Cossacks' deputies. All local power should belong to these soviets: not to the atamans and generals, but to the elected representatives of the toiling Cossacks. . . . An attempt is being made to frighten you with rumors that the soviets want to take away your land. Who is trying to frighten you? The rich Cossacks, who know that the Soviet regime wants to put the landowners' land into your own hands. . . . Are not you yourselves, toiling Cossacks, suffering from poverty, oppression, and a shortage of land? How many Cossacks are there who have no more than four or five desyatinas per household? And next to them are Cossack landowners who have thousands of desyatinas of their own land and who, in addition, grab the Voisko lands and tracts. Under the new Soviet law the lands of the Cossack landlords are to be conveyed, without compensation, to the toiling Cossacks, the impoverished Cossacks. . . . And so, Cossacks, choose whom you will stand up for. For the Kornilovites and Kaledinites, for the generals and rich men? Or for the soviets of peasants', soldiers', workers', and Cossacks' deputies?[5]

Two days later, the Council of People's Commissars published an appeal to the workers of the Soviet Republic in which it condemned Kaledin's revolt on the Don and that of Dutov in the Urals. A state of siege was declared "in all those regions in the Urals, on the Don, and in other localities where counter-revolutionary detachments have appeared." Meetings with leaders of counter-revolutionary uprisings or attempts at mediation were prohibited. Kaledin and Dutov were outlawed, and any aid to them "on the part of the local inhabitants or railroad personnel" was prohibited. At the same time the Council declared that "any toiling Cossack who threw off the yoke of the Kaledins, the Kornilovs, and the Dutovs, would be accorded a brotherly welcome and requisite support from the Soviet regime."[6]

Two weeks later, on December 13, the Council published the following decree-appeal "to all the toiling Cossacks":

By the authority of the revolutionary workers and peasants, the Council of People's Commissars declares to all the toiling Cossacks of the Don, the Kuban, the Urals, and Siberia that the Workers' and

Peasants' Government has set for itself the urgent task of resolving the land question in Cossack regions in the interests of the toiling Cossacks and all toilers on the basis of the Soviet program and, taking into account all local and everyday conditions, in agreement with the vote of the local toiling Cossacks. At the present time the Council of People's Commissars decrees:

1. The revocation of compulsory military service for Cossacks and the replacement of permanent service with short courses of study at stanitsy.

2. The assumption by the government of all expenses for supplying uniforms and equipment to Cossacks called up for military service.

3. The abolition of weekly duty for Cossacks at stanitsa headquarters, winter exercises, inspections, and camps.

4. The establishment of complete freedom of movement for Cossacks.[7]

Although in December 1917 the Soviet government did not yet control any considerable military forces, it took all military measures possible under those conditions to put down the counter-revolution on the Don. To combat Kaledin, Red Guard detachments were sent from Petrograd and Moscow, while detachments of revolutionary sailors, individual military sub-units, and some Cossack units were sent to the borders of the Don Region. The main base for the attack was organized in the Donets Basin under the leadership of V. A. Antonov-Ovseyenko.

Thus the Cossacks were faced with a choice that could not be put off: either to "defend" their region against the Soviet detachments, taking upon themselves responsibility for a civil war; or, together with the Soviet detachments moving on the Don Region, to rise up against Kaledin, against the volunteer army formed on the Don, against all the groups of Cadets, Octobrists (Constitutionalists), and Right SR's who had come to the Don to shape it into a solid base for the Russian counter-revolution. Under these conditions a deep split among the Don Cossacks into enemies and supporters of the Soviet regime was inevitable; and that split manifested itself early in 1918.

January 4 witnessed the opening, in Tsaritsyn, of a congress of

delegates from individual Cossack combat regiments who supported the platform of the Soviet regime. A conference of representatives of the toiling Cossacks began on January 7 in Voronezh.
But the most representative congress of the front-line Cossacks was
convened on January 10 at the stanitsa of Kamenskaya, in the Don
Region. This congress was also attended by those who had taken
part in the Voronezh Conference of Working Cossacks. All in all,
twenty-one Cossack regiments, five batteries, and two reserve
regiments took part in the Kamenskaya Congress. Also present
were representatives of the Donets miners and the Moscow Council
and Party Committee.[8]

The Kamenskaya Congress elected a Don VRK (Military Revolutionary Committee) headed by Sub-Cornet F. Podtelkov and
Ensign M. Krivoshlykov, who were pro-Bolshevik. After resolving
to organize a workers' regime, the Don VRK sent the following
ultimatum to the Voisko government:

1. As of today, January 10, 1918, all authority in the region of the
Don Voisko over the Voisko units and the conduct of military opera-
tions passes from the Voisko ataman to the Don Cossack Military
Revolutionary Committee.

2. As of January 15 of this year, all partisan detachments operating
against the revolutionary forces will be recalled. They will be disarmed, as will all volunteer units, cadet schools, and schools for
ensigns; and all members of these organizations not residing in the
Don Region will be sent out of that region to their place of residence.

3. The city of Novocherkassk will be occupied by Cossack regiments
as ordered by the Military Revolutionary Committee.

4. The members of the Voisko Circle are divested of their authority
as of January 15 of this year.

5. All police forces sent by the Voisko government to the mines and
plants of the Don region will be recalled.

6. Stanitsy and villages throughout the Don Region will be informed
that the Voisko government has voluntarily abdicated its authority in
order to avoid bloodletting, and that authority is being immediately
transferred to the Regional Cossack Military Revolutionary Committee
pending formation in the region of a permanent regime of workers for
the entire population.[9]

Thus two power bases and two regimes were formed in the Don Region: the Don Military Revolutionary Committee in the stanitsa of Kamenskaya, and the United Voisko government of the Don Region in Novocherkassk.

These dramatic events, so decisive for the Don region, are portrayed in Book Five of Mikhail Sholokhov's *And Quiet Flows the Don*. In his novel, Sholokhov provides a vivid picture of the Kamenskaya Congress of the Front-Line Cossacks, the creation of the VRK, and portraits of the chief leaders of that committee. General Kaledin attempted to break up the Don VRK by sending to Kamenskaya several military units under Captain Chernetsov. But the greater part of the rank-and-file Cossacks went over to the VRK. The hard-fought battles between the Chernetsov detachment and the Cossack units of the VRK, supported by Red Guards, ended in the defeat of the Kaledinites. Already the struggle was an extremely harsh one. And Sholokhov describes gruesome scenes of the physical annihilation of all captured officers from a Kaledinite detachment, and of Chernetsov himself, on orders from Podtelkov and with his participation. Of course, in times of revolution and civil war, judgments on captured commanders of the warring sides have almost always been swift and harsh. But Sholokhov does not conceal the fact that these reprisals on the unarmed prisoners provoked a protest among some of the combat Cossacks, including Grigory Melekhov.

Even before the Kamenskaya Congress, the Soviet regime had been proclaimed in the stanitsa of Morozovsk in the First Don District, and in the main centers of the Ust-Medveditsa District. On January 17, under the leadership of A. G. Selivanov and A. M. Seliverstov, there was an uprising in the stanitsa of Uryupinsk; and the Soviet regime was also established throughout the Khoper District. At that time, one after another of the Don stanitsy recognized the authority of the Don VRK. On January 19 insurrectionary workers seized power in Taganrog. Those Cossack regiments which still recognized the authority of Kaledin went over to the VRK. A number of Red Guard detachments and groups of revolutionary sailors came from various directions to support the insurrectionary Cossacks in the Don Region. Seeing such a manifest about-face among the Cossacks, generals Kornilov and Alekseyev, heading up the volunteer army, decided to leave the Don Region and the city of Rostov and go to the Kuban to join forces with other White Guard volunteer units. After telegraphing his decision to Kaledin, Kornilov ordered his army to prepare to march. General Kaledin was left without any combat-ready units to defend Rostov and Novocherkassk.

On January 29 Kaledin summoned the Voisko government and announced that he was divesting himself of his authority as Voisko ataman, since he considered the situation hopeless and did not want any more bloodletting. That same day he shot himself.

The agony of the Kaledin government, however, continued for several weeks. The Voisko government refused to capitulate, and tried to organize the defense of Rostov and Novocherkassk. General Nazarov was elected Don ataman. The Small Circle, which had convened at Novocherkassk and was attended chiefly by representatives of the wealthy southern stanitsy, passed a resolution "to defend the Don to the last drop of blood." The Voisko Circle ordered general mobilization, set up military tribunals, and called upon the newly formed Cossack detachments to move to the front immediately.[10]

But the mobilization was ineffective and yielded the Voisko ataman only a few thousand Cossacks. And these hurriedly formed Cossack detachments could not hold back the advance of the VRK units and Red Guards. On February 23 Lenin sent the following telegram to V. A. Antonov-Ovseyenko: "Urgent. To People's Commissar Antonov at his temporary headquarters. Take Rostov today at all costs. Lenin."[11]

This order from Lenin was carried out the following day. And the next day the 27th and 10th Cossack Revolutionary Regiments entered Novocherkassk. General Nazarov was arrested, along with the presidium of the Small Circle, which had convened there. Only a few detachments of White Guards—among them the largest detachment under the campaign ataman, General Popov, with 1,500 sabers, five field pieces, and forty machine guns—retreated into the Salsk steppes. The Kaledinites had been successfully destroyed. By the beginning of March, the Soviet regime had been proclaimed in all cities and large stanitsy of the Don Region.

As the supreme authority in the region, the Don Cossack VRK recognized the TsIK (Central Executive Committee) of the Russian Soviet Republic as the supreme authority in the land. On February 19 the VRK decreed that it would merge with the Military Revolutionary Committee of the non-Cossack population, which had been formed in November 1917 in Rostov. F. Podtelkov was elected chairman of the new, united Regional VRK of the Don Region, and S. I. Syrtsov was elected deputy chairman. This new revkom soon moved to Rostov-on-Don, which now became the capital of the Don Region.

On February 28 Lenin sent the following telegram to Antonov-Ovseyenko:

Petrograd. Our warm greetings to all you dedicated fighters for socialism: greetings to the revolutionary Cossacks. In reply to your telegram from Novocherkassk, we state: the authorized Congress of Urban and Rural Soviets of the entire Don Region should work up its own draft law on the agrarian question and submit it for approval by the Sovnarkom. That would be better. I do not oppose the autonomy of the Don Region. The geographic boundaries of that autonomy must be determined by agreement with the population of the adjacent zone, and with the Autonomous Republic of the Donets Basin. We cannot send you any delegates: we are all up to our ears in work. We ask you to send a representative to the Council of People's Commissars, or to name someone at your discretion.[12]

Elections to the soviets were soon held in the stanitsy, villages, and volosts of the Don Region and elections to the district soviets followed. By March 23 the Don Regional VRK proclaimed the founding of a Don Soviet Republic.[13]

In this newly founded Soviet republic, elections of deputies to the First Congress of Soviets of the Republic were held in late

March. G. K. Ordzhonikidze, a member of the TsK RKP(b) who had come from Moscow, was in general charge of the congress. On April 10 he reported from Rostov by direct wire to Moscow:

The congress opened yesterday. All 750 delegates were in attendance. Comrade Kovalev, a Cossack Bolshevik, was unanimously elected chairman. Eleven of our people and nine Left SR's were named to the presidium. Lenin and Liebknecht were elected honorary chairmen. I greeted the congress in the name of the Sovnarkom and the TsIK. The viewpoint of our Left Communists, defended here by Syrtsov, was rejected almost unanimously today at a fractional session. Immediate problems will be discussed tomorrow. The congress has proclaimed itself the supreme Soviet authority on the Don.[14]

The Congress of Soviets elected a TsIK of the Don Republic with representatives from all districts. V. S. Kovalev was elected chairman of the TsIK, and F. G. Podtelkov became chairman of the SNK of the Don Republic. S. I. Syrtsov was elected his deputy and Commissar for the National Economy. M. Krivoshlykov was named People's Commissar for Administration.

Philip Mironov also took an active part in establishing and strengthening the Soviet regime in his native Ust-Medveditsa District.

As has been said, on January 17, 1918, the 32nd Don Cossack Regiment, under Mironov's command, reached the stanitsa of Sebryakovo in the Ust-Medveditsa District. Shortly before Mironov's regiment reached Sebryakovo, the workers' settlement of Mikhailovka, adjacent to the stanitsa, had been the scene of bloody events. Insurrectionary Cossacks, together with a group of Red Guards, had killed most of the officers of the 5th Don Cossack Reserve Regiment quartered in the settlement. In Mikhailovka and its environs there was a wave of shootings (most of them unnecessary and pointless) of arrested officers, some of whom were even shot in the hospital. All this engendered dissatisfaction with the actions of the revkom among the population.

Mironov was resolutely opposed to unnecessary violence. He feared the shootings would compromise the Soviet regime on the Don. At his insistence a new revkom was elected in Mikhailovka, with Squadron Commander Alayev of the 32nd Regiment as its chairman.

On January 22, Mironov, with a group of Cossacks from his regiment and members of the Mikhailovka Revkom, arrived at the stanitsa of Ust-Medveditsa to organize Soviet rule there. Speaking at a meeting in his native stanitsa, Mironov called for solidarity between the Cossacks and the working masses of Russia as the only guarantee of saving the Don Region and its inhabitants.

A few days later, a local printing establishment published an appeal, written by Mironov, from the Regimental Committee of the 32nd Regiment to all Cossacks of the Ust-Medveditsa District:

Citizen Cossacks! The time has come when we must correct a frightful mistake made by our delegates to the Voisko Circle. . . . This mistake has cost many thousands of human lives. And if we do not now set out to correct it immediately, more streams of human blood will flow, and our native steppes will be littered with tens of thousands of corpses. And instead of blessing us, our descendants will curse us. For whom? For what?

Look around you. The war on the foreign front is dying down; yet your sons and grandsons are still mobilized, rather than being busy with their plows and harrows with a view to the approaching spring. The economy is collapsing, and our huts are threatened with a frightful famine. We have lots of paper money, but what is it worth? What can it be used for? Life in this country has come to a standstill because of a fratricidal civil war.

All the generals, deprived of their authority; all the landowners whose lands have been taken away by socialism; the capitalists, whose capital has been taken away by socialism; the industrialists, from whom socialism has taken away plants and factories and given them to the working class; all the bourgeois whom socialism has deprived of their gay and idle life—all these have fled to General Kaledin and our Voisko government. This Cadet (and perhaps monarchist) general has betrayed the interests of the working people and sided with the capitalists and landowners of the bourgeois class. THAT IS THE CAUSE OF THE CIVIL WAR! Enough deceit! Enough mockery of us Cossacks! . . . The earth has begun to quake under the feet of General Kaledin and the entire

Voisko government. They did not manage to deceive the combat troops! Military revolutionary committees have already been formed in the stanitsy of Ust-Medveditsa, Kamenskaya, and Uryupinsk, and in the settlement of Mikhailovka. Those committees do not recognize the authority of General Kaledin and the Voisko government, and they demand their complete removal. . . . Away with the civil war from the banks of the Don! Down with those who instigated it: General Kaledin, his comrade Bogayevsky, and the golden-tongued Ageyev!

In this same appeal Mironov tried in his own way to explain the differences among the socialist parties of Russia to the Cossacks, who were still quite illiterate politically. In so doing, he displayed a manifest preference for the Bolsheviks:

The socialists are divided into many schools or parties.
There is the Popular Socialist Labor Party.
There is the Socialist Revolutionary Party, which in turn is split up into Right and Left SR's.
There is the Social Democratic Party, with two main branches: the Mensheviks and the Bolsheviks.
"What is this?" you ask. "They believe in the same thing, but they have split up?"
It's quite true that they believe in the same thing, but they believe in different ways.
Remember one thing: the final goal of all these parties is to rebuild society on those principles required by socialism.
But the parties follow different paths toward that final goal.
For example: the Popular Socialist Party says: "We will finally give you land, and freedom, and the rights of the people in fifty years."
The Right Socialist Revolutionary Party says: "We will give the people all this in thirty-five years."
The Left Socialist Revolutionary Party says: "We will give the people all this in twenty years."
The Menshevik Social Democrats say: "We will give the people all this in ten years."
But the BOLSHEVIK Social Democrats say: "Go to the devil with all your promises! Land and freedom and rights and power to the people right now! Not tomorrow, and not in ten, twenty, thirty-five, or fifty years!
"EVERYTHING TO THE WORKING PEOPLE, AND EVERYTHING RIGHT NOW!"

Oh! ! . . . What have we come to, without even noticing it? TO THE
BOLSHEVIKS! . . .

And it makes a person shiver all over, from head to toe—not us, but
the landowners, and the capitalists, and their defenders: General Kaledin, Bogayevsky, Ageyev, and the whole Voisko givernment.

After all, the Bolsheviks are taking everything away from them and
giving it to the people. And they are telling them: "Enough of living
idly, enjoying yourselves, and living off the fat of the land in foreign
countries! Try working and earning your bread in the sweat of your
brow."

So I repeat: the BOLSHEVIKS demand that land, freedom, rights, and
power be put into the hands of the working people immediately. They do
not accept the gradual satisfaction of their demands. They do not even
accept any unity with the other parties—especially the bourgeois
parties. In all their actions, they are extremely direct, and do not
accept even the slightest changes in their programs.[15]

When they first came back to the Don Region, the Cossacks
of the 32nd Regiment resolved not to demobilize until the end of
the struggle against Kaledin. But they were unable to carry out
this resolution. Almost all the Cossacks in the regiment were from
stanitsy along the Medveditsa River. They were eager to go home.
It was therefore decided that for two weeks, one-third of the Cossacks would be sent on leave to their native stanitsy. Few of those
furloughed, however, returned to the regiment. Their renewed
closeness to their families, the persuasive arguments of fathers and
grandfathers, and the agitation carried on by priests and some of
the officers had their effect on the mood of the Cossacks, who were
weary from a long war. Three weeks later, Mironov decided to
disband the regiment and let the Cossacks go home. But he again
called upon them to rally under the banner of their revolutionary
regiment in the event of a threat of counter-revolution.

The Soviet regime was soon triumphant throughout the Ust-
Medveditsa District. Mironov was elected a member of the District
Executive Committee and Military Commissar of the Ust-Med-
veditsa District.

As military commissar of the district and a member of the
executive committee, Mironov constantly traveled through the dis-

trict, helping to strengthen the Soviet regime in the area. He made speeches and wrote leaflets that were printed at a press in Ust-Medveditsa and then distributed throughout the district. It was not until March 1918 that a district organization of the RKP(b)—as yet only a small one—was set up in Ust-Medveditsa.

Some of the local Communists mistrusted Mironov, both as an officer and as a former member of the Popular Socialist Party. Nor were they all pleased by Mironov's popularity among the Cossacks. On the other hand, Mironov sometimes criticized members of the District Executive Committee and certain Communists for individual abuses (distributing rectified alcohol confiscated from the local warehouse, drinking up requisitioned wine, getting cloth from the military crafts school). He protested the arrest of the district prosecutor and members of the court, declaring that hasty repressions "cannot strengthen Bolshevism." As he wrote in his memoirs eighteen months later:

On the whole, the members of the District Executive Committee were far from popular—not only among the Cossacks but among the peasant population. . . . Unfamiliar with the life of the working masses, they followed a false path, assuming that unjustified repressions would strengthen the influence and authority of the Soviet regime. Just the opposite happened; and the advocates of counter-revolution hastened to take advantage of it, showing up these blunders—and what were often evil examples—in the eyes of the disconcerted Cossacks.[16]

By early March 1918, the Soviet regime held sway throughout almost the entire Don Region, but this pre-eminence proved to be temporary and unstable. Hardly had the First Congress of Soviets on the Don proclaimed the founding of the Don Soviet Republic, when the very existence of that republic was threatened.

The rapid defeat of the Soviets on the Don in the spring of 1918 was brought about by many unfavorable circumstances, both internal and external.

For one thing, the Bolshevik Party was still numerically weak on the Don. Party organizations existed mostly in the cities and in workers' districts. The Council of People's Commissars of the Don Republic, established in Rostov, was active chiefly in the cities. Its activity embraced Rostov first of all, then Taganrog and Novocherkassk. In most of the stanitsy, nothing was known of the appeals by the SNK of the Russian Republic to the working Cossacks, who were unaware of the SNK's December decree abolishing compulsory military service for them. There were too few Bolshevik representatives in the region to distribute and explain these documents. The ataman's authority still prevailed in some of the southern stanitsy, and these became a support and base for developing anti-Soviet forces. And in many other stanitsy and villages the Soviet regime was established only as a matter of form—there were many hangers-on in the revkoms and soviets, the bosses often being wealthy Cossacks and people from the previous administration, together with proponents of the Right SR's and the Cadet Party. On March 26, 1918, the Sovnarkom of the Don Republic sent the following instructions to local organizations:

Rostov-on-Don. To the Taganrog District Soviet and Revolutionary Committee; to town, plant, factory, mine, stanitsa, volost, rural, and village soviets and revolutionary committees: Former gendarmes, officers, Cadets, kulaks, and other counter-revolutionaries who are manifest enemies of the new Soviet regime of the toiling people are by chance or happenstance being included in local soviets. The presence of such persons in a soviet of deputies is inadmissible.[17]

In many districts, however, there was neither the time nor the cadres to implement these instructions.

The SNK and the TsIK of the Don Republic did not have the time to work out a clear and concise program for revolutionary reforms in the Don Region. All strata of the region's population were especially interested in the question of land reform. Although in many declarations of the central and regional soviets it was clearly stated that the land allotments of the working Cossacks would not be affected by the reforms, in certain districts and volosts demands were heard—and resolutions passed—to assign land to the peasants and aliens from holdings of landowners and the Voisko reserve and also by redistributing Cossack lands. These rash demands for equalizing land tenure for all Cossacks, peasants, and aliens touched off fear and dissatisfactions among the middle Cossacks, who did not want to yield any of their land to the native peasantry and the aliens, or to the poor Cossacks. This aggravated class discord in many districts, which was quickly exploited by intense anti-Soviet propaganda.

There were no Bolshevik agitators in the stanitsy, but there were only too many agitators from among the officers, the kulaks, the clergy, the "old men" of reactionary leanings, etc. The anti-Soviet underground tried in every way to frighten the Cossacks. It took advantage of Cossack illiteracy, of their being ill-informed, spreading all kinds of fictions about the Soviet government in Moscow, its plans, its policies, and exaggerating the individual mistakes of local Soviet organs and revkoms.

Many of the Red Guard detachments which had come to the Don from Moscow, Petrograd, the Donets Basin, and other regions left the Don after Kaledin's defeat. The Cossack regiments, batteries, and squadrons that had returned to the Don from the front broke up. After overthrowing Kaledin, the Cossack soldiers dispersed to their homes and set to work restoring farms that had been ruined during the war and preparing for spring sowing. By the end of March 1918 the SNK of the Don Republic had almost no army to maintain order or to defend the revolutionary regime.

Tension and dissatisfaction increased in the stanitsy and villages. At that time, under the onslaught of the German forces, many Red Guard detachments were retreating from the Ukraine through the Don Region toward Voronezh and Tsaritsyn. The railroads were jammed with slow-moving troop trains. Detachments of the demobilized Tsarist Army were also moving through the Don Region toward the east. It was not uncommon during this retreat for livestock and foodstuffs to be requisitioned arbitrarily, which of course further aggravated discontent among the Cossacks. The White Cossack detachment that had retreated to the steppes, and whose numbers had grown noticeably, speeded up its actions in March. Counter-revolutionary uprisings broke out in a number of stanitsy: the Cossacks overthrew the organs of the Soviet regime, which were still weak, and again elected atamans. In *And Quiet Flows the Don*, Sholokhov, describing uprisings in dozens of villages and stanitsy, tells how the entire Tiraspol Detachment of the 2nd Socialist Army was destroyed in retaliation for outrages by the Red Guards of that detachment who, demoralized by their retreat, had robbed the Cossacks and raped their women as they passed through the farms in the Don Region.[18]

By the end of March, bands of insurrectionary Cossacks were combining into larger units, providing the foundation for the White Cossack Don Army, the command of which was soon taken by General Krasnov.

During these same weeks the volunteer army returned to the Don; it had failed to take Ekaterinodar and had lost its former commander, General Kornilov, in the Kuban. This army, under the command of General Denikin, considerably strengthened the counter-revolution in the Don.

By April, anti-Soviet uprisings encompassed most Cossack villages and stanitsy. The ruling clique of generals and officers used persuasion and, when that failed, deceit, fright, and terror. Punitive detachments were sent to those stanitsy and villages unwilling to join the uprising. Individual Cossacks of revolutionary leanings who spoke out against forced mobilization in the White Army were beaten, imprisoned, and even shot. The Krasnovites dealt harshly with those accused of "sympathizing with Bolshevism."

The precarious position of the Don Soviet Republic turned critical when the German Army, moving eastward through the Ukraine, approached its borders. Without formally breaking the Treaty of Brest-Litovsk, the Germans were striving to annex new territories in Russia. They occupied the Ukraine, transferring authority to their puppet, Hetman* Skoropadsky. German forces occupied the Crimea, and also strove to overrun the Don Region and seize the Caucasus. At a time when the volunteer army was looking for help from the Entente, the leaders of the Don counter-revolution were counting on aid from the German Army, figuring on both weapons and direct military support from the German imperialists. While the volunteer army generals and officers were saying it was imperative to restore a Russia that was "one and in-divisible," the ringleaders of the newly formed Don Army were aiming for an independent and "sovereign" Don Republic—or rather, Don State—under the protection of Wilhelm II. (We shall see later that a considerable part of the Krasnovites defended the principle of a monarchist government.)

By April, the atamans of some stanitsy were appealing to the Germans for aid. Later that month, with the support of General Krasnov and the counter-revolutionary Cossack leaders, sizable German Army forces invaded the Don Region and moved on Ros-tov and Taganrog.

The unification of the Don counter-revolution paved the way for a Provisional Don Government and a single command for the White Cossack Don Army. On April 22 the staff of the campaign ataman issued the following appeal to the Don Cossacks:

The time has come when there are no longer any doubts—when one can say that God stands not for force but for justice, and that the brigandage of the Red Guard is coming to an end. Our little handful of Cossacks has boldly risen in defense of their own honor, and that of their wives and daughters, and in defense of property of the stanitsy and farms. The Don Cossacks have awakened from the feverish sleep of falsehood, which confused them, and have sided with their cam-paign ataman. Everyone living in the Don Region is hereby informed that the campaign ataman is appealing to the populace, for the last time, to immediately quit the ranks of the Red Guard, to hand over their

* The equivalent, for the Ukrainian Cossacks, of "ataman" for the Don Cossacks; i.e., "chieftain."—Translator's note.

weapons and return to their peaceful occupations, and in every way to help purge the region of tyrants. Everyone is hereby informed that the volunteer army, reinforced by the Kuban Cossacks, has come from the south to support the loyal sons of the Don—that same army which, together with the Cossacks of Egorlykskaya Stanitsa, has been battling the Red Guard since April 19. From the west and the north the Ukrainian *gaidamak** regiments are hot on the heels of the Red Guard; and the gaidamaks have already taken the stanitsy of Millerovo and Kamenskaya. The Red Guard is now hurriedly moving through Rostov to the south, leaving the Don Region. In order that those who have strayed from the path and been weak in spirit should not later experience painful disillusionment and bitter regrets, the staff of the campaign ataman confidently affirms that no one who at this moment—sincerely and honorably, without any hesitation—lays down his arms and quits the ranks of the Red Guard will be prosecuted or punished. The Don Cossack does not seek revenge; and he once again makes a brotherly appeal to everyone.

In the future all individuals and settlements found in the ranks of the Red Guard will be declared traitors to the common people's cause of the entire Don Region, and will be treated harshly as enemies of the entire people. . . . Each Cossack who after this appeal remains in the ranks of the Red Guard will be deprived of his Cossack allotment of land. Each peasant who joins the ranks of the Don forces fighting against the Red Guard will be granted all the rights of a Cossack, since the rights in a region should belong only to those who defend it. Brothers! You may be sure that a desire for peace and order for all compels us to wage war against the Red Guard with all the harshness merited by these tyrants.[19]

The critical military situation compelled the Soviet leaders to curtail the work of the First Congress of Soviets of the Don Republic. An Extraordinary Defense Committee headed by G. K. Ordzhonikidze was named to defend Rostov. But the enemy pressed hard, and there were not enough forces to defend Rostov and Taganrog. By the end of April, when German forces invaded the Don Region, the Soviet regime hung on only in the large cities, in the workers' settlements and stanitsy along the railroad, and in

* Special cavalry units of the Ukrainian Nationalist Army.—Translator's note.

the northern districts of Ust-Medveditsa and Khoper. To combat the German invaders and White Cossacks, the TsIK and SNK of the Don Republic decided to set up a special commission for mobilizing the Cossacks of the northern districts in the Red Army. On May 1 this commission, heading up a detachment of one hundred twenty men, left Rostov by train for the northern districts. The train carrying an expedition headed by Podtelkov was moving very slowly, and he decided they should go the rest of the way on horseback and in carts. But where they were going waves of counter-revolutionary uprisings were moving faster than Podtelkov's expedition. Ten days after leaving Rostov his detachment was surrounded and imprisoned. Only a few men managed to escape. The others were shot, except for Podtelkov and Krivoshlykov, who were hanged.

But even before the disastrous Podtelkov expedition, German units and White Cossacks had taken Taganrog and Novocherkassk; and on May 8, after a two-day battle, the Germans entered Rostov-on-Don.

On May 11 a so-called Circle for the Salvation of the Don gathered in Novocherkassk. At this Circle, General Krasnov was elected the new Don ataman, to replace General Nazarov, who had been shot.

By the end of May the White Cossack Don Army numbered about 20,000. Krasnov declared a general mobilization in the name of the Circle for the Salvation of the Don, and he soon tripled the size of his army. The Don Army had about 200 field pieces, more than 600 machine guns, and 20 aircraft. On the reasonable assumption that the front-line Cossacks would not want to fight beyond the boundaries of the Don Region, Krasnov began to recruit young Cossacks who had not been in the war to form a special shock group intended to march on Moscow. He planned to organize this attack jointly with the volunteer army.

The victory of the counter-revolution in the Don Region unleashed the White Terror—especially in the towns and worker districts. Krasnov went so far as to reject any sharing of authority with representatives of the non-Cossack population. He welcomed the occupation of the Don Region by the German Army and concluded an agreement with Germany on supplying the Don Cossacks with German weapons and ammunition in exchange for grain, livestock, and raw materials. In a speech before the Voisko Circle, Krasnov said:

> When a house is burning, you don't go to the next village to get a pail of water if there is a full pail of water ready at hand. . . . I have entered into talks with the Germans. Thanks to the very skillful policy of General Cheryachukin in Kiev, and of Paramonov and Lebedev in Rostov, we have obtained field pieces, rifles, and cartridges in exchange for wool and grain. . . . But the Donets Basin and the Taganrog District were occupied by the Germans. The Ukraine, despite all my arguments and my old friendship with the hetman, has not let go of them; and the struggle for them threatens to end in a bloody conflict. . . . Under these circumstances, for the sake of saving the Don Region I wrote to Emperor Wilhelm. I wrote him as a sovereign writes to his equal. I pointed out to him the chivalric sentiments of both warring peoples— the Germans and the Don Cossacks—and asked his cooperation in achieving our recognition as an independent state, in the transfer to us of the Taganrog and Donets districts, and in supplying weapons to us. In exchange for this I promised that the Don Voisko would not use its weapons against the Germans, that with respect to them it would observe neutrality, and that it would sell to them on a priority basis that surplus of its products usually sold abroad. . . . The letter produced results. A treaty has been signed between the Ukraine and the Don. By its terms the Great Don Voisko is recognized as an independent state, and all the lands of the Don Voisko remain inviolate. For this treaty we are obliged to the great pressure of the German Command on the Ukraine. We have obtained weapons. . . .[20]

By the summer of 1918 General Krasnov had gained control of the entire Don Region and proclaimed it an independent state. But he had no intention of stopping at that. The Don Army, under the command of Krasnov and Denisov, moved out of the region and launched an attack on Voronezh and Tsaritsyn, striving to capture these important strategic centers of Soviet Russia. In doing this, Krasnov was not merely "securing" his own state. He had set himself the ultimate goal of overthrowing the Soviet regime and restoring the monarchy, drawing on support from the German Army and other anti-Soviet forces in the country.

The Soviet losses in the Don Region and Krasnov's army moving south coincided with the Czechoslovak Corps revolt* and the Soviet regime's overthrow in a great part of the Urals, Siberia, and the Volga Region. Soviet Russia unexpectedly found itself encircled by fronts, civil war becoming the chief factor in the life of the young Soviet state. Henceforth Communist programs had to be subordinated to military problems, and primarily to the creation of a combat-ready and disciplined Red Army. To the fullest extent of his abilities, Philip Mironov took part in accomplishing this task.

* In March 1918, after the signing of the Treaty of Brest-Litovsk, the Czechoslovak Corps set out for Vladivostok on the Trans-Siberian Railroad. Their ultimate intention was to embark at Vladivostok for Western Europe so as to reenter the war against the Central Powers on the western front. The Soviet government at first agreed to this strategy, but some two months later, at a time when some of the Czechoslovak troops had reached Vladivostok and the rest were strung out along the Trans-Siberian Railroad, Trotsky ordered their internment as prisoners of war, thus precipitating their "revolt."—Translator's note.

PHILIP MIRONOV: RED ARMY COMMANDER

[June 1918 · March 1919]

In the rapidly developing anti-Soviet uprising on the Don, the northern districts of Khoper and Ust-Medveditsa held out longer than the others. But in late April 1918, detachments of White Cossacks began appearing in the Ust-Medveditsa District. As military commissar and chief of staff, Mironov took immediate steps to defend the stanitsy and farms in the district. There were many volunteers; but the shortage of weapons and cartridges was severe. And there was no single command. Mironov proposed combining all Red Guard detachments into a single military unit but his views were disregarded: the influence of partisan-style warfare was still potent.

The Cossacks of some stanitsy and villages in the northern districts, under the influence of counter-revolutionary propaganda, began revolting. A "Council of Free Stanitsy and Villages of the Ust-Medveditsa District" announced its refusal to carry out orders of the Soviet regime. Underground counter-revolutionary groups and small partisan detachments were formed in Ust-Medveditsa.

In late April a high school student, B. Podpolsky, shot in the head S. Ya. Rozhkov, chairman of the Ust-Medveditsa Revkom. Another terrorist fired three shots through the window of Mironov's home, but missed. One underground terrorist group was exposed and its members arrested and shot by order of the revkom.

In early May the White Cossacks moved close to the stanitsa of Ust-Medveditsa, which was put under martial law. Its garrison, under the command of Mironov, was small—only some one hundred sixty men.

On May 12 a large detachment of White Cossacks approached the stanitsa. After a skirmish it became clear that the enemy had a considerable advantage in numbers, and that the stanitsa would have to be abandoned unless help were forthcoming from Mikhailovka. But word came from Mikhailovka that it would be two days before the Red Guard detachment could reach Ust-Medveditsa. Mironov ordered the stanitsa evacuated. Some of the Cossacks went over to the Whites, and some Red Guards fled.

Earlier, a group of truce envoys from the neighboring stanitsy had come to see Mironov. He called on them to refrain from a fratricidal war among Cossacks, but it was precisely during this parley that word came of the beginning encirclement of the stanitsa. Keeping the truce envoys as hostages, Mironov with a small detachment of Red Guards retreated in haste toward the Don. One other Red Guard detachment remained in the stanitsa. A Cossack reported to Mironov that all those Red Guards had surrendered to the White Cossacks; and Mironov believed him without double-checking. Therefore, without waiting for the other detachment, he and his troops crossed the Don and retreated toward Mikhailovka. At this point he ordered the release of the truce envoys. The detachment of Ust-Medveditsa Red Guards that had remained in the stanitsa was captured by the insurrectionary Cossacks.

A. Savostyanov, chairman of the Mikhailovka Revkom, demanded that Mironov explain why he had abandoned Ust-Medveditsa. Without examining the situation, he almost had Mironov shot as a former Tsarist officer.

Many Red Guard detachments and groups were assembled in Mikhailovka at this time; but there was no single military command as the White Cossacks drew near to Mikhailovka. The District Executive Committee entrusted Mironov with defending the settlement and its environs. Mironov put into effect a large-scale program for strengthening the defenses. He personally led the Red Guards in attacks, wrote appeals to the Don Cossacks, visited many villages and stanitsy to encourage Cossacks to join the Red Army. In his memoirs Mironov wrote of his fears for the fate of the Don Region and Cossack property:

I said they should put down the counter-revolution on the Don with their own forces and not let Red Guards from Russia enter the struggle. I said people would come who were unfamiliar with the historical and everyday conditions—people who would look upon the Cossacks as a counter-revolutionary element. Days of horror and violence would set in, and we would have ourselves to blame.[1]

On May 25, V. S. Kovalev, chairman of the TsIK and commander of the Don Soviet Republic forces, named Mironov to replace Fedorov as commander of the Ust-Medveditsa District forces.

Heading up the defense of the entire district, Mironov proclaimed the mobilization of the Cossacks. And he called upon the 32nd Don Cossack Regiment, with which he had returned to the Don from the Rumanian Front, to join the Red Army. Most soldiers responded to his appeal. In the first half of June Mironov had under his command a total of about four thousand men. But they were short on weapons—especially artillery and machine guns. At Mironov's insistence, I. A. Sdobnov, a friend of his childhood and youth, was named his chief of staff. Sdobnov too, since the first days of the October Revolution, had taken the side of the Soviet regime. A. G. Golikov was named commander of artillery for the Ust-Medveditsa War Zone.

After the fall of Rostov the government of the Don Soviet Republic had moved to Tsaritsyn, and then to the stanitsa of Velikoknyazheskaya. I. A. Doroshev was elected chairman of the SNK, and V. S. Kovalev remained chairman of the TsIK.

As early as June, Mironov's troops had carried out several successful operations. About this time defense operations in the south of the country were entrusted to the Military Commissar of the Northern Caucasus Military District (SKVO) and the staff of the Voronezh Sector of the Western Curtain. The chief of the SKVO staff in Tsaritsyn was one Nosovich, a former major general in the Tsarist Army. In the spring of 1918, this general had wanted to flee to the volunteer army. But the underground Moscow Section of the volunteer army instructed him to join the Red Army. Sent to Tsaritsyn as a military specialist, Nosovich also received instructions from anti-Soviet underground centers in Moscow to sabotage Bolshevism by every possible means. Later, after he had fled to join Denikin, Nosovich wrote in a report to him: "My chief function consisted in exposing to the Cossacks first one flank of the combat sector, then another (and in making everyone quarrel among themselves)."

But Mironov refused to carry out several clearly treasonous orders from Nosovich. In one battle, Mironov's detachments provided decisive support for the 1st Soviet Division under the command of V. I. Kikvidze, which had fallen into an extremely difficult position because it followed Nosovich's orders.

In late June the District Executive Committee called a congress of the stanitsy and volosts not yet taken by Krasnov's forces. This congress showed that as yet the Bolsheviks had very little influence among the Cossack population: the majority of the delegates were SR's, Mensheviks, or Cadets. The presidium of the congress raised the question of discontinuing the civil war and holding "peace talks" with Krasnov. A "peace delegation" was chosen, and went to White Guard command headquarters for talks. But at that time the White Cossacks were stepping up their pressure and artillery fire on Mikhailovka. On orders from Mironov, the settlement was declared in a state of siege, and the congress was dissolved.

This unsuccessful congress once again demonstrated the tremendous importance of explaining to the Cossacks the aims and tasks of the October Revolution and of the Soviet regime. And once again Mironov wrote letters to all the Cossacks of the Don Region, exposing Krasnov and calling upon the populace to support the Soviet regime. For example, when he learned of Krasnov's agreement with the German Command, he wrote a long "Open Letter" to the combat Cossacks and soldiers of the Don Region in which he said, *inter alia*:

This Cossack-German alliance was concluded by General Krasnov, formerly commanding officer of the 10th Regiment and then in command of the 2nd Cossack Composite Division.

In his Order No. 1 he says: "Our enemies of yesterday, the Austro-Germans, have crossed the frontiers of the Voisko—of our native Don Region. They are our allies against the Red Guard and for restoration of complete order on the Don."

This order means savagery and horror!

Cossacks! . . . If any of you agrees with General Krasnov that the Austro-Germans are our allies—for conquering us!—he is an ally of the Germans. There is no place for such a Cossack on the Don, among the stanitsy and villages we love so well. . . . I personally will surrender my weapons to General Krasnov and his German allies only along with my head, after having first had his head and those of the Germans . . . if the 32nd Regiment will help! . . .

In those districts of the Don Region occupied by the Germans, we now hear:

"Good day, Your Excellency!"

"Yes, Your Excellency!"

"No indeed, sir! . . . Quite so, Your Honor!"

"About face! . . . Forward march!"

Once again the Cossacks are under the general's lash and German drill. And with this comes servitude. . . .

Front-line Cossacks and front-line soldiers! Enough of sleeping! Enough of doubting! . . . Each moment of delay brings closer to our necks the yoke of the German General Krasnov—the yoke of the bourgeoisie! . . .

Forward, comrades of the front line, for the salvation of our native land and freedom! . . .

Commander of the Revolutionary Forces of the Ust-Medveditsa District, Citizen-Cossack P. Mironov.[2]

Mironov devoted special attention to stopping illegal searches and requisitioning among the Cossacks. When the inhabitants of the stanitsa of Archad told him of an illegal search, he promulgated "Order No. 8 to the Revolutionary Forces of the Ust-Medveditsa Front," which stated:

. . . I appeal to the comrades who committed this violence to reveal their names. In this way they will show that they committed the act out of inadvertency. And only in this way can they be pardoned in the name of the Revolution. . . . Some comrades have failed to realize the whole gist of the ideals of the Revolution. They take the liberty of using violence on peaceable inhabitants, which far from helping the toiling people actually brings ruin to them. It disgraces the name of the defenders of the Revolution and increases the number of the latter's enemies. If this is repeated, or if the comrades who committed the act do not reveal their names and those who know these madmen cover up for them, in six hours I shall divest myself of all authority and resign from the command of such an army.[3]

After this appeal, the guilty parties themselves came to Mironov's headquarters.

In his appeals, distributed by the thousands throughout the stanitsy and farms of the Don, Mironov cited instances of Krasnov's violence against ordinary Cossacks, of times he had deprived them of their rank and requisitioned livestock and grain. These appeals were an important influence in changing the mood of the ordinary Cossackry.

The crucial role played by Mironov in the fate of the Don Cossacks during the spring of 1918 is recorded in *And Quiet Flows the Don*. In the first edition of this novel, Part Six began with the words:

In April 1918 a great split took place in the Don Region. The combat Cossacks of the northern districts—the Khoper, Ust-Medveditsa, and partially the Upper Don—went with Mironov and the retreating units of the Red Guards, while those from the southern districts drove hard against the borders of the region. The Cossacks from the Khoper District went with Mironov almost to a man; those from the Ust-Medveditsa District to the extent of about half; and those from Upper Don in negligible numbers.

Describing the June battle in the northern districts of the Don Region, Sholokhov wrote:

> In the north the stanitsa of Ust-Medveditsa passed from hand to hand. First it was taken by Mironov with a detachment of Cossacks and Red Guards who had joined him from the villages of the Glazunovskaya, Novo-Aleksandrovskaya, Kumylzhenskaya, Skurishenskaya, and other stanitsy. But an hour later he was driven out by a detachment of White partisans under the officer Alekseyev. . . . In the north, Cossacks from the Upper Don District rolled like thunder from one stanitsa to another. Mironov retreated to the boundary of Saratov Province.

But in the editions of Sholokhov's novel which appeared after 1933, Mironov's name was deleted both from the passages quoted above and from many other passages of the novel.

In late June Krasnov's forces attacked. They cut the Povorino-Tsaritsyn railroad line and occupied several stanitsy, including Velikoknyazheskaya. Krasnov's chief aim was to take Tsaritsyn to cut off the central industrial regions of Soviet Russia from the southern regions and unite the forces of the counter-revolution in the east and south of the country. Through Nosovich's fault, Mironov's detachments had not received any weapons, but Mironov, nonetheless, began to prepare his forces for a mid-July attack. On July 18, in a battle near the village of Shashkin, one of Mironov's detachments destroyed a large unit of White Cossacks. Mironov was wounded by a shell fragment, but remained at his post directing the battle operations. The White Cossacks retreated with great losses, and many were taken prisoner.

Mironov ordered that the dead and wounded White Cossacks be loaded on carts and sent through the lines to the territory occupied by Krasnov's forces. He also ordered the release of all prisoners, who were instructed to accompany the carts. In the occupied stanitsy and villages Mironov held meetings and assemblies, after which individual Cossacks and entire squadrons came over to his detachments.

The attack on the Ust-Medveditsa sector considerably eased the situation in Tsaritsyn, since Krasnov was obliged to withdraw several regiments from the Tsaritsyn front to throw against Mironov. However, the staff of the SKVO, headed by Nosovich, did not support Mironov's operations, and forbade Kikvidze's division to go to the support of the Ust-Medveditsa front. After hard-fought battles Mironov's forces had to retreat, although heavy losses were inflicted on the enemy.

In his report to the SKVO staff, Mironov wrote:

> The results of my attack were tremendous. Before I had no cavalry. Now 450 Cossack cavalrymen who came over to our side are in forward positions facing the enemy. Among those who have joined me are 100 Cossack cavalrymen and 50 infantrymen from the villages of Krasny, Kozlov, Sedov, Pichugin, and others of the Novo-Aleksandrovskaya Stanitsa. These Cossacks are valuable not for their. quantity but for their quality. . . . They know that their property will be plundered by counter-revolutionary bands and their families tortured; yet they join the struggle for the toiling people. I now have a Cossack cavalry regiment consisting of four different draft contingents which must be armed with Maxim or Colt machine guns . . . upon which I urgently insist in the name of the Revolution.[4]

Mironov also reported both to Tsaritsyn and to Voronezh on some important repositionings of Krasnov's units—but neither the staff at Tsaritsyn nor at Voronezh paid attention.

The Red Army was lacking in experienced commanders, weapons, and ammunition. The majority of the units still had elected commanding officers. Frequently the orders of senior commanders were submitted to general meetings for discussion, and quite often rejected. Chaos also reigned in the higher echelons. For example, Mironov's group of forces was subordinated at times to the SKVO staff in Tsartisyn, at other times to the Military Council of the Voronezh Region. The Red Army had only just begun to make the transition from recruiting volunteers to mobilization, and many soldiers were poorly trained. On the other hand, General Krasnov led a well-organized force with many experienced officers. Also, the German Army sent several of its crack units to the Don Region and provided Krasnov with a large quantity of weapons and ammunition.

Mironov's great skill as a commander and his personal bravery were demonstrated in the July battles on the Ust-Medveditsa front. The Don counter-revolutionaries, however, were sparing no effort to discredit Mironov: he was described in print as a traitor, a bandit, a drunkard. A large price was placed on his head. In many of his speeches and orders General Krasnov demanded of his subordinates that "if they catch Mironov and Sdobnov" they should hang them without trial.[5] And yet Krasnov himself once said to some of his close acquaintances: "I have many officers, but not one Mironov."

Many rumors about Mironov were circulating among the commanders and commissars of the Red Army. Few knew of his revolutionary actions from before the October Revolution. But much emphasis was placed on his class status as a Cossack and his high military rank as a lieutenant colonel in the Tsarist Army. All this not only offended Mironov but hampered his work.

In late July the former Colonel Bagrationov, commanding officer of the 1st Frolov Soviet Division, went over to the Whites, acting on orders from Denikin's secret agents on the SKVO staff, Nosovich and A. N. Kovalevsky. This enabled Krasnov's forces to take the stanitsa of Archad, which put Mironov's forces, then responsible for the Ust-Medveditsa combat sector, in an extremely difficult position. Krasnov concentrated superior forces under the command of generals Fitskhalaurov and Kuznetsov against Mironov, and Mironov and Sdobnov telegraphed the Military Council of the Northern Caucasus District for help. Mironov also asked the Saratov Military Commissariat for reinforcements.

Not having received a reply from either Tsaritsyn or Saratov, Mironov sent a telegram to Trotsky, People's Commissar for Military and Naval Affairs. The telegram read:

Military. Top priority. To Military Commissar Trotsky. The situation of the Revolution on the Don is critical. General Krasnov is bending every effort to defeat me at the stanitsy of Archad and Sebryakovo. In this area the fight against the counter-revolutionaries is being carried on by mobilized soldiers and Cossacks from the district. The counter-revolutionaries have moved mobilized Cossacks from the

Cherkassk, First Don, Don, and Upper Don districts into this area. If the situation is saved here, it means saving the Revolution on the Don. To achieve this, we must give up the idea of combatting the counter-revolution with volunteer forces. It is imperative to recognize the principle of mobilization, and to declare it in the neighboring provinces of Saratov and Tambov. I request urgent instructions to send us reinforcements. Also to send us an aircraft and two armored cars by special train.

Front Commander Mironov. Chief of Staff Sdobnov.[6]

Mironov received no reply from Trotsky, but Podvoisky sent the following telegram:

Have just received reliable information that the forces pressing on you do not exceed 1,800. There is no regiment of Cherkess,* only groups. Cannot send reinforcements today, since we are strengthening Sivers, whose forces are battered. When this is done, we shall send reinforcements, but not for at least 36 hours. You must hold on.[7]

Mironov had just learned that his father had died, that for "betraying the Don" he, Philip Mironov, and his family had been deprived of their Cossack rank and all their property was confiscated. His wife and children were in hiding on a remote farm.

But there was no time to grieve or take offense: bitter fighting had broken out along almost the entire front around Mikhailovka. Mironov and Sdobnov fought a skillful defensive battle, but their situation weakened steadily. To make matters worse, the units of Mironov's forces were not wholly under the command of a single officer. In the squadrons, companies, and regiments, soldiers' committees were functioning. Pro-SR soldiers and Cossacks often ran the show in a number of regimental and company committees. They called upon the Red Army men not to carry out any orders without first discussing them at general meetings.

Furthermore, the idea of concluding an armistice with Krasnov's forces was being discussed among the men. A number of small subunits left their positions in midbattle and went over to the enemy.

---

* Ethnic Circassians.—Translator's note.

All of which left the forces under Mironov's command threatened with encirclement.

On July 30 Mironov issued the order to retreat, outlining the situation that had developed and pointing out the enemy's clear superiority in numbers and the threat of encirclement. The deadline of thirty-six hours specified in Podvoisky's telegram had long since expired, and no help had come from anywhere.

In his order, Mironov said:

> To remain in Mikhailovka at a time when the enemy is trying to throw an iron ring around it is unthinkable. . . . At this moment the counter-revolutionaries have taken several stanitsy in the rear and are effecting the mobilization of ten census lists [*perepisei*]. In order to prevent this, to establish contact with the Center of the Soviet Republic, and—most important—to deny the enemy an early opportunity of rushing his newly mobilized forces to the water artery (the Volga) and cutting off communications between Tsaritsyn and the Center, in the name of the Revolution I call upon all units to withdraw to the village of Bolshoi.[8]

The withdrawal was very difficult but was accomplished with few losses. The Red Army men were joined by refugees from Mikhailovka and other settlements and, together with the baggage train, this added up to about two thousand carts. In order to avoid battle under unfavorable conditions, they traveled at night and on back roads.

During their retreat toward Saratov Province, Mironov's detachments were renamed a brigade. On August 1, 1918, this new brigade counted seven battalions of infantry, six squadrons of cavalry, a battery of artillery, a machine-gun company, and a company of engineers. The brigade comprised 4,510 men, about 1,000 horses, 9 field pieces, and 20 machine guns. Thus during six weeks of fighting, the size and armament of Mironov's detachments had grown considerably.

The Red Army's abandonment of the Povorino-Tsaritsyn railroad line had complicated Tsaritsyn's situation, creating an encirclement threat for this strategic center in southern Soviet Russia. Lenin was extremely perturbed by the possibility of losing Tsaritsyn, for whose defense J. V. Stalin was responsible during those summer weeks. Stalin, however, was not really familiar with the general situation on the southern front at this time. He may also have been misinformed by such persons as Nosovich and Kovalevsky, who were secretly working for the defeat of the Red Army. In a letter to Lenin dated August 4, Stalin outlined the unfavorable situation which had developed in the south, saying it was due to:

1. The fact that the veteran, the "well-off muzhik," who in October was fighting for the Soviet regime, has now turned against the Soviet regime. (With all his soul he hates the grain monopoly, the fixed prices, the requisitions, and the struggle against the *meshochnichestvo.**)

2. The Cossack composition of Mironov's forces. (The Cossack units that call themselves Soviet cannot, and do not want to, wage a resolute struggle against the Cossack counter-revolution. Entire regiments of Cossacks have gone over to Mironov so that, after receiving weapons, they could familiarize themselves with the positioning of our units and then go back over to Krasnov, taking entire regiments with them. Mironov has three times been surrounded by Cossacks, since they knew everything about Mironov's sector and—naturally—crushed him.)

3. The detachment structure of Kikvidze's units, which leaves no possibility for communications or the coordination of actions.

4. The isolation—resulting from all this—of Sivers's units, which have lost support on the left flank.[9]

Everything Stalin said about Mironov's forces was based on a patent misconception. Mironov and his detachments were not crushed: they had retreated in orderly fashion, after first having worn out the enemy in strenuous battles.

Stalin had introduced a myth about Mironov that became firmly implanted in the minds of many high-ranking military and political

---

* Petty speculators in grain and produce, which was carried around in a bag (*meshok*)—hence the sobriquet.—Translator's note.

workers. In June and July of 1918, Mironov's forces had received no reinforcements or weapons, although they were supplied to Kikvidze's division (for example) in rather large quantities. And there were instances when Mironov had no weapons to furnish to Cossacks who had come over to his side; they had to be sent off to their homes.

As Krasnov's forces advanced, Mironov's troops were directed to defend the much-sought-after railroad lines from Elan-Kamyshin to Krasnyi Yar. But Mironov, realizing that the chief aim of Krasnov's army was to take Tsaritsyn, proposed to Podvoisky that he organize vigorous offensive operations in this area.

The enemy forces facing us [he wrote to Podvoisky] are such that we should launch an attack against him all along our front so as to compel those forces moving on Tsaritsyn to withdraw back to the north, and those moving on Povorino to pull back to the south and east. After all, he has only a curtain-zone in front of him; and we too are trying only to cover ourselves with a curtain-zone rather than trying to expose his forces in front of us. This is an impardonable mistake. On the basis of personal observation I have reached the necessary conclusion that in a few days we must attack in order to ascertain his forces in this area, and to draw him toward us. . . . I take the liberty of informing you that the tactic of fighting without leaving the railroad is extremely harmful and dangerous, and that passive defensive warfare will never lead to victory. . . .

In the name of the Revolution I ask you to consider my detachment always ready for combat. But I also ask you not to fragment it, so as not to put me and my comrades in a position inviting defeat. Do not refuse to send reinforcements of two battalions or more, so that I can deal a strong blow to the enemy. . . . Please believe that I have a wealth of experience which was appreciated by the high command of the old regime, and that it pains me to see the counter-revolution triumph because of our blunders and lack of talent. . . .

Brigade Commander Mironov[10]

But Mironov did not get the help he asked for. Podvoisky, obviously irritated by Mironov's sharp criticism, sent him the following telegram:

Sebryakovo. To Mironov. I suggest that you not overload the telegraph with superfluous words and reply accurately and briefly to questions. Under autocracy you could do and say what you wanted. But today you are obliged to obey without demur the representatives of the Worker-Peasant Soviet Regime, and not to take the liberty of using expressions which are inadmissible vis-à-vis members of the government.[11]

Mironov, not to be outdone, likewise sent Podvoisky a very sharp telegram. Needless to say, this skirmish only harmed the common cause.

Although he had not received reinforcements, Mironov decided to organize an attack in his sector on his own, without violating the order to defend the railroad line. The attack was launched on August 9 and developed successfully. Mironov's brigade—in a battle that lasted three days—crushed the Krasnovite units opposing it and took several populated areas, including the settlement of Orekhovka. Hundreds of enemy soldiers and Cossacks were killed and wounded, and more than a hundred Cossacks were taken prisoner. As he had done before in battles with the Cossacks, Mironov assembled the prisoners and made an impassioned speech to them, calling upon them to discontinue the fratricidal civil war. The prisoners were given copies of an appeal to the working Cossacks signed by Lenin, Sverdlov, Makarov, and Danilov—the last two being members of the Cossack Committee of the VTsIK. Once again Mironov ordered that carts be provided to carry the dead and wounded, and that prisoners accompany them back to the position of the Krasnovite units. As they were leaving, he told them: "You can tell all Cossacks about everything you heard here."

The successful operations of Mironov's brigade (which Stalin had thought was crushed) caused great alarm at Krasnov's headquarters. Several Cossack regiments were withdrawn from the Tsaritsyn-Kamyshin sector and thrown against Mironov. Mironov's brigade defended itself vigorously against the superior enemy forces. But his repeated requests for reinforcements went unanswered. He received conflicting telegrams from Charnavin and

Podvoisky, as well as from Sytin, all of whom misconstrued the situation in the forward areas.

Among the rank-and-file Cossacks of Krasnov's units, Mironov's popularity had grown. He had escaped the most difficult situations; and far from shooting Cossack prisoners, he had sent them back to their units. Moreover, the Don Cossacks did not want to fight outside the boundaries of their own region. In Krasnov's Cossack regiments, discipline weakened and desertions increased. Many Cossacks went home or went over to Mironov. On September 2, Mironov took advantage of this mood and ordered his brigade to launch a new attack. In six days of fighting he was able to move ahead well, again taking the settlements of Orekhovka and Danilovka, and many other populated areas. Hundreds of Cossacks, including Mironichev, commanding officer of the 12th Cossack Regiment, went over to Mironov.

The demoralization of the White Cossacks was also indicated by a telegram from Fitskhalaurov dated August 21, 1918, in which he stated, *inter alia*:

. . . During the taking of Orekhovka, at a time when troops of General Tatarkin's cavalry detachment were supposed to deal a decisive, final blow to Mironov, Cossacks from the stanitsy of Razdorskaya, Malodelskaya, Sergeyevskaya, and Eterevskaya refused to follow orders. And within the hearing of their commanders, a number of Cossacks shouted: "Long live Mironov!" During a decisive engagement these same Cossacks told their officers they didn't see why they should fight against Mironov; that they had lived well under Mironov; that the officers should make the attack, since they needed it more. The Cossacks from the stanitsy of Ilovlya and Kachal [Kalach?]—both the World War veterans and the "old men"—manifested even more insolence and treason toward our units. They said they did not know what they were fighting for; that they had a better life with the Red Guard; and they behaved in a provocatory manner toward our forces. I request that you report the foregoing to the Great Voisko Circle immediately, and take appropriate steps against such traitors to our entire Cossack population.[12]

On September 14 Mironov's brigade renewed the attack and inflicted great losses on the enemy, capturing many prisoners and much matériel in three days of fighting. The brigade suffered losses of its own in these battles, and certain sub-units went over to the Krasnovite side, but as a whole the brigade grew in size, from defections of Krasnovites. Mironov had also received permission to mobilize in the volosts, villages, and stanitsy occupied by the brigade, so that by September it had 7,500 men, 18 field pieces, and 40 machine guns. The brigade was renamed the 1st Mironov Medveditsa Soviet Division.[13]

Meanwhile, Red Army units dealt a crushing defeat to Krasnov's forces near Tsaritsyn. The Soviet forces advanced into the Tsaritsyn area, capturing the stanitsa of Ilovlya in the northern sector of the front, together with Kalach in the west. Soviet troops moved forward in the southern sector as well and the Don Cossack Army had to withdraw to the Don.

On September 28 the presidium of the VTsIK awarded Mironov the Order of the Red Banner for distinguishing himself in battle. Mironov was the third Soviet commander to be given this award.[14]

That autumn the Soviet government and the Communist Party concentrated on creating a combat-ready Red Army. The changeover from a volunteer army to military mobilization was made everywhere, rapidly increasing the size of the Red Army. A Revolutionary Military Council (RVS) of the Republic was created with Leon Trotsky at its head. Along with many active Party workers, thousands of military specialists from the old Tsarist Army were brought in to work in the Red Army. These latter constituted the basic staff cadres of the new army. Clear lines were drawn among the fronts. The numerous ill-assorted detachments and armed groups were formed into regiments, divisions, and armies. Strict measures were taken to strengthen discipline in the army and eliminate vestiges of partisan-style warfare.

For example, the RVS of the Republic ordered the formation of a southern front, to include the formations of the Bryansk, Kursk, Voronezh, Povorino, and Balashov-Kamyshin sectors, the forces of the SKVO, and of the Astrakhan Group. All military sub-units in these sectors were combined into five armies. Mironov's division was made a part of the 9th Army, under the command of Party worker Knyagnitsky. The chief of staff of this army was the former Colonel Vsevolodov, a member of a secret White Guard organization.

Krasnov's losses in September 1918 were not decisive. By mid-October Krasnov and Denisov had regrouped and strengthened their army, and again went on the attack, aiming to capture Tsaritsyn. Also, General Denikin's volunteer army won some important victories in the Northern Caucasus. As early as August 1918, Denikin's forces had taken Ekaterinodar and Novocherkassk. After some difficult battles, the volunteer army managed to advance farther to the east, taking Grozny and Vladikavkaz and surrounding Stavropol. The 11th Army, operating in this area, had to retreat with heavy losses.

In the autumn months of 1918 Germany suffered several major defeats on its western front. Revolution was imminent in Germany and morale among German troops occupying the Ukraine, the Don, the Crimea, and part of the Caucasus was withering. But the Entente nations began extensive activities in the south of Russia. England and France had assembled large forces to expand the intervention against Soviet Russia. Mironov's division, now named the 23rd Infantry Division, continued fighting fiercely throughout October in Ust-Medveditsa. But among the command staffs and units of the Red Army, there were still quite a few former officers who were secretly collaborating with the White Guard. Attacks launched against Krasnov failed and, in fact, the White Cossacks managed to capture the town of Borisoglebsk and the Liski railroad station. A critical situation now existed along the entire front. On the southern front, the Voronezh area was extremely unstable; commanders did not execute orders, troops deserted and morale was low. Although Mironov regularly supplied headquarters with information on the disposition of his forces, Vsevolodov, chief of staff and a man who was later to prove himself a traitor, never acknowledged receiving them. Mironov, in turn, disputed orders that were either impossible to execute or would place his division in an extremely difficult position. This hardly increased his popularity with the RVS and the staff. Mironov's dissatisfaction culminated in his telegraphing Trotsky on December 9: "Imperative we discuss the question of combatting the counter-revolution, but I cannot leave the division. Request you visit the division."[15] Trotsky did not come; but he summoned Mironov to Headquarters. Commissar Kovalev went in Mironov's place and spent ten days at Headquarters "weathering a great battle with Trotsky." Kovalev was convinced that Trotsky, like many other military leaders of those days, distrusted Mironov.

In late November and early December, despite all the shortcomings in the leadership of the army, Mironov's division, acting jointly with Kikvidze's division, carried out several vigorous offensive operations. In a battle lasting many days that developed in their sectors, they delivered the White Cossacks a stiff defeat, overrunning White positions all along a large front. Mironov's division took many prisoners, predominantly Cossacks from Miguli, Kargi, and Veshenskaya. Mironov called upon the prisoners to stop fighting the Red Army and disperse to their homes. After a talk with Mironov, the commanding officer of the 28th Cossack Regiment agreed to leave the front with his entire regiment. This episode was decisive in changing Cossack attitudes in the sectors of the 8th and 9th armies. Those Cossacks who returned from Mironov's "imprisonment" began to agitate vigorously for discontinuing the civil war.

In December 1918 the entire southern front made ready for a decisive attack against the Don Army. The armies of the front received considerable reinforcements—troops, commanding officers, and political workers—and additional equipment and ammunition. Lenin issued a directive to the RVS in which he said: ". . . nothing for the west, a little for the east, and everything (almost) for the south."[16]

In December the position of Soviet Russia eased considerably. A revolution had begun in Germany, and the regime of the Kaiser was overthrown. Accepting defeat, Germany concluded an armistice on the western front. German units were leaving the territory of the

Don, the Caucasus, the Ukraine, the Crimea, Belorussia, and the
Baltic area. The Soviet government denounced the Treaty of
Brest-Litovsk, Krasnov's army was no longer being supplied with
German weapons and ammunition. To the leaders and representatives of the Entente, Krasnov began to send one message after another, begging England and France to send equipment, weapons,
uniforms, and money to the Don and also three or four army corps,
promising to "liberate" all of Russia in three or four months. He
proposed the immediate dispatch to Novocherkassk of "skilled generals of French, British, or American forces so that they could visit
the fronts and look over the troops; so that they could get a correct
notion both of the Don Army and of the very nature of the struggle
against Bolshevism."[17]

The Entente did not object to helping the Don Army, but the
Allies insisted on combining all of the White Guard armies in the
south of Russia under the command of Denikin, the representative,
in British opinion, of the Russian armies operating against the Bolsheviks.

Discord between the White generals and the delay in obtaining
aid from the Entente created a favorable moment for launching
a general attack on the southern front. Moreover, the many months
of heavy fighting against the Red Army, which by the end of the
year was numerically superior to the White armies in the south,
influenced the loyalties of the Cossacks—especially in the poorer
northern districts of the Don Region. In April and May of 1918
many Cossacks of the Khoper and Ust-Medveditsa districts, and
some of those from the Upper Don District, had left the Red Army.
These men were now again fighting in its ranks.

Further to encourage Cossacks to join the Red Army, Trotsky,
chairman of the Revolutionary Military Council of the Republic,
signed an appeal especially aimed at the officers of Krasnov's and
Denikin's armies.

The forces of Krasnov and Denikin have reached a dead end. Thousands of inexperienced and politically immature officers, addicted to old

bourgeois-monarchist prejudices, at first believed Krasnov's talk about patriotism and saving the country, and followed him. He used them to create special officers' units, converting them into gendarmes with whose help he exacted obedience from mobilized Cossacks and soldiers. The Cossacks are perishing, the mobilized peasants (often half naked) are perishing, the officers deceived by Krasnov are perishing. Today a considerable part of them have realized that they have reached a dead end. Many of them would be willing to leave the plague-infected Krasnov camp and come back to Soviet Russia with their heads hanging low. But they fear the just reprisals of the revolutionary regime—they fear vengeance for the blood they have spilled. Unquestionably, their crimes are great. . . . But the revolutionary people is magnanimous toward those of its enemies who have acknowledged their crimes before the people and are ready not only to lay down their arms but to serve honorably in the ranks of laboring Russia. . . .

In the name of the supreme military authority of the Soviet Republic I declare: every officer who, either individually or at the head of his unit, voluntarily comes over to us from the Krasnovite camp, will be exempted from punishment. If he shows by his actions that he is ready honorably to serve the people in either a military or a civilian capacity, he will find a place in our ranks.

Down with the traitor Krasnov, who has deceived the toiling Cossacks—who has deceived many former officers!

Long live peaceful collaboration among workers, peasants, toiling Cossacks, and all honorable citizens who regardless of their past are ready to serve the people selflessly![18]

But it was Philip Mironov who, on the eve of the decisive battles on the southern front, wrote an especially large number of appeals to the Cossacks. Thousands of these leaflets were disseminated among the Krasnovite Cossacks. According to subsequent acknowledgments by the generals and other officers of Krasnov's army, Mironov's letters and appeals had a substantial effect on the morale of that army. Mironov's appeals were directed not only to the Cossacks in Krasnov's army overall, but also to specific individual units. For example, in one appeal he said:

Brother Cossacks of the Bokovo-Kargi Regiment, it is time to come to your senses. It is time to stack your rifles and talk, not in the language of those rifles but in the human tongue—the same one in which each of us talks with his dear ones. . . . Let's remember the Carpathians, the Dvina, the Pinsk Swamps, the Germans, the Austrians, the Bulgarians, the Turks, the Hungarians . . . We fought hard against them, but we all asked from time to time: When will this damned war end? When will we get home to our dear ones? And those with a little more sense asked: Why is the German, let's say, or the Bulgarian my enemy? Did he take something from me? Or I from him? Or was the earth too crowded for us? From the day we were born we had never seen each other. And we never would have seen each other all our lives. But somebody dragged us toward each other, put rifles in our hands, and commanded "Fire!" Tens of millions of people perished from that "Fire!" And other tens of millions were left cripples. . . . Human blood flowed for more than four years. The first ones to wake up from that trance were we Russians. And we grabbed the Tsar—the main culprit in the war, and the number one landowner in Russia—and we gave it to him! We breathed easily during those first days, but the remaining landowners and capitalists did not relax. They had to accumulate more gold out of human blood. Up popped Kerensky, the errand boy of the capitalists, shouting that the war should be fought to a victorious end. And up popped generals Kornilov, Kaledin, and the other loyal allies of Kerensky and the bourgeoisie. But the Bolsheviks, the Party of the people, who served neither capital nor the generals but the really poor people of the countryside, were not napping. In 1914 this Party was against the war; but at that time it was weak. It took a revolution to make people open their eyes. And when they opened their eyes they saw that the Bolsheviks were right, and they went along with them. That's why we are strong. . . . When they had ended the war, the Bolsheviks went after the main culprits in the war: the landowners, the capitalists, the generals, and the priests. They took away all the landowners' land and turned it over, without compensation, to the toiling people. They took away all the capitalists' money, plants, and factories, and declared it the property of the people. And not only that: all those debts to foreign capitalists that the Tsar had heaped on the neck of his "loyal" people were declared by them to be canceled (i.e., abolished); and they refused to pay them. . . . Then General Krasnov, in order to save the landowners' land and the capitalists' money, and his own power, under the pretext of saving Russia—which had allegedly perished at the hands of the Bolsheviks—called the Germans into the Don Region. Russia had indeed perished, but what Russia? Tsarist Russia. The Russia of the landowners. The Russia of the generals. The Russia of the priests and the noblemen. But our toiling Russia—peasant and Cossack Russia—is alive and will live for a long time if you, dear fellow Cossacks, come to your senses and help to suppress the generals, the landowners, and the entire bourgeoisie.

Those scoundrels did not succeed in continuing the war for the interests of capital, so they started one on the Don. The Germans spent several months in our country. They hung around in the midst of the Russian Revolution, and their eyes were opened. They saw that among them, too, the Tsar, the capitalists, and the landowners were the ones to blame for the war. And they threw them out of their suffering country. . . . So change your minds, brother Cossacks, before it's too late. Do you really want to fight the whole world? Haven't you had enough? We're not your enemies; those who command you are. . . .

I hereby issue a call to all officers, promising immunity in the name of the Revolution. And to those who sincerely repent, I promise service. Service to the people, and not to capital. Citizen officers! Enough of deceiving yourselves and deceiving the Cossacks! . . . The Allies will not come to your aid. The workers' revolution is breaking out everywhere. . . .

Come to your senses, men of Bokovskaya and Kargi. It is still not too late. There is still time to redeem your terrible sin of rebellion in May 1918 and put out the fire.[19]

As early as December 1918, a change in morale among the poorer Cossacks was increasingly manifest: troops were refusing to carry out the orders of Krasnov's officers. In late December, in the region of Boguchar, several Cossack units left the White front and dispersed to their homes.

On December 30, 1918, K. Mekhanoshin, a member of the RVS of the Southern Front, reported to the RVS of the Republic:

Available information on the Don Army indicates that its demoralization is progressing rapidly, lowering its fighting efficiency day by day. We are now encountering only isolated offensive operations in those areas where a small group of punitive detachments is concentrated. The other Cossacks fight under pressure from them, and only within the territory of the Don Region. But with each passing day the ranks of these detachments are thinning, and their influence over the other Cossack regiments is weakening. There can be no question of reviving the old spirit of the Don, since their leader, Krasnov, does not have a broad base of authority.

Mekhanoshin further stated that the Cossacks were refusing to be drafted, despite strict punitive measures, and that on certain sectors of the front desertion had become a mass phenomenon.[20]

In the early days of January 1919 seven stanitsy, headed by Veshenskaya, rose up against Krasnov and massacred their officers. On January 5 a stanitsa assembly in Veshenskaya voted to send a delegation for talks, to disband the punitive detachments, and to release those arrested under Krasnov's rule. The 28th Don Cossack Regiment abandoned its position near Kalach and went to Veshenskaya to find Krasnov and deal with him. Order No. 1 issued by this regiment and the stanitsa of Veshenskaya stated that the working Cossacks were taking power into their own hands, and that their first goal was to destroy the nest of traitors, plunderers, and bandits—the Krasnovites.

The situation in the south had plainly developed in favor of the Red Army; and the RVS of the Republic issued an order to launch a new general attack against the Don Cossack Army.

At this time, Mironov, while retaining control of his 23rd Division, was also named commander of the 16th; the 15th Division was subordinated to him as well. Thus a group of shock troops was created in the 9th Army—soldiers who formed the advance guard of a developing attack. On January 17, Mironov's group broke through into the Whites' rear area and, after defeating them, took the stanitsa of Uryupinsk. Having cut off sizable units of Whites between Filonovo and Borisoglebsk, his troops then advanced rapidly toward the south along both banks of the Khoper River, mopping up the Krasnovites in the Khoper and Ust-Medveditsa districts and gaining a bitter victory at the stanitsa of Skosyrskaya.

Krasnov at this time was issuing slanderous bulletins against Mironov in an attempt to sully his reputation. Although the Red Army's advance through the Cossack regions was accompanied by some excesses—illegal requisitioning, and outbreaks of bitterness and violence—a minimum of such incidents occurred in the areas where Mironov's shock group was operating. As in previous battles, Mironov, true to his word, had ordered all Cossack POW's to disperse to their homes. In one of his orders he wrote:

For the triumph and strengthening of the Revolution, I demand that all Red Army men and officers deal humanely with the local inhabitants. I prohibit arbitrary requisitioning, plundering, and violence of any kind. Please do not stain the red banner of labor. All those committing acts of violence will be punished immediately.[21]

Although it had been defeated in the northern sectors of its front and had almost entirely lost the Khoper and Ust-Medveditsa districts, the Don White Cossack Army continued its advance on Tsaritsyn, striving to swing the balance in its favor by capturing this very important strategic center. By mid-January the White Cossacks had reached the approaches to Tsaritsyn. Krasnov's artillery shelled the outskirts of the city, and some units crossed on the ice to the left bank of the Volga. Units of the 10th Army offered strong resistance, but the situation was becoming steadily more critical. Then Mironov's shock group, advancing rapidly, crossed the Don and together with other units of the 9th Army moved deep into the Don Region. The rear of the Tsaritsyn group of White Cossacks was threatened. Krasnov had to pull back many of his crack regiments and throw them against Mironov's advancing units. This created favorable conditions for the 10th Army in Tsaritsyn to attack. Its assault was launched in mid-February and developed successfully, with the divisions under B. M. Dumenko and D. P. Zhloba especially distinguishing themselves.*

The fact that units had been pulled back from Tsaritsyn and thrown against Mironov's divisions did not stop the latter's rapid advance. By the end of February, in several sectors of the front, Mironov's divisions had crossed the northern Donets, and the staff of the composite group made preparations for an attack on the capital of the region, Novocherkassk.

The collapse of the White front on the Don is confirmed by

---

* S. M. Budenny commanded a brigade in Dumenko's Composite Cavalry Division and distinguished himself by his boldness and resourcefulness. But published studies of recent years have unjustifiably ascribed all the successes of this division to Budenny's leadership.

many documents from the defeated side. On February 2, 1919, General Krasnov wrote to General Denikin:

Under the influence of malicious propaganda put out by the Bolsheviks from the north . . . the northern front of the Don Army is rapidly collapsing. Units under Major General Savateyev are withdrawing to the Don, Archada, and Medveditsa rivers without offering any resistance. The officers are again spreading terror with arrests, tearing off epaulets, and violence. The exhaustion of ten months of fighting in the complete isolation of the northern front, the bitter cold waves of these months, the snowstorms, the deep snow, and the lack of footwear and warm clothing have completed their job of demoralizing the Cossack masses. The poison of mistrust has become too strong. In the best case, troops take their arms and go home. In the worst case, they go over to "Comrade Mironov," who promises them the paradise of the Soviet regime and heaps of gold. If this fire spreads beyond the Don—where, in the Donets, the First Don, the Second Don, and (especially) the Taganrog districts there is more than enough combustible material among the peasant masses—by March we will be back where we started a year ago, and a year of bloody fighting will be reduced to nothing.
Your Excellency, we are at the breaking point! If help is not furnished to the Don now, I am afraid that it will be so shattered by my enemies that in the spring it will be necessary to use foreign forces to win the Don back from Mironov.[22]

In his memoirs, General Denikin wrote:

The Don Army, which had reached Liski and Kamyshin demoralized and completely disorganized, was in full retreat toward the northern Donets and the Sal. The feeling of fatigue and hopelessness affected not only the Cossacks but even a part of the Don intelligentsia. The Soviet forces were advancing almost without stopping, moving on Novocherkassk. The Circle, the ataman, and the government pointed out the mortal danger threatening the Don and asked for help. . . . In December 1918 the Don Army had more than 50,000 men, but only 15,000 retreated beyond the Donets. The Reds applied increasing pressure in the direction of Novocherkassk; and by February they had already crossed the Donets in several places between the Don and the Southeastern Railroad.[23]

The defeat of the Don Army and its retreat beyond the Donets created the impression in the Republic RVS that a decisive victory had been won on the southern front. Speaking in late February in the Palace of the Union in Moscow, Leon Trotsky bluntly declared that February had been a decisive month and that Krasnov's army was almost nonexistent. Many of the reserve troops intended for the southern front were shifted to Petrograd to oppose the troops of General Yudenich. Most of the orders for greatcoats and uniforms for the southern front were reissued for the eastern front.

But it soon became clear that Trotsky's optimistic declarations were premature. In January, in the Northern Caucasus, the volunteer army had dealt a crushing defeat to the units of the 11th Army operating in this area. Denikin had succeeded in dismembering this army and breaking up its leadership. In the winter, its remnants began to retreat across the barren steppes toward Astrakhan. Only a minority of the troops survived the march. Most of them perished from typhus, the freezing cold, or the enemy's bullets. In January 1919 G. K. Ordzhonikidze, Extraordinary Commissar for the South of Russia, reported to Lenin that the 11th Army no longer existed.

Having taken the entire North Caucasus, Denikin began to transfer his crack units to the Don. On February 14, Denikin came to Novocherkassk to attend a meeting of the Great Voisko Circle. The delegates to the Circle, having discussed the situation on the Don, expressed their lack of trust in General Denisov, commanding the Don Army, and General Polyakov, his chief of staff, and demanded their removal. When Krasnov declared he could not work without Denisov and Polyakov, the Voisko Circle decided to remove him from his position as Don ataman. General Bogayevsky was elected as the new Don ataman, and General Sidorin became commander of the Don Army. Previously, that army had refused to recognize the authority of Denikin. But as early as January it recognized him as Supreme Commander of all White forces in the south of Russia. Both Bogayevsky and Sidorin were advocates of joining forces with the volunteer army. The Voisko Circle also recognized the supreme authority of Kolchak and his so-called Russian government. This put an end to the "independent and sovereign Don government." Under the command of the new generals, the Don Army began to put itself in order.

In late February a thaw settled on the Don. Roads were washed out, and the ice began breaking up on the northern Donets. All bridges and other means of crossing the Don had been destroyed by the Whites in their retreat. The Red Army's advance was stalled and the White Cossacks regrouped to build up their forces. Also, there was a sharp increase in aid furnished by the Entente to the White Guard armies in the south. Weapons and ammunition were sent to the Don, and the volunteer army shifted most of its troops to that region. Everything testified to the fact that the decisive battle between the Red Army and the White armies in the south was still in the future. And just when the units of the Red Army were preparing to renew their temporarily halted attack, the shock group of the 9th Army, which had advanced farthest and was only one or two days' march from Novocherkassk, received an order: Philip Mironov was to give up his command and report for duty at General Headquarters; i.e., with Trotsky.

During the civil war the personality of a commander often had great significance, since in many cases a detachment previously formed by that commander served as the basis for a brigade or division. This certainly applied to the 23rd Division, which in the 9th Army was called "Mironov's Division." Mironov's troops had great faith in their commander and responded to his leadership. Mironov also enjoyed considerable popularity and authority among other units of the 9th Army's shock group. Under these conditions, the transfer or replacement of a commander had to be especially well-grounded to avoid a sharp drop in his unit's efficiency. It is therefore pertinent for us to examine the reasons for Mironov's removal from the 9th Army shock group command at one of the most decisive moments of military operations in the south.

Let us consult the record.

As he advanced toward the south, Mironov was supposed to appoint military commandants in the liberated districts and stanitsy. But at that very time the political organs of the army and the Party leadership in the region were selecting—in the liberated districts, stanitsy, and villages—military revolutionary committees or revkoms which had great powers. For example, comrades Savostyanov, Fedortsev, and Ruzanov were appointed to the revkom in the Ust-Medveditsa District. These Communists had served well in establishing the Soviet regime on the Don in 1918. But their incompetence on the front led to several conflicts between Mironov, military commissar of the Ust-Medveditsa District, and the district executive committee in the first months of 1918. After the retreat from the Don in summer 1918, Savostyanov panicked and called for the disbandment of all units of the Red Army. This elicited a sharp rebuke from Mironov. Fedortsev and Ruzanov, assigned to one of Mironov's units, left his brigade, and Mironov considered them deserters. It is therefore not surprising that when he learned of the proposed membership of the Ust-Medveditsa Revkom, Mironov sent the following telegram to the RVS of the Southern Front on February 11, 1919:

The entire Ust-Medveditsa District, with the exception of two or three stanitsy and volosts, has been cleared of counter-revolutionary bands. The situation requires the immediate restoration of revolutionary authority to regulate the political and economic life of the district. In view of this I request the appointment, as extraordinary district commandant, of Comrade Karpov (a Communist), deputy chief of staff of the 23rd Division, who is temporarily filling that position. Comrades Savostyanov, Fedortsev, and Ruzanov, proposed by Division Political Commissar Dyachenko, cannot be given authority in the district because of the way they behaved at a critical moment in the Revolution. Today the Revolution is strong. All the sluggards are crawling out into the sunlight, and making blotches on it.[24]

But Mironov's telegram had no effect: the previously designated district revkom was approved by the RVS of the Front, and the Donburo of the RKP(b). (This bureau had been created in 1918 to direct the underground activity of Bolshevik organizations on the Don.) Later S. Syrtsov, chairman of the Donburo, wrote in one of his notes for a report:

The work of the revkom of the Ust-Medveditsa region, which consists of three members (Fedortsev, Ruzanov, Savostyanov), has gone very badly. In terms of their abilities and outlook, these local workers were poorly qualified for responsible work. But the complete lack of workers in the Ust-Medveditsa region made it necessary to settle for them.[25]

The confirmation of Fedortsev, Ruzanov, and Savostyanov as the members of the revkom in the district liberated by Mironov's units set the stage for a conflict between Mironov, commanding the shock group, and the Ust-Medveditsa Revkom.

The conflict broke out after Mironov appointed Comrade Danilov as military commissar in Ust-Medveditsa. In the rear of the army in the field, the military commissar was supposed to deal with the military units' requirements. Though he was appointed by the troop commander, his success depended upon cooperation with the revkom. However, the Ust-Medveditsa District Revkom demanded the replacement of Danilov because, they alleged, he was "spineless" and lacking in foresight. Fedortsev, chairman of the revkom, proposed that a local Communist, Ivan Biryukov, be named temporary military commissar instead. A telegram containing this proposal was sent to the RVS of the Southern Front, with a copy to Mironov. When he received it, Mironov exploded. In his reply to Fedortsev he said:

I request that you not meddle in my affairs, but together with Savostyanov and Ruzanov come to the front and take up a rifle, as deserters from the front, and help beat the enemy. Ten poods of sugar have been found in Biryukov's possession—something that disturbs the local inhabitants. Your recommendation was a bad one. I have seen both you and Rudnev drunk, and you aren't even thinking of overcoming that drunkenness.

Group Commander Mironov[26]

At the same time I. Sdobnov, chief of staff of the 23rd Division, sent Fedortsev a telegram with a formal order to come from Mikhailovka to Ust-Medveditsa and "bring with you all instructions for organizing authority in the district." It should be noted that Mironov had formal grounds for intervening in the

activity of the local revkom. In October 1918 a district congress
had been held in the settlement of Danilovka. It was attended by
representatives of the northern stanitsy, villages, and settlements
of the Ust-Medveditsa District, and representatives of several
thousand deserters from this district and from military units of
the 23rd Division. Mironov was among those elected to the executive committee at this congress; and the congress entrusted him,
after the capture of Mikhailovka and Ust-Medveditsa, with the
restoration of the Soviet regime in these regions.

Fedortsev, however, refused to report to Mironov. His reply
was as follows:

> To Comrade Mironov. In reply to your telegraphed order to come
> to Ust-Medveditsa from Mikhailovka, the revkom states for your infor-
> mation that it has been appointed by the Political Department of the
> Southern Front and the Donburo of the RKP(b), to which it is entirely
> subordinate, and that only those orders and instructions originating from
> the aforementioned organizations are binding upon the revkom.[27]

But Mironov was unwilling to see people he considered inept
holding power in his home district. Impetuously, he sent Fedortsev
the following telegram:

> In the name of the Socialist Revolution I protest against your re-
> maining in power—along with Ruzanov and others—and demand that
> you report to me at headquarters. If this order is not complied with, I
> shall subject you and your people to personal arrest, and then I shall
> take up this matter with the staff of the 9th Army and with all those
> authorities to which you refer. Beware of the Revolution. It will not
> forgive you those moments you remember all too well. Once again I
> order you to report.
>
> Group Commander Mironov[28]

As was to be expected, the revkom filed a complaint against
Mironov with the Donburo and the Political Department of the
Southern Front. Naturally, the situation required an investigation
into the nature and causes of this conflict. There were a great many
such conflicts, inevitable under conditions of a civil war, between

commanders of Red Army combat units and local authorities. But the Donburo and the RVS of the Southern Front immediately took the side of the revkom without making any investigation. Moreover, Syrtsov asked Trotsky to remove Mironov from the Don Region, hinting that Mironov, as a Cossack, could not fight unreservedly against the White Cossacks. This was patent slander, since Mironov's units had particularly distinguished themselves in the winter battles on the Don. I. Khodorovsky and V. Gittis, members of the RVS of the Southern Front, also requested that Trotsky "get Mironov away from his native stanitsy and send him to another front, even if he has to be promoted." At the same time, they sent the following letter to the RVS of the 9th Army:

> Mironov, commanding the 23rd Division, with the evident approval of Political Commissar Butago, who signed his messages to the revkom, disregarding Instructions ##178, 195, and 225 of the RVS of the Southern Front, has crudely meddled in and hampered the affairs of the Ust-Medveditsa Revkom. He has protested against the authority of the revkom, and has demanded that members of the revkom report to headquarters to explain themselves, threatening in the event of noncompliance to subject the entire group to personal arrest. Mironov is unfamiliar with the work of the revkom. His behavior, and especially that of the political commissar, is helping to strengthen the counterrevolution. Take immediate steps to create normal conditions for the work of the revkom. Issue the appropriate instructions to Butago, explaining the inadmissibility of his behavior. Report on the results. . . .[29]

The request from Khodorovsky and Gittis to transfer Mironov from his native stanitsy, "even if he has to be promoted," revealed the real reasons for the removal of Mironov from command of the 9th Army's shock group. It was precisely during these weeks that the policy of "decossackization," with all its frightful consequences, was implemented in the liberated territory of the Don Region behind the field armies. Those who initiated and carried out this policy quite rightly assumed that Mironov would never go along with it. And they were striving to see that this popular commander was removed "away from his native stanitsy."

Trotsky's telegram ordering Mironov to report immediately to

General Headquarters was sent on February 18. But Knyagnitsky, commanding the 9th Army, held it up at his headquarters for ten days. He could not make up his mind to forward Trotsky's order to Mironov, whose group was then carrying out difficult offensive operations. G. Sokolnikov, a member of the RVS of the Southern Front and of the TsK RKP(b), also protested against Mironov's transfer. In a conversation with Knyagnitsky over the direct wire Sokolnikov said:

> I ask you to send Trotsky the following telegram in my name: "Upon returning from the front, I learned that Mironov, commanding the 23rd Division, had been summoned by the supreme commander for a new assignment. I categorically state that the departure of the division commander at the present time is impossible. I request that it immediately be deferred until a time to be fixed by the RVS. Sokolnikov, member of the RVS of the Southern Front."[30]

But Trotsky did not cancel his instructions. They had to be obeyed. After receiving his orders, Mironov went home to Ust-Medveditsa for a few days, then traveled to Serpukhov to take up his new assignment. The RVS of the Army gave him a silver-encased sword for skillful leadership of troops, and the Republic RVS presented him with a gold watch with chain. The 23rd Division was awarded the Red Banner.

It should be added that Mironov's recall was not cleared with the Cossack Section of the VTsIK. A few months after the events described above, Stepanov, head of the Cossack Section of the VTsIK, and Makarov, commissar of that section, set forth in a report the reasons for Mironov's recall, as follows:

> Mironov had no Communist cells, and he took a suspicious attitude toward the commissars, as was the case in Kikvidze's division. But he was a good strategist and a good military specialist. He got out of the most difficult situations with small losses, which made him popular with the Cossacks. But the entire population liked him (both the Cossacks and the non-Cossacks: the peasants of Saratov Province greeted him with hospitality). The discipline in his command was excellent. Under

him there was no theft, armed robbery, or forcible requisitions. His units did not offend the religious sentiments of the population. In general, the population did not see his units as enemies, and thus it was attracted to the Soviet regime. Mironov was all the more respected in that this was not the case in the units operating close to his; in Kikvidze's division, for example. Owing to the lack of discipline in those units, the population took a hostile attitude toward them. It was for this reason that the RVS of the Southern Front, taking Mironov's role into account and wishing to make use of him as a man whom the masses followed, entrusted greater forces to him, naming him commander of a special group consisting of two divisions.

It should be noted that he brilliantly justified the hopes placed in him. In a short time, during January and February 1919, moving in the vanguard of the 9th Army, he reached the southern Donets River without much resistance from the Krasnovite White Guards, since most of the Krasnovite regiments willingly surrendered to him as one who had special prestige both among the Red Army men and the laboring Cossacks in the White Guard camp.

But the greater his popularity grew, and the closer he came to Novocherkassk, the greater was the dissatisfaction in the rear, owing to the clumsy building of the Soviet regime, the groundless requisitions, the mass shootings, etc. . . . Mironov sharply criticized individual Communist workers for their mistakes and tactlessness (for example, his speech in Ust-Medveditsa). This circumstance, and the fact that he was suspected of Bonapartism, explains why the RVS of the Southern Front transferred him to the western front—something of which the Cossack Section of the VTsIK was not informed. After Mironov's removal morale in his units dropped, owing to lack of skill in command and other causes.

The military situation on the southern front, which as late as spring had been so favorable for the Red Army, had altered decisively by the end of May 1919. On the eastern front the Red Army had won decisive victories over Kolchak's armies and the latter, demoralized and beaten, had begun hurriedly to retreat beyond the Urals, a situation completely different from the southern front.

All the plans of the Red Army command in the south were disrupted by an uprising of the Cossacks on the Upper Don. Attempts to put it down failed. Skillfully maneuvering their divisions, the Upper Don Cossacks defeated the greater part of the units thrown against them, most of which had been hastily formed.

Deprived of reliable communications with the rear, those units of the Red Army that had stopped on the bank of the northern Donets River could not advance. This enabled the White armies on the Don and in the Northern Caucasus to restore order in their battered units and reinforce them with new mobilizations. General Denikin was given overall command of the main armed forces in the south of Russia. Moreover, in the spring of 1919 the Entente, using the Black Sea route, supplied the volunteer army and the revived Don Army with a variety of equipment, including tanks, aircraft, and a huge quantity of uniforms and ammunition. In the White armies, shock groups were created for the purpose of breaking through the front and into the rear of the Red Army.

The attack of the White armies under Denikin's command began in May 1919 and developed successfully. At the juncture of the southern and Ukrainian fronts, Denikin's army broke through into the northern regions of the Donets Basin.

Shortly after Mironov's recall, P. E. Knyagnitsky, commanding the 9th Army, was also recalled and replaced by the former Colonel Vsevolodov. He ordered the 16th Division transferred to the 8th Army. The 23rd Division was ordered to hold a very broad front. After issuing several orders complicating the position of the Red Army, Vsevolodov went over to the White Guards.

THE POLICY OF "DECOSSACKIZATION" ON THE DON AND ITS CONSEQUENCES

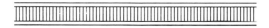

[January · June 1919]

The Soviet regime's defeat on the Don and in other Cossack regions in the first half of 1918 engendered discussions, among the leaders of both the Don Republic and the TsK RKP(b), concerning the means of further building up the Soviet regime in Cossack regions, and concerning the overall attitude of the proletariat dictatorship toward the working Cossacks.

On June 1, 1918, Lenin signed a decree of the Sovnarkom on organizing the Soviet authority in the Cossack regions. This decree stated:

1. All Cossack regions and voiska are regarded as individual administrative units of local Soviet entities (provinces).
2. Jointly and on a basis of equality with the laboring peasantry and workers living on Cossack lands, the laboring Cossacks have the right to organize Soviet authority in the form of:
    (a). Voisko or oblast (depending upon the type of province) soviets of Cossacks', peasants', and workers' deputies.

(b). Raion or okrug (depending upon the type of district) soviets of Cossacks', peasants', and workers' deputies.

(c). Stanitsa or settlement (depending upon the type of volost) soviets of Cossacks', peasants', and workers' deputies.

The representatives of the Cossackry in the VTsIK will form a section which will delegate its members in all People's Commissariats to settle questions concerning Cossack regions (oblasti) and voiska. . . .[1]

Clearly, this new SNK decree did not provide for the future creation of autonomous soviet republics in Cossack regions. It remained consistent with the basic principles of Soviet authority— the election of local and central organs of authority by participation of the entire laboring population of the given region.

In August 1918 the Don Soviet government informed Lenin and Ya. M. Sverdlov that it had decided to wind up its affairs. In September the presidium of the VTsIK accepted the report from the Don Soviet government and decreed its activity terminated.

Hoping to unify the Cossack factions in combatting the counter-revolutionary Krasnov regime and to win working Cossacks over to the Soviet regime, the SNK RSFSR passed a decree on September 3, 1918, on organizing a new Soviet Don Voisko. This decree authorized the creation of a Campaign Circle to administer legal authority and direct the organization of the Don armed Soviet forces.[2] However, neither the new Campaign Circle nor the new Soviet Don Voisko was ever created. But the decree itself played up the principle of an alliance between the proletariat and the laboring Cossackry.

That same September, the Donburo of the RKP(b) was formed to direct the underground movement in Don towns and stanitsy. It was headed by S. I. Syrtsov, a twenty-five-year-old Bolshevik from Rostov and a party member since 1913. Syrtsov had gained considerable experience among the workers of Rostov and Nakhichevan, but despite his claims of expertise on "the Cossack question" he was poorly acquainted with the socioeconomic and political problems of the Cossack regions.

Deciding the means of Soviet reconstruction on the Don became an increasingly pressing concern as the Red Army grew stronger and liberation from German occupation and the Krasnovite regime grew nearer. Opinions were sharply divided.

For example, V. S. Kovalev, former chairman of the TsIK of the Don Soviet Republic, stated in a report to K. A. Mekhanoshin, a member of the RVS of the Republic and the Southern Front, that the Cossacks must be won over by evidence of the Soviet regime's social justice and not by force of arms. He proposed preserving the Don Region's autonomy by creating a regional government of Communists and non-Party men who had shown themselves loyal to the Soviet regime. He recommended K. Mekhanoshin, S. Syrtsov, and Mironov (the others to be provided by the TsK). For individual stanitsy Kovalev suggested maximum utilization of former workers of soviets that had previously fled from Krasnov. ("In this way we will show that we are not introducing anything new but merely restoring the Soviet rule.")[3] The Cossack Section of the VTsIK shared Kovalev's views in a policy thesis adopted after the liberation of some Cossack districts from the White Guards.[4]

Mironov voiced his opinion on the means of reconstruction in a memorandum to the Republic RVS in March 1919. He warned against the fanaticism of the Cossacks, which he felt could be curbed by taking into account the historic, ethnic, and religious traditions of the Cossack population. He counseled against using force to persuade Cossacks to join the Soviet cause. However, he did suggest making sure that counter-revolutionary elements did not succeed in obtaining power and that "enlightened politicians" exercised power in the executive branches of district congresses.[5]

Such a view was, however, opposed by the Donburo, headed by S. Syrtsov. A "Left Communist" in the recent past, Syrtsov was a man inclined to extremes. He was enraged at the Cossacks, who had twice compelled him—along with the leaders of the Rostov Communists—to flee from Rostov.

In his letters to the TsK RKP(b), Syrtsov rejected the notion of autonomy for the Don or of dividing the Don Region into provinces like those in the rest of Russia. He was against any electoral Soviet authority on the Don, claiming that the Communist organizations in that region were still too weak and that without their leadership "the Cossack population would elect soviets which, not being strictly Party, would not be at the proper level and hence not long-lived, and at the first pressure from Krasnov would melt like wax." In areas liberated from the Krasnovites, he proposed appointing extraordinary commissars from among the Communists (including those brought in from outside) invested with special powers.

He wrote to the TsK:

Considering that a considerable part of the Don Region by its very nature is hostile to the socialist regime, individual sympathetic elements are drowning in the sea of ignorance of the bourgeois-Cossack mass. (The "laboring revolutionary Cossackry" exists more as a propaganda formula than as a reality.) It would be a mistake to allow that mass itself, economically homogeneous, to build local organs of power.

Although he had a poor understanding of the agrarian problems of the Don Region, Syrtsov wrote the following with aplomb:

The peculiarities of the agrarian problem in the Don Region consist in the fact that the peasants, with their hunger for land, have had to covet not the landlords' holdings (which are relatively small in this area) but the Cossacks'. Although they are a minority of the population in the Don Region, the Cossacks own most of the land (in the form of voisko, stanitsa, and Cossack allotments). . . . . Huge tracts of land have been sold for almost nothing by the Voisko government to the horse-breeders, who on this virtually free land have organized vast agricultural establishments [ekonomii]—veritable "wheat factories." . . . The agrarian revolution on the Don must consist in the complete destruction of the economic basis of the Cossackry; and that includes the Cossack allotments, along with all other kinds of monopolies and privileges. The abolition of this "allotment agriculture," the transformation of voisko tracts into state-owned tracts (which will be administered by state proletarian organs) . . . [will remove] all economic dividing lines between the peasants and the Cossacks. The big ekonomii (which, admittedly, have been severely damaged during the civil war) must be transformed into model Soviet farms. . . . Such are our principles, although of course they are still only tentative and not yet systematized. The main thing is that the Soviet regime will not defer to Cossack land tenure but, taking advantage of the results of the civil war, will abolish the economic basis of the "Russian Vendée." Unfortunately, it will be necessary to settle the agrarian question on the Don without having available either literary or statistical materials, since the materials on that subject which had been gathered with such great difficulty were destroyed in the retreat from the Don Region.[6]

Syrtsov thus proposed transforming the big farms on the Don into model Soviet farms, and solving the land problems of the peasantry and aliens at the expense of Cossacks. Syrtsov misinformed the TsK in saying that the Cossacks constituted a minority of the population in the Don Region and that the ignorant "bourgeois-Cossack mass" predominated among the Cossacks. In the rural areas on the Don the Cossacks constituted the majority of the population. And among the Cossacks, the poor and middle farmers—i.e., the working Cossackry—considerably outnumbered the kulaks and big landowners.

Knowing well that his proposed "complete destruction of the economic basis of the Cossackry" would meet with stubborn resistance, Syrtsov insisted on the use of massive terrorism in the Cossack districts and areas.

His viewpoint was supported by other members of the Donburo. Thus the following conclusion was drawn about V. S. Kovalev's report: "Kovalev's fear of bullets and his strong penchant for exhortation are an old disease of the Bolshevik Cossacks (the idea of 'settling things peacefully' with 'their own people')—a kind of short-sighted weakness . . . since in the final analysis this took the form of talks with the counter-revolutionaries, and the latter dealt harshly with those fools who thought they could kill the counter-revolution with talks." Rejecting Kovalev's reasonable proposal to include not only Bolsheviks but loyal non-Party Cossacks in the government of the Don Region, A. A. Frenkel wrote: "The Donburo flatly rejects any idea of a government involving non-Party people."[7]

Moreover, the Donburo, alleging that Kovalev was "liberal" and "soft," insisted on removing him from any future executive work in the Don Region.*

At that time the Organization Section of the TsK RKP(b) was headed by Ya. M. Sverdlov, secretary of the TsK and chairman of the VTsIK. After considering the Donburo's proposals, the section adopted Syrtsov's viewpoint. Rather than set up electoral organs of the Soviet regime in the liberated areas of the Don Region the section chose to create revkoms with extraordinary powers. The Donburo and the RVS of the Southern Front were charged with general administration of the district and stanitsa revkoms; and a Civil Government Section, or *Grazhdanupr*, was established under the RVS. This section was staffed with army political workers. But its actual director was Syrtsov, who had come to it from the Donburo. Thus he was to exercise the basic authority in the liberated areas of the Don Region.

The relatively small number of local Bolsheviks working in the newly created revkoms were soon joined by about three hundred Komsomol and Party members from cities and regions in the central part of Soviet Russia, from the Donets Basin and Tsaritsyn, and from the political sections of the 8th, 9th, and 10th armies.

One of the first tasks facing the new organs of power on the Don was to carry out *prodrazverstki*—i.e., to requisition stocks of grain from kulaks and wealthy Cossacks in order to supply both the industrial regions of the country and the Red Army. The revkoms registered the property and land of the White Guard officers and kulaks who had fled south with the Don Army. Here and there attempts at organizing Soviet farms on the basis of the nationalized holdings of landowners were made. But very soon this work in the liberated Cossack districts gave way to massive Red terrorism and "decossackization" in the Don Region, as set forth in a special di-

---

* Kovalev, whose health had been undermined by many years of exile in Tsarist times and by intensive work in Soviet organs on the Don and in the Red Army, died in the spring of 1919.

rective of the TsK RKP(b). The ruinous consequences of such policies soon made themselves felt in the whole situation on the southern front.

The word *terror* in Latin means "fright" or "horror." It usually refers to the systematic or massive use of violence, up to and including the physical annihilation of the enemy. The usual aim of terror is to frighten large groups or entire strata and classes of people, and compel them to retreat and make concessions. It is well known that in time of revolution, it is primarily the ruling classes—either overthrown or under threat of being overthrown—who resort to terrorism. Almost every upsurge in revolutionary struggle is accompanied by terrorism against the masses. But in the first stages, the revolutionaries too occasionally resort to terrorism against the enemies of the revolution.

Marxism by no means rules out revolutionary violence, whether it be used to overthrow the old regime or to put down resistance by the enemies of a victorious revolution. Nor does Marxism eschew the use of such an extreme form of violence as terrorism. As early as 1901 Lenin wrote, in his article "What to Begin With?": "As a matter of principle we never refuse, and cannot refuse, to use terrorism. It is a form of military action that may be completely suitable and even necessary at a certain moment in battle, when the forces are in a certain state, and under certain conditions."[8]

Although the overthrow of the Provisional Government was effected by means of violence, on the whole the revolutionary coup in Petrograd was accomplished rather easily and with few victims on either side. Also, the counter-revolutionary actions of the cadets (*yunkers*) and certain military units led by Kerensky and Krasnov were countered with little difficulty. Actually, those measures of compulsion used by the new government against its opponents cannot be called terrorism.

Against its political enemies the new regime showed restraint and even magnanimity. The majority of those members of the Provisional Government arrested on the night of October 25 (O.S.) were quickly released. After the initial setbacks in his "offensive" on Petrograd, Kerensky fled and was soon abroad. General Krasnov was arrested but soon released, since he had given his "word of honor" that he would not fight against the Soviet regime. The majority of cadets were also disarmed and released.

Actually, terrorism on a relatively broad scale was not used by the Soviet government until the late spring and summer of 1918— against the kulaks and well-to-do peasants who were sabotaging the supply of grain to the starving cities and undermining the grain monopoly that had already been established by the Provisional Government. In the cities the Red Terror did not become extensive until September 1918, after the murder of M. S. Uritsky, chairman of the Petrograd ChK, and the attempt on Lenin's life. On September 5, 1918, because of these things, the SNK RSFSR passed the following decree:

The Council of People's Commissars, having heard the report of the Extraordinary Commission for Combatting Counter-Revolution on the activities of that Commission, finds that in the given situation securing the rear areas by means of terrorism is a direct necessity; that in order to strengthen the activity of the All-Russian Extraordinary Commission and give it greater regularity it is necessary to assign to it the greatest possible number of responsible Party comrades;

that it is necessary to secure the Soviet Republic against class enemies by isolating them in concentration camps;

that all persons involved with White Guard organizations, plots, and mutinies are to be shot;

that it is essential to publish the names of all those shot, and the grounds for applying this measure to them.[9]

In the critical situation of autumn 1918, temporarily isolating class enemies in the Red Army's rear and shooting people who organized mutinies became a harsh necessity, although in a number of cases, as in Petrograd, the Red Terror assumed an excessive scope and unjustifiably cruel forms.

By the end of 1918, however, when it became clear that the

Czechoslovaks had been defeated on the eastern front and when revolution had begun in Germany, the Red Terror diminished almost everywhere. The petty-bourgeois masses began to move toward agreement with the Soviet regime, and Lenin called upon the Party to take advantage of this movement to try and reach agreement with the middle peasants, "the handicraftsmen, the tradesmen, the workers placed in the most petty-bourgeois conditions, with office workers, officers, and the intelligentsia in general. There is no doubt," Lenin said, "that our Party frequently displays a lack of skill in taking advantage of this veering on their part, and that this lack of skill can and must be overcome and transformed into skill."[10]

Lenin was to reiterate his point at a meeting of Party workers in Moscow on November 27, 1918.

You know [Lenin said] that throughout Russia during the Czecho slovak advance . . . the great majority of the Mensheviks and SR's were on the side of the Czechoslovaks, the Dutovites, and the Krasnovites. This situation demanded of us the harshest struggle and the terroristic methods of that war. However that terrorism was condemned by people from various points of view—and we heard such condemnation from all vacillating Social Democrats—for us it was clear that that terrorism was provoked by the intensified civil war. It was provoked by the fact that all the petty-bourgeois democrats had turned against us. They were waging war against us by various means—by means of civil war, subornation, and sabotage. It was these conditions that made terrorism necessary. Therefore we must not repent of it or repudiate it. All we must do is to understand clearly what conditions in our proletarian revolution made for the sharpness of the struggle. Those special conditions consisted in the fact that we had to act against patriotism; that we had to replace the Constituent Assembly with the slogan "All power to the Soviets!"

But now, at the end of 1918, a profound reversal is taking place in the situation and attitude of the entire petty bourgeoisie. It has become disenchanted with Anglo-French and American imperialism, which has proven to be no better than German imperialism, and which is playing the role of the strangler of Russia's freedoms. The petty bourgeoisie sees that the "Allies" are becoming the chief enemy of Russian independence, and its patriotism is impelling it in the direction of the

Soviet regime. For Russia cannot and will not be independent unless
the Soviet regime is strengthened.

That is why this reversal is taking place. And in connection with it
we are now faced with a task: to define our own tactics. That person
would be very mistaken who had the idea of advancing this slogan of
our revolutionary struggle in that period when there could not be any
truce between us, when the petty bourgeoisie was against us, when our
firmness demanded that we use terrorism. Today this would not be firmness but merely stupidity, an inadequate understanding of the tactics
of Marxism, since the tactics of Marxism are determined by class relations. . . . Today, when these people (i.e., the petty bourgeoisie) are
beginning to veer toward us, we must not turn away from them merely
because previously our slogan in leaflets and newspapers was different.
And when we see that they are veering toward us, we must rewrite
those leaflets, because there has been a change in the attitude of those
petty-bourgeois democrats toward us. We must say: "Come on in. We
are not afraid of you. If you think we can act only by means of
violence, you are mistaken. We could come to agreement."[11]

The new attempts at accommodation applied as well to the Don
Region, especially in its northern districts, where in early 1919 the
great part of the working Cossacks had turned away from Krasnov
and the generals' counter-revolution and had begun to support the
Soviet regime. The Cossack regiments there were successfully leaving the front exposed, surrendering their weapons to the advancing
Red Army and dispersing to their homes. It was especially important for the Bolsheviks to reach agreement with the working Cossacks in that region, and even to make certain concessions, so that
the poor and middle-level Cossack masses might have an opportunity to reconsider their position, and then take a firm stand for the
Soviet program. But nothing of the kind was done.

At the end of January 1919, on the basis of a report from the
Donburo, the Orgburo of the TsK RKP(b) promulgated a directive
on "decossackization," which was sent "to all responsible comrades
working in Cossack areas." This directive stated:

Recent events on various fronts and in Cossack areas, together with
our advance deep into Cossack settlements and the demoralization

among the Cossack forces, impel us to issue instructions to Party workers on the nature of their work in these areas. Taking into account the experience of the civil war against the Cossacks, it is necessary to recognize the unique correctness of the most pitiless struggle against all upper strata of the Cossackry, by means of their extermination to a man.

1. To carry out *large-scale terrorism* against the wealthy Cossacks, exterminating them to a man; to carry out pitiless, large-scale terrorism against all Cossacks who have taken any part, direct or indirect, in the struggle against the Soviet regime. With respect to the middle Cossacks, it is necessary to apply all measures providing a guarantee against any attempt on their part to again oppose the Soviet regime.

2. To confiscate grain and compel the collection of all surpluses at indicated points. This applies to grain and to all agricultural foodstuffs.

3. To take all steps to render assistance to indigents being resettled from other areas, organizing the resettlement where this is possible.

4. To establish equality between aliens and Cossacks as regards land and in all other respects.

5. To effect complete disarmament, and to shoot any person on whom weapons are found after the deadline for turning them in.

6. To issue weapons only to reliable elements from among the aliens.

7. To leave armed detachments in the Cossack stanitsy pending establishment of complete order.

8. All commissars assigned to Cossack settlements are to show the greatest firmness and carry out the present instructions to the letter.

The Central Committee decrees that Narkomzem, acting through the appropriate Soviet agencies, must carry out its obligation quickly to work out detailed steps for the large-scale resettlement of indigents on Cossack lands. TsK RKP(b).[12]

We do not know any details about the discussion and adoption of this directive by the TsK. One may conclude that the TsK's circular letter of January 29, 1919, was adopted on the basis of a report from the Donburo of the RKP(b). There is no evidence that this directive was discussed in the Politburo or anywhere outside the Orgburo of the TsK. It is quite obvious that Sverdlov, who was not only chief of the TsK's Orgburo but chairman of the VTsIK, did not clear this directive with the Cossack Section of the VTsIK. That section was presented with a fait accompli, and

in the months that followed, it protested against the January directive. The Orgburo's directive on "decossackization" was apparently
not cleared with Lenin. As we know, Lenin, speaking at the Seventh
Congress of the RKP(b), said that "in this work [i.e., in the work
of the TsK's Orgburo] we have been compelled entirely to rely
upon—and we had every reason to rely upon—Comrade Sverdlov,
who has often made decisions on his own."[13] Also, in his speech at
the extraordinary session of the VTsIK on the day of Sverdlov's
funeral, Lenin said that Sverdlov "directed very important sectors
of work in all their aspects and on his own."[14] One may therefore
assume that the TsK's directive of January 29 on the "work" in the
Cossack areas was adopted *on his own* by Ya. M. Sverdlov, who
also signed the covering letter for that directive.

But local workers could not have known about these peculiarities
in the work of the TsK RKP(b), when particular orders and directives, extremely important in terms of their consequences, were
promulgated by the responsible members of the TsK. For the Party
officials working in the Cossack areas the circular letter of January
29 was a binding decree of the TsK. And it perplexed and bewildered many of them.

The January decree conflicted with all preceding decrees of the
SNK RSFSR on work in the Cossack areas. Also, it completely
contravened the recent (December) formal declarations of the
SNK, the VTsIK, and the RVS to the effect that the Soviet regime
would not punish those Cossacks and Cossack officers who voluntarily left Krasnov's army. Only a short time before, the SNK and
the VTsIK had solemnly promised the Cossacks that the Soviet
regime would not encroach upon the foundations of the Cossack
way of life; that the Cossacks would be allowed complete independence in arranging their lives; and that the lands of the working
Cossacks would not be affected by new land legislation. Also, in
a proclamation signed by Lenin and Sverdlov, it was stated that the
Soviet regime would not try to break up the Cossacks' military
(*stroyevoi*) and economic way of life. That same proclamation
stated that the right to land in the Cossack areas would be recog-

nized only in the case of toilers *permanently* (*osedlo*) living on the voisko territories. The new directive revoked all those appeals, decrees, and promises.

While the Soviet regime's desire to punish counter-revolutionary enemies was understandable, the directive in fact condemned the entire Cossack population. For, under Krasnov's conscription in the summer and autumn of 1918, the majority of the adult males in the Cossack areas had in fact served in his army. And the remaining Cossacks had helped Krasnov's army with deliveries of provisions. Thus, all were affected by the directive, which ordered in paragraph one "pitiless, large-scale terrorism against all Cossacks who have taken any part, direct or indirect, in the struggle against the Soviet regime." Nor was there any clear formulation of the concept of the "wealthy Cossacks," whom the new directive proposed to "exterminate to a man." Compared to the peasantry of Russia, the middle Cossacks could easily be considered "wealthy" in that they had more land and livestock. Even the demand to exterminate Cossack kulaks down to the last man was unnecessarily harsh. For in all other Russian provinces, the dispossession of the kulaks in 1918 provided for the confiscation of surplus land and equipment from the kulaks but not by any means for their physical annihilation. Only certain kulaks were shot.

The large patriarchal families, which accorded great respect to old Cossacks, constituted one trait peculiar to the Cossack areas. The conservative and even monarchistic convictions of the old Cossacks, who had once faithfully served the "Tsar-batyushka," were no secret. It was absurd to demand of the "older men" that they renounce their conservative convictions or their deep commitment to the Orthodox religion. And it was even more absurd to punish and shoot older Cossacks because they had spoken out against the new Soviet system. A paragraph in the January directive concerning the immediate establishment of equality "as regards land and in all other respects" between the Cossacks and the "aliens" was politically premature. In effect, the aliens were placed above the Cossacks, since they were armed with the weapons the Cossacks were forced to surrender. But even more hasty and erroneous was a paragraph in the directive on "quickly" working out measures for the massive resettlement of indigents from other provinces of Russia on Cossack lands.

The promulgation of the circular letter of January 29, 1919, was a gross political mistake. It was in essence a crime against the Revolution. Beyond basic political or moral considerations, the implementation of the January directive in Cossack areas, where the entire male population was armed and was skilled in the use of those weapons, where in the stanitsy and villages mobilization could be effected at precise times and provide dozens of infantry and cavalry regiments—in that situation the directive on "decossackization" and mass terrorism inevitably meant an uprising of the Cossacks. And such rebellion threatened not only the southern front but all the Revolution's gains.

The circular letter signed by Sverdlov dismayed many local Communist workers, eliciting protests from them. Since the organs of Soviet power had not yet taken form in the liberated zones, there were few Communists in those areas—not even enough to staff the revkoms. G. Sokolnikov, a member of the TsK and the RVS of the Southern Front who was working on the southern front, telegraphed his displeasure to Moscow on February 10 and noted that it would be to the Soviet regime's advantage to utilize the labor potential of the older Cossacks for public works.

Not only did the Donburo not protest the January 29 directive of the TsK (it forwarded the TsK's circular letter to chairmen of district revkoms for implementation), but the Donburo also sent an accompanying directive of its own to all revkoms in liberated areas, reiterating the TsK's harsh measures:

With a view to the most rapid liquidation of the Cossack counter-revolution and to preventing possible uprisings, the Donburo proposes to effect the following through appropriate Soviet agencies:
1. In all stanitsy and villages, immediately to arrest all prominent representatives of the given stanitsa or village who have any authority, even though they are not involved in counter-revolutionary actions, and send them to the raion revolutionary tribunal as hostages. (Those con-

victed must be shot, pursuant to the TsK directives.) 2. When publishing the order to turn over weapons, to announce that if any weapon is found on anyone after expiration of the period stipulated, not only the possessor of the weapon but several hostages as well will be shot. 3. Persons with a Cossack title who are not Communists can in no case serve on revkoms. If the foregoing is violated, raion revkoms and the organizer of the local revkom will be held liable. 4. Under the responsibility of the revkoms, to draw lists, by stanitsy, of all fugitive Cossacks (this also applies to kulaks); to arrest all of them without exception and send them to raion tribunals, where the extreme penalty must be applied.[15]

In order to expedite the terrorism and expand it the RVS of the Southern Front decided to set up, in addition to the raion revolutionary tribunals, temporary military field tribunals* in all regiments of the Field Forces.[16]

The creation of the regimental tribunals and the raion revolutionary tribunals (i.e., beginning about the end of February 1919) paved the way for a frightful campaign of terrorism in the Don Region. Most of the time the tribunals dealt with cases on the basis of lists. Sometimes it took only a few minutes to consider a case. And the sentence was almost always the same: shooting. Those shot included not only wealthy Cossacks who had remained in the stanitsy and on the farms but middle and poor Cossacks who had recently served in Krasnov's army or had publicly expressed dissatisfaction with the actions of a revkom. Old Cossacks from various families were shot. Officers who had voluntarily laid down their arms were shot. Even Cossack women were shot. The tribunals handed down verdicts on the basis of unverified denunciations. In most cases no witnesses were called and sentences were executed immediately. Among the victims of this terrorism, only a minority were active counter-revolutionaries. The guilt of the majority was negligible, and many were completely innocent.†

* *Voenno-polevye tribunaly*: Usually translated as "(drumhead) courts-martial." But in this case civilians were being tried.—Translator's note.

† S. P. Starikov, one of the authors of this book, was head of the revkom in one Cossack stanitsa. Since March 1919, he had also been a member of the bureau of the Ust-Medveditsa organization of the RKP(b). He recalls

Of course the terrorism was not uniformly extensive in all districts and stanitsy. For example, while few were shot in the Ust-Medveditsa District, the Upper Don District suffered from an especially violent campaign of terrorism. Hundreds of Cossacks were shot in the course of a few days in the stanitsy of Miguli, Kazanskaya, and Shumilinskaya.

In his novel *And Quiet Flows the Don*, M. Sholokhov tells how the rich Cossacks, officers, and ordinary Cossacks were shot and how all the Cossackry resented these shootings. At a village meeting, the armless Aleshka Shamil says:

This is the way I see it. If I'm wrong, then I'm wrong—and tell me straight out. I'll tell you right off what all of us Cossacks are thinking, and why we have a grudge against the Communists. . . . You, Comrade, said you wouldn't go against the poor Cossacks, who aren't your enemies. You're against the rich ones, and you're brothers with the poor ones. Then tell me: Is it true they shot the people from our village? I won't speak up for Korshunov. He was an ataman, and all his life he'd ridden on other people's backs. But why did they shoot Avdeich the Liar? And Matvei Kashulin? Bogatyrev? Maidannikov? And Korolev? They were just like the rest of us—ignorant, simpleminded, and couldn't figure things out. They'd learned to hold plowhandles and not books. Some of 'em couldn't even read and write. And even if they said something bad, did you have to shoot 'em for that? You grabbed the ones who talked like fools, and punished 'em. But you're not even touching the merchants! . . . The ones you shot maybe would've driven their last bull out of the barnyard to save their own skins, but you didn't ask 'em for tribute. You took 'em and wrung their necks.[17]

---

that on one occasion a tribunal came to the stanitsa, and the chairman ordered that a pit for burying one hundred fifty people be dug during the night. The younger male Cossacks slipped off and hid in the steppe and the nearby woods. But the chairman of the tribunal ordered the arrest of the old men and the women. The tribunal had an armed detachment of thirty to forty men. But the revkom had a detachment of seventy to eighty men; and Starikov, assembling his detachment, refused to allow the innocent people in his stanitsa to be tried unfairly. But this was by no means the case everywhere.

Sholokhov even shows that the Bolshevik Stockman's explanations that Avdeich the Liar had been shot because he "spread propaganda so they could overthrow the Soviet regime," and that Matvei Kashulin had done the same thing, while Maidannikov had "put on epaulets and shouted in the streets against the regime," produced no impression on the village meeting.

In another passage in the novel an old man of the Old Believers sect tells Stockman:

You've squeezed the Cossacks, and made fools of yourselves. If you hadn't, your power would have lasted forever. There are a lot of fools among you. . . . I'm sure you know that yourself. You've shot people. Today it's one man. And tomorrow, before you know it, it's another. . . . Who wants to wait for his turn?

And later the old man tells how, at the stanitsa of Bukanovskaya, illiterate old Cossacks were shot merely because they were once elected honorary judges in the stanitsa court and sat there "just so people could see them."[18]

But Sholokhov writes about all this as merely an abuse of power by local revkoms. Moreover, one gets the impression that only a few dozen Cossacks were shot in the Don Region. Before the early thirties Sholokhov could not say anything more; and for what he did say he suffered considerably. The journal *Oktyabr* refused to publish Book Three of the novel because it allegedly justified the Cossack counter-revolutionary uprising. In 1931 Sholokhov testified to Gorky by letter:

Certain "orthodox chiefs" of RAPP who have read Part VI have accused me of trying to justify the uprising by giving instances where the Cossacks of the Upper Don were badly treated. Is that true? Without exaggerating, I depicted the harsh conditions that preceded the uprising. And I deliberately left out certain incidents which were among the proximate causes of the uprising, such as the shooting, without any trial, of sixty-two old Cossacks in the stanitsa of Miguli, and the shootings in the stanitsy of Kazanskaya and Shumilinskaya, where the number of Cossacks shot in the course of six days reached a solid total of more than four hundred.[19]

The repressions were especially cruel in the stanitsa of Morozovsk, where Boguslavsky, chief of the Expeditionary Section of
the 10th Army, headed up the revkom. According to G. Donskov,
chief of the Food-Requisition Section of the Morozovsk Raion
Revkom, Boguslavsky had scarcely taken up his work with his revkom when he received a telegram from Musin, chief of the Don
Department, in which the Morozovsk Revkom was accused of softness in implementing the dictatorship of the proletariat. After receiving this telegram, Boguslavsky got drunk, went to the jail, and
got a list of prisoners. In numerical order he called out sixty-four
Cossacks then in the jail, and shot them all in turn. Subsequently
Boguslavsky and the revkom members Trunin, Tolmachev, Vasilev,
and Volkov continued massive reprisals against the Cossacks, summoning them to the revkom or to their homes. The resentment provoked by these shootings without trial was so great that when the
staff of the 9th Army passed through the stanitsa of Morozovsk the
army's Political Section, together with the Donburo member I.
Doroshev, ordered the arrest of the entire Morozovsk Revkom to
hold an inquiry. Even this brief inquiry revealed the savage reprisals by the revkom members against the residents of the stanitsa
and the surrounding villages. As many as ninety corpses of Cossacks and their families were found in Boguslavsky's front yard
alone. Another one hundred fifty corpses were found in various
places outside the stanitsa. Many of those murdered were innocent
and should have been released. Boguslavsky, Trunin, and Kapustin,
business manager of the revkom, were shot after being sentenced
by the tribunal of the 9th Army. Other members of the revkom
received long prison terms and were deprived of rights.[20]

These mass shootings of Cossacks, the arbitrary requisitioning of
livestock and grain (very often from middle and poor Cossacks),
and the confiscation of working livestock directly from the field,
ignited a spontaneous uprising of all the Cossacks of the Upper Don
District—an uprising that later encompassed some of the stanitsy
in the Ust-Medveditsa and Khoper districts.

It is significant that the uprising began on the night of March 11–
12 in the stanitsy of Kazanskaya and Veshenskaya. The Cossacks

of Veshenskaya had recently risen up against Krasnov, massacred some of his officers, left the front, and dispersed to their homes to help establish the Soviet regime. When units of the Red Army approached Kazanskaya, almost all the inhabitants came out to greet the army with "bread and salt."* The meeting called to celebrate the liberation of the stanitsy from Krasnov's forces was attended by more than ten thousand inhabitants. A resolution passed at the meeting stated:

> The Soviet regime has shown itself to be . . . an honorable and militant defender of the interests of workers, peasants, and Cossacks. We stand guard for that regime, pledging to repulse without mercy the minions of the Russian and Allied capitalists. Away from our Don, White bloodsuckers!

The same meeting adopted a "greeting to Lenin," in which the Kazanskaya Cossacks wrote:

> Our warmest greetings to you, Vladimir Ilich, steadfast fighter for the interests of the working people! We are taking our place, once and for all time, under the Red banner, which is in your hands. Long live the policy of carrying out the ideas for which the proletariat arose in October.[21]

And now the inhabitants of Kazanskaya and Veshenskaya, along with thousands of Cossacks from other stanitsy and villages, were taking up arms to put an end to the power of the Communists and the revkoms. Within a few days after the beginning of the uprising there were more than fifteen thousand men in the ranks of the resurgent detachments; and their number steadily increased. By the end of April the insurgent army had doubled.

At the time, *Donskaya pravda*, which had only recently begun publication, viewed the uprising as the result of a plot by officers and kulaks.† In one item it stated: "There has been an uprising of

---

* Traditional tokens of Russian hospitality.—Translator's note.

† Needless to say, the kulaks, the former atamans who had been in hiding somewhere, and some of the officers willingly joined the uprising. On the whole, however, it was undoubtedly spontaneous, with middle and poor

White Guards in the stanitsy of Kazanskaya and Veshenskaya. Former officers, atamans, kulaks, and sergeants, the big bosses of the Krasnov regime, by means of a number of inflammatory leaflets and actions, have instigated the inhabitants to rise up against the Soviet regime." (*Donskaya pravda*, No. 9, 1919.)

The insurgent Cossacks' hope of building a people's regime on the Don without Communists and without generals, without Reds and without Whites, was very soon dissipated. For the majority of the insurgents, finding themselves encircled and experiencing an extreme shortage of weapons and ammunition, it soon became clear that their uprising could succeed only with support from the Don Army and the volunteer army, which had passed over the Donets. Permanent communications by aircraft (obtained from the Entente) were established between the command of the insurgents and the staff of the Don Army and the Voisko Circle. The Don Army, only recently demoralized and discouraged, was overjoyed by the news of the uprising in the Red Army's rear.[23]

The Veshenskaya uprising exacerbated the situation along the entire southern front. Movements of troops and munitions to the front were disrupted, and some of the forces had to be pulled back and used against the insurgents. Various units were hurriedly shifted from central Russia to the Don to put down the insurrection. Moreover, it seemed likely the uprising would spread to the Khoper and Ust-Medveditsa districts. G. Sokolnikov, a member of the TsK RKP(b), hurried to Moscow to report to the TsK on the dangerous situation that had developed on the Don.[24]

However, it was not until March 25, 1919, that the Donburo

Cossacks constituting the majority of the insurgents. Almost the entire population of the Upper Don District took part in the rebellion. The terrorism practiced by the Donburo had temporarily unified all the Cossacks: the rich and poor, the officers and rank-and-file. This social cross-section involved in the Veshenskaya uprising is described very well in Sholokhov's novel.

The Cossacks' disillusionment with a regime they had at first welcomed is clearly indicated in their proclamations.[22]

sent a telegram to its subordinate revkoms and army political sections instructing Party workers to discontinue the use of massive
terrorism.

Immediately notify responsible Party and soviet executives in the
area that the Central Committee has revised its directive and instructs
Party workers to discontinue the use of massive terrorism. Do absolutely nothing that might aggravate relations and lead to an uprising.
Economic measures, especially requisitioning, must be applied cir-
cumspectly and cautiously. When it is impossible to haul out foodstuffs,
there is no need to seize them and cause distress to the inhabitants. The
removal of individual harmful counter-revolutionaries is of course essential. The Veshenskaya uprising must be suppressed resolutely and
mercilessly. But repressions must not be extended, without grounds, to
other stanitsy that have not been insurgent. Greater harshness must be
used on the southern Cossacks, but without exceeding the limits. No.
974. SYRTSOV.[25]

It was not until April 22, 1919, that the RVS of the Southern
Front passed these instructions on to the units under its command.

With a view to combatting successfully the counter-revolution on
the Don, it is ordered that the following be rigorously adhered to: with
respect to peaceable inhabitants, do not resort to terrorism; prosecute
only active counter-revolutionaries. Impose very strict prosecution for
arbitrary requisitioning. Make thorough arrangements to pay for legal
requisitions and deliveries of carts, not allowing the requisitioning of
carts and not allowing the requisitioning of working livestock. Absolutely prohibit the exaction of tribute. The organized imposition of
extraordinary taxes is to be effected only by special permission of the
RVS of the Southern Front. . . . Pursuant to the present order, the
following orders are canceled: the order from the RVS of the Southern
Front, dated February 5, 1919, on setting up regimental tribunals; and
the order dated February 15, 1919, on confiscating horses and carts
from the Cossack population. Confiscation is to be effected within the
limits of actual need and by means of legal requisitions, with prompt
payment. The present order is to be immediately forwarded by telegraph to all divisions, regiments, and the peaceable population. No.
3448, RVS of the Southern Front.[26]

But these belated instructions and orders were poorly implemented. In the first place, severe shortages of foodstuffs, vehicles, and horses for the Red Army units arose after the Veshenskaya uprising. But the only thing the Red Army commanders had at their disposal to pay for the grain and property requisitioned from the Cossacks was a highly inflated paper currency which few people took seriously. For want of any other kind of money, it was necessary in some cases to pay the inhabitants in the currency issued by the Krasnovite authorities. Secondly, the successful development of the Veshenskaya uprising made for hostility toward the Cossacks in the Donburo and in the RVS of the Southern Front, leading to harsh attacks on insurgent Cossacks and inhabitants of the stanitsy and villages that supported the uprising. For example, a few days after the beginning of the Veshenskaya uprising, S. Syrtsov sent the following telegram to I. Reshetkov, a member of the Donburo who had fled from Veshenskaya to the village of Monastyrshchina:

Get in touch with Comrade Malokhovsky's detachment of the 8th Army, which has been detached to put down the counter-revolutionaries, and assume leadership of political affairs. For each murdered Red Army man or member of a revkom, shoot one hundred Cossacks. Prepare prisoner-convoying points for sending the entire male population, from age eighteen to fifty-five inclusive, to forced labor in the Voronezh Province, Pavlovsk, and other areas. Order the guard commanders to shoot five men for every escapee, making the Cossacks keep check on one another by way of a mutual guarantee.[27]

I. Yakir, a member of the RVS of the 8th Army, who had distinguished himself in the winter battles on the Don front and was the second person after Blyukher to receive the Order of the Red Banner, wrote the following in the spring of 1919 in one of his letter-orders:

Not a single divisional commissar furnished information on the number of executed White Guards, whose complete extermination is the only guarantee of the stability of our gains. . . . Uprisings will continue to break out in the rear of our forces unless we take measures eradicating even the thought of such developments. These measures are: the complete extermination of all insurgents, the immediate shooting of all those bearing weapons, and even the quota-based extermination of the male population. There must be no pourparlers with the insurgents.[28]

It is not surprising that the insurgent Cossacks did not believe the proclamations addressed to them and the leaflets proposing that they voluntarily lay down their arms. They went on fighting hard. And, since they knew the terrain well and were helped by their families, they did serious damage to the Red Army units sent to put down the insurrection.

In his detailed description of the outbreak and development of the Veshenskaya uprising in *And Quiet Flows the Don*, Sholokhov does not conceal the extreme bitterness of the struggle on both sides. He tells us that when Grigory Melekhov gives the order to kill the Red Army POW's, the inhabitants of the villages beat to death the Red Army men and commissars being taken through those villages under guard. But Sholokhov also writes about the cruelty of the Red Army men. Thus we read in his novel:

After the murder of Stockman, and after Mishka [Koshevoi] had heard the rumor that Ivan Alekseyevich and the Elanskaya Communists had been killed, Mishka was possessed by a fierce hatred for the Cossacks. When an insurgent Cossack fell into his hands, he no longer thought, no longer listened for the faint voice of mercy. With eyes blue and cold as ice, he would stare at him and ask: "Have you fought against the Soviet regime?" And without waiting for an answer, no longer looking at the prisoner's face, pallid with fear, he would cut him down. He would cut them down without pity! Not only did he cut down prisoners, but he would set a torch, called a "red rooster," to the roofs of homes in villages abandoned by the insurgents. And when, having broken through the burning fences, the fear-crazed cows and bulls ran bellowing out into the street, Mishka would shoot them down point-blank with his rifle. He waged an uncompromising, pitiless war against Cossack satiety, against Cossack treachery, against that indestructible and stagnant way of life that for centuries had gone on under the roofs of comfortable homes. . . . On that day he and his comrades burned down a hundred fifty homes in the stanitsa of Kargi. Somewhere in a merchant's warehouse he found a can of kerosene. He went around the square, leaving behind him the acrid smoke and flames which had engulfed the handsome, painted frame houses of the merchants and priests and the wealthy Cossacks' homes.[29]

For that matter, entire villages were often burned. Sholokhov tells how the same Mishka Koshevoi shot the helpless Uncle Grishaka from the kulak family of the Korshunovs. And how Mitka Korshunov, who had served in a punitive detachment in the White Cossack forces, upon his return to the village strangled and cut down Koshevoi's mother and younger brothers and sisters out of his desire for vengeance.

In an attempt to justify itself in the eyes of higher authorities, the Donburo, in a series of letters and decrees, tried to explain the campaign of terrorism it had unleashed and to show that the Veshenskaya uprising had occurred not because massive terrorism had been initiated in the liberated areas but because the terrorism had not been carried out with sufficient decisiveness.

For example, A. A. Frenkel, a member of the Donburo and a delegate to the Eighth Congress of the RKP(b), presented a report to the congress on the causes of the Veshenskaya uprising in which, *inter alia*, he said the following:

Because of the immediate employment of terrorism, because of the frictions between the military authorities and the revkoms, because we permitted the existence of an elective body that was infiltrated by counter-revolutionaries, an uprising took place on the night of March 11–12 in the stanitsy of Veshenskaya, Meshkovskaya, Kazanskaya, and Miguli, and the villages of Solonets and Shumilino. The ring-leaders of the uprising had mobilized Cossacks from the age of sixteen to sixty; and there were also Cossack women in the ranks of the insurgents. The latter got hold of weapons that had been hidden and, after seizing our weapons and depots, were well equipped with all kinds of weapons. The campaign slogan for the uprising is "AGAINST THE JEWISH COMMUNISTS," who are committing plunder, murder, and rape. And in their proclamations the ringleaders propose to "TAKE

THE SOVIETS INTO OUR OWN HANDS." Military actions have already been undertaken against the insurgents, and the uprising will be put down. But this uprising shows that until there is an iron Soviet regime on the Don the terrorist tactic of exterminating the greatest possible number of Cossacks will not of itself suffice, since you can't exterminate all the Cossacks, and under these conditions the uprisings will continue. Together with this method, there remains the large-scale application of the more radical terrorist tactic indicated in the same directive of the TsK but not yet implemented; namely, the dispossession of the Cossacks (decossackization) and their mass resettlement in the interior of Russia, with the introduction of alien laboring elements to replace them. This is the best way of eliminating the Cossacks. But these measures can be undertaken only by the Center, where a special commission for dealing with this question should be set up. And we must start to work on this immediately.[30]

On April 8, 1919, the Donburo passed a resolution completely ignoring the new instructions from the RKP(b) in which it defended the former policy of terrorism. This resolution stated in particular:

All this poses the urgent problem of the complete, rapid, and decisive extermination of the Cossackry as a special economic group, the destruction of its economic foundations, the physical annihilation of Cossack officials and officers and all the Cossack upper strata in general, the dispersion and rendering harmless of rank-and-file Cossacks, and their formal liquidation.[31]

Also in April, summarizing the "positive results" of the Donburo's activity, S. Syrtsov wrote in a memorandum:

The victories of the Red Army have made the peasants confident, and they are beginning to carry out reprisals against the Cossacks. . . . Under the influence of the peasants, the revkoms are beginning to rename the stanitsy and khutora [Cossack villages] volosts and villages. . . . In many stanitsy and khutora, the word "Cossack" is going out of use. . . . The stanitsy in the Millerovskii Raion are empty of people. The Cossacks and their families, taking some property with them, have gone off with the retreating army, knowing that those who remain behind have harsh reprisals in store for them. . . . The general conditions compel us, by way of meeting the peasants halfway (except for the very top strata), to make them our supporters in the job of liquidating the Cossacks.[32]

On April 21, 1919, the following telegram was sent from the train of the commander of the southern front to the TsK RKP(b):

Izyum, April 21, 1919, 1100 hours. The Donburo claims that the uprising was not due to the implementation of the original directive, which allegedly "was not in fact implemented." The Donburo is in error. I have at hand official figures authenticating the fact that the directive was carried out on a huge scale in a region which precisely corresponds to the locus of the current uprising. So far as I know, the Donburo has in no way revoked the [earlier] change in policy, which fact is fully in line with its view that the original policy was not yielding results. I am completely unaware of any instructions issued by the Donburo to the Don Party organizations on the political struggle against the spread of the insurrection, or any literature specially put out by the Donburo to that end.[33]

Unfortunately, during these same weeks the Sovnarkom of the RSFSR adopted several hurried resolutions that were not carefully thought out. For example, on April 24, the Sovnarkom promulgated a decree on organizing the resettlement of impoverished peasants from the central provinces of Russia to the Cossack areas. Soon the first resettled persons began to arrive in the most densely populated and poor lands in the northern districts of the Don Region. Hostility immediately arose between the resettlers and the Cossacks.

May 1919 witnessed the formation of a regional revkom that included S. Syrtsov, A. Beloborodov, and certain other Communists. This revkom continued to insist on implementing "decossackization" and on forcibly breaking up the Cossack way of life and its economic foundations. Syrtsov even demanded that the Don Region be dismembered, and that some of its districts be transferred to the Tsaritsyn and Voronezh provinces. Local revkoms were instructed to replace districts (*okrugi*) with raions;

and it was categorically prohibited to use the word "Cossack" or to wear Cossack-style stripes on uniform trousers. Protests against this stupid policy reached Lenin, and on June 3 he telegraphed the RVS of the Southern Front and told them to be indulgent toward insignificant local customs.[34]

Although in March 1919 the Cossacks in the Khoper and Ust-Medveditsa districts did not support the Veshenskaya uprising, throughout the spring of 1919 the campaign of terrorism was waged in these districts too, especially in the Khoper District. This was done despite the fact that in the past it was precisely the Khoper District that, compared to the other districts, had provided the greatest percentage of Cossacks for the Red Army. M. V. Nesterov, a Party member from the Zamoskvoretskii Raion of Moscow who was sent for economic work to the Khoper District, later wrote in a memorandum to the Cossack Section of the VTsIK:

Having been sent by the VSNKh to the Don Region to organize councils of the national economy, I had for almost two months an opportunity to become familiar not only with economic life in the conquered area but with political life as well. I was in the stanitsa of Uryupinsk, the center of the Khoper District. At that time, Uryupinsk was about 250 to 300 versts from the front. It had no soviet, but a civil administrator of the Don Region was appointed. The revkom and the Party organization were likewise not elective but appointed from above. The Party bureau was headed by a man who knew absolutely nothing about the Cossack way of life, and could not even begin to understand it. In his own words he followed some kind of instructions from the Center, and those instructions from the Center were understood to mean that terrorism involved the complete extermination of the Cossacks. . . . Out of a population of 300,000, there were about one hundred Party members. Many Party members had no idea of the Party program and some of them had recently been Right SR's, Bund members, etc. According to the Party bureau's chairman Vyborkov, it worked in complete harmony and contact with the revkom, and fully approved its policies.

But in my view the revkom's policy markedly diverged from the general line of the central institutions. In the past, under the Tsarist regime, I had known the Cossacks as people who loved freedom, who even in those days had their own elective body, and who were used to collectivism in work. (Even today one can find families of twenty-five to thirty persons working on communistic principles without hiring manpower and cultivating large tracts of land.) But now I found the Cossacks downtrodden, terrorized, afraid of saying a word too much to a stranger, taking a hostile attitude toward local authorities and the way they did things, sitting around in the villages afraid to show up in the district stanitsa because their horses might be taken away from them and they might be shot. And the shootings there were frightful. The revolutionary tribunal shot old Cossacks, sometimes without a trial and on the basis of a denunciation from the local tribunal or slanderous remarks by a neighbor. They shot illiterate old men and women so feeble they could scarcely drag their legs along. And they shot Cossack sergeants, not to mention officers. According to the local authorities, all this was done on instructions from the Center. Sometimes as many as sixty or eighty persons were shot in one day. The guiding principle was: "The more we kill, the sooner Soviet power will be consolidated on the Don." There was not a single attempt to approach the Cossacks in a practical way, to reach an agreement peacefully. There was only one approach: the rifle and the bayonet. Almost every day one could witness a scene of savagery when a batch of prisoners were taken out of jail to be shot. The healthy ones carried the sick; and the guards, with rifles and revolvers, cleared people from the street along which the procession was passing. Everybody knew that the prisoners were doomed to die. I often noticed tears in the eyes of Soviet sympathizers when they witnessed such scenes. They were outraged, and asked whether it could really be true that the Soviet regime was doing such a terrible thing. They didn't believe it. . . .

During searches, agents of the revolutionary tribunal and the authorities would seize all kinds of houseware, such as glasses and spoons, often for their own use. All this was done before the eyes of the Cossacks, who were indignant and conceived a grudge against the Soviet regime. They suffered and they waited for some kind of salvation from the local tyranny. Some were waiting for inspectors to come from Moscow, others were waiting for the advance of the White Guard Don Army.

Nor was the situation any better with regard to the policy on procuring foodstuffs. A certain Goldin was head of the Foodstuff Procurement Section. His view of the Cossacks was as follows: the

Cossacks were his enemies—prosperous, and wielders of whips. And until all the Cossacks were slaughtered and the Don Region settled by an alien element, no Soviet regime would exist there. Hence the order to show no mercy to the Cossacks. Agents armed with rifles roughly broke into huts without explaining the principles of the Soviet system, and demanded grain, livestock, butter, eggs, etc. All this requisitioning was irresponsible and unorganized. Sometimes they took milk cows off to slaughter. . . . There was one case in the stanitsa when thirty head of cattle were requisitioned for slaughter, including twelve cows that were with calf. The Cossacks warned that they were with calf when the slaughter of them was begun. One could cite many more instances of unjust treatment of the Cossacks by local authorities. But all these instances have had, and have, a single basis: an incorrect approach to the Cossacks.

In conclusion I should say that all this unfortunate experience in the Don Region must quickly change our policy toward the Cossacks. . . . It is not with words, and not with rifles, that we must teach Communism to the Cossacks. Rather, by example and by deeds must we make them loyal allies of the Soviet regime. And this can be done.[35]

The same kind of thing was reported to the Cossack Section of the VTsIK by another Moscow Communist, K. K. Krasnushkin, who on June 3, 1919, arrived in the Khoperskii Raion from the Sokolnicheskii Raion of Moscow on a mission to strengthen the Party organization in the stanitsa of Uryupinsk. In June 1919 Krasnushkin worked in the People's Court Section under the revolutionary tribunal, and also served as a jurist and business manager for the revkom. Beginning on June 14, he was chairman of the City Party Committee, which enabled him to get a good grasp of affairs in the raion in a short period of time. Krasnushkin was astounded by the state of affairs. Having noted that Party work in the Khoperskii Raion was unsatisfactory, he went on, in his report, to say the following about Soviet work in the raion:

There were numerous factors in Soviet work in the Khoperskii Raion that rendered it completely unsatisfactory: (a) the fact that absolutely all really responsible workers were appointed by Grazhdanupr; (b) the remoteness of Grazhdanupr from the Don Region both geographically (the town of Kozlov) and in terms of its membership (an element foreign to the Cossacks); (c) an insufficiently strict selection of responsible workers, whereas strictness was essential, especially since the electoral principle is in abeyance; (d) a very limited number of responsible workers, so that one and the same person has had to head up two or three sections at once; (e) a lack of guidance materials in the sense of instructions and directives; (f) owing to the above factors, a complete failure to understand the tasks of the Soviet regime on the part of both Grazhdanupr and the local authorities.

Meanwhile, deprived of reliable communications with the rear, those units of the Red Army that had stopped on the bank of the northern Donets River could not advance. This enabled the White armies on the Don and in the Northern Caucasus to restore order and reinforce their battered units. Moreover, in the spring of 1919 the Entente was able, using the Black Sea route, to supply the volunteer army and the revived Don Army with tanks, aircraft, all other kinds of equipment, and a huge quantity of uniforms and ammunition.

The attack of the White armies under Denikin began in May. At the juncture of the southern and Ukrainian fronts, Denikin's army broke through into the northern regions of the Donets Basin. In the Don Region, the Don Army went over to the attack. General Mamontov's corps broke through into the rear of the 10th Army, and a shock group of the Don Army under the command of General Sekretov broke through the front of the 9th Army and moved along the railroad line in the direction of Kazanskaya Stanitsa. On June 7 Sekretov's cavalry group linked up with the insurgent army from the Upper Don District. The 9th Army, its ranks badly thinned, began to retreat rapidly to the north. The 23rd Division, until recently so successfully commanded by P. K. Mironov, also retreated toward the north. On June 7, 1919, I. A. Sdobnov, chief of staff of the 23rd Division and Mironov's closest friend, committed suicide after first seriously wounding his wife. Although the report on this tragic event states that the reasons for Sdobnov's suicide were not known, it is not difficult to imagine what drove Illarion Arsentyevich Sdobnov to that act of desperation.

One after another, the stanitsy of the Ust-Medveditsa and Khoper districts were occupied by the White Cossacks. In many cases this was preceded by an uprising of Cossacks in the stanitsy and villages, and their defection to the Don Army, which also absorbed the disbanded divisions of the insurgent Cossack army. The White Cossack forces crossed the Don and, bypassing Tsaritsyn in a rapid movement, came out on the Volga in the area of Dubovka. The retreat of the 8th, 9th, and 10th armies became increasingly disorderly.

By the end of June the White Guards had occupied the entire Donets Basin, the Crimea, a considerable part of the Ukraine, and the entire Don Region. Kharkov fell on June 24, and by June 30 units of the Red Army had to abandon Tsaritsyn. During the next few months Denikin's forces moved into the central regions of Soviet Russia and took Belgorod, Kursk, and Voronezh. In September Denikin ordered a further advance, having already assigned his army the immediate task of capturing Moscow. Never in the course of the entire civil war had Soviet Russia been in such a critical position.

Of course there were many causes for these grievous failures of the Red Army. But chief among them was the mistaken and extremely harmful policy of decossackization, which had driven a great part of the Cossacks into the ranks of the White armies. Lenin wrote that it was precisely the Cossackry "that alone has made it possible, and is making it possible, for Denikin to create a major force."[36] And in fact, in May and June of 1919, twenty-six cavalry divisions were operating on the side of the Whites on the southern front. These were mostly Don, Kuban, and Terek Cossacks.

It may be confidently stated that it was only the serious mistakes made by the Donburo and the TsK RKP(b) in the spring of 1919 with respect to the Cossacks, together with a number of similar mistakes vis-à-vis the middle Cossacks in the southern areas of the Ukraine, that prevented the Red Army from victoriously concluding the civil war in 1919. It was precisely these political mistakes that enabled the enemies of the Red Army and the Soviet state to prolong the civil war for another year—and cause great damage to the young Soviet Republic.

PHILIP MIRONOV
AT THE HEAD OF
THE DON CORPS

[June · September 1919]

VII Upon receipt of Trotsky's orders proposing a "more responsible appointment," which directed him to report promptly to field headquarters in Serpukhov, P. K. Mironov turned over command of his 23rd Division to A. Golikov and, after a brief stay in his native stanitsa of Ust-Medveditsa, reported to the Republic RVS. In mid-March 1919, RVS Chairman Trotsky was in Moscow, so that Mironov had to go there. It was in Moscow that Mironov and Trotsky became personally acquainted and had a talk. It was immediately apparent that Trotsky had no clear plans for using Mironov's services. In the course of their talk he proposed that Mironov form a Cossack cavalry division consisting of six regiments. Mironov agreed, and on March 15 the Republic RVS promulgated a decree to that effect.

After receiving his new papers, Mironov went to Kozlov to get the fifteen million rubles allocated for mobilizing the Cossacks in the new division (chiefly for the horses they would bring with them).

But the idea of Mironov's forming a Cossack cavalry division was resisted by the Donburo and most members of the RVS of the Southern Front. Both Syrtsov and Khodorovsky, a member of the RVS of the Southern Front, sent Trotsky a number of dissenting telegrams insisting that Mironov be removed from the Don Region. Mironov was the object of all kinds of unfounded and unverified accusations: arbitrariness, attempts to liquidate the Soviet regime in the Ust-Medveditsa District, and even an attempt to "drive the adventurers out of the Donburo, and Trotsky along with them." Apparently these telegrams had the desired effect on Trotsky, for they prevented the new division from being formed. At Kozlov, Mironov was greeted coldly and did not receive any part of his allowance. He was delayed there in idleness for more than a week and was refused permission to go to the Don Region. Instead, he was ordered to Serpukhov, where he was to report to I. I. Vatsetis, Supreme Commander of All Armed Forces of the Republic. There, too, he was received with great reserve and was assigned the position of Deputy Commander of the Belorussian-Lithuanian Army. He soon went to Smolensk to take up his new duties. Mironov considered his new appointment as a kind of exile. In one of his personal letters he wrote that he "did not know the real reasons" for his removal from the Don Region, but "could surmise them."

Those dramatic events in the Don Region described in the preceding chapter had taken place while Mironov was far from the Don. He learned of some of them from newspapers and letters sent by friends. But apparently he was not yet aware of the general character and huge scope of the bloody drama that had unfolded on the Don.

During this period the Belorussian-Lithuanian Army did not carry out any active military operations, which of course prevented Mironov from demonstrating his talents as a commander. In the meantime, severe battles were being fought on the southern front, with the situation growing more and more unfavorable for the Red Army. Its divisions and regiments were retreating under the onslaught of the Don Army and the volunteer army. The Don Expeditionary Corps, organized to put down the Veshenskaya uprising, was in fact defeated by the insurgents; and its commander, T. S. Khvesin, showed that he lacked both presence of mind and organizational ability.

On June 10, 1919, G. Ya. Sokolnikov proposed to the Republic RVS that Mironov be appointed commander of the Expeditionary Corps. The next day, Trotsky sent the following telegram by direct wire to Moscow:

> Moscow. To Silyansky. Sokolnikov insists Mironov be appointed commander of the Expeditionary Corps. I do not object. Get in touch with Serpukhov. If affirmative, summon Mironov immediately. June 11, 1919.
>
>   RVSR Chairman Trotsky.[1]

Supreme Commander Vatsetis agreed with Sokolnikov's proposal, and Mironov reported immediately to the RVS of the Southern Front. After picking up his orders Mironov left immediately for the Don Region. At that time a chaotic and demoralized mobilization was in progress in those northern districts of the Don not yet occupied by the White Cossacks. Mironov's arrival radically changed the situation. He helped mobilize the Cossacks in the Khoper District and in his name a considerable part of the Cossacks were mobilized in the Ust-Medveditsa District. In whatever stanitsy Mironov met with groups of mobilized Cossacks, they organized meetings and called upon the Don Cossacks to wage a resolute struggle against the advancing forces of Denikin. Party member E. Efremov, who at that time was working on the southern front, later wrote in his report to the Cossack Section of the VTsIK:

> ... Mobilization was effected in the Don Region in June. So that it might be more successful, the RVS announced this mobilization in the name of Comrade Mironov, who was popular among the Don peasants and Cossacks. The call-up went fairly well. Comrade Mironov's

appearance in some stanitsy had the result that they yielded a full contingent of mobilized Cossacks. In other stanitsy, which Comrade Mironov was not able to visit, the Cossacks created disturbances. Rumors circulated among them that Mironov was not alive, that they were being deceived. As a result a smaller number of Cossacks was mobilized. . . . The RVS sent an order to evacuate the mobilized Cossacks to Lipetsk. The Cossacks made a disturbance. Mironov arrived and quieted them down. He organized a huge meeting. In his speeches I detected a desire to meet the Communists halfway, to work with them in friendship and harmony. . . . He expressed the hope that with the newly arrived Communist comrades he would defeat Denikin. . . . Comrade Zaitsev and I asked Mironov to come to the apartment for a snack. In a friendly talk, in the presence of Comrade Skalov, a member of the RVS, I gradually drew Mironov out and got to know him. He was very well disposed and merry. . . .[2]

In mid-June the Expeditionary Corps was renamed the Special Corps, with Mironov as its commander.

On June 19, 1919, Mironov and V. Trifonov, commissar of the Special Corps, went to the region of Buturlinovka, where the corps command was located. But after taking over the corps from Khvesin, its former commander, Mironov became convinced that the corps did not in fact exist as a battle-ready unit. He found that the troops lacked training and equipment and that morale was extremely low. He informed Trifonov of the situation.

After having taken over command of the Special Corps and familiarizing myself with the situation, personnel, and state of the units, I report that combat conditions are extremely trying, in view of the very extended front and the shortage of personnel in the units (some regiments have no more than eight riflemen). . . . Owing to a lack of training and esprit de corps, many units are markedly unstable and . . . when passing through their own stanitsy, Cossack squadrons defect to the enemy. . . . Under these conditions, when the units have been exhausted by many successive engagements, have suffered heavy casualties, and have lost many officers and commissars in battle, their psychological resiliency is very slight and they can be used only as a light screening detachment behind which we must proceed promptly to form and train new units. It is impossible to carry out any combat missions with these troops without an appropriate breathing space. According to the latest report from the commander of the 2nd Division, there were no more than 150 rifles [bayonets]* in each brigade.

Mironov, Commander of the Special Corps.

Trifonov, member of the RVS.[3]

At this same time Mironov was studying developments on the Don. He unearthed the details of the Veshenskaya uprising and questioned Cossacks about its causes. Mironov clearly saw the beginning of the retreat, and here and there even the collapse of the southern front. Some panic-stricken staffs were retreating to the north, abandoning trainloads of wounded, arms, ammunition, and military property. Many stanitsy were jampacked with thousands of resettled peasants who had been brought to the Don from the provinces of Voronezh, Tambov, and Penza and had become stranded en route owing to the advance of Denikin's forces.

On June 24, Mironov expressed his distress and set forth proposed solutions in a telegram to Moscow and Kozlov.

To: Citizen Trotsky, Chairman of the Revolutionary Military Council.

Copy to: Citizen Lenin, Chairman of the Council of Defense.

Citizen Kalinin, Chairman of the TsIK, or his deputy.

The RVS of the Southern Front at Kozlov.

In appointing me commander of the Special Corps, the RVS of the Southern Front stated that this former Expeditionary Corps was strong; that it comprised up to 15,000 riflemen (including up to 5,000 trainees), and that it was one of the best fighting units of the front. If the same information was given to you, I consider it my revolutionary duty to report the complete contradiction between such information and the actual state of affairs. I find this inadmissible, since, regarding the information as something positive, because of it we close our eyes to the real danger and, lulled, do not take prompt steps. And if we do take steps, it is too late. I have stood, and still stand, not for the covert

---

* *Shtyki* ("bayonets") was conventionally used as a synonym for "troops" in giving the size of a unit. (Cf. "sabers" for cavalry units.) But in this case, given the very small number for a brigade, it would seem the actual weapons are meant.—Translator's note.

construction of social life in accordance with a narrow Party program, but for publicized construction—construction in which the people take a lively part. (In this matter I do not have the bourgeoisie and the kulak elements in mind.) Only such construction evokes the sympathy of the peasant stratum and of part of the authentic intelligentsia.

I report that the Special Corps has about 3,000 riflemen for a front extending over 145 versts. The units are exhausted. Except for three classes, the trainees have shown themselves to be beneath criticism. And of those thousands of stalwart young men there remain only a few miserable hundreds [or squadrons] and tens. The Communist Regiment has deserted. There were men in it who didn't know how to load a rifle. The Special Corps can play the role of a screening unit. Its position is being saved right now only because mobilized Cossacks are being brought in from the Khoper District. General Denikin's expectations with regard to that district have proven wholly unfounded. But as soon as the White Guards correct that oversight the Special Corps, as a screen, will be broken through. It is not merely that the activities of certain revkoms, special sections, and a number of commissars have provoked a general insurrection on the Don: that insurrection threatens to overflow the peasant villages all over the republic in one broad wave.

If I tell you that at public meetings in the villages of Novaya Chigla, Vekho-Tishanka, and elsewhere people openly shout "Give us a Tsar!" you will understand the mood of the peasant stratum that has provided such a large percentage of deserters forming detachments of Greens.* The uprising in Ilovatka and on the Pers [?] River is still muted; but the great ferment in most districts of Saratov Province threatens the cause of social revolution with complete collapse. I am not a Party man. But I have given too much of my energy and health to the struggle for social revolution to stand idly by while General Denikin on his horse "Kommuniya" tramples the red banner of labor.

Looking ahead mentally, and seeing the ruin of the social revolution (since there is nothing to make one optimistic, while as a pessimist I have rarely been mistaken), I consider it necessary to recommend the following measures as urgent. First, to reinforce the Special Corps with a fresh division. Second, to transfer to it the 23rd Division as the basis for the future might of a new army with which I and divisional commander Golikov will personally take the initiative into our own

* The Greens were bands of deserters who opposed both the Whites and the Reds.—Translator's note.

hands again so as to provide scope for the other divisions and armies; or else [third] to name me commander of the 9th [Army], where my military prestige is high. Fourth, the political situation in the country makes it imperative to call a popular assembly—and not merely a Party assembly—to cut the ground from under the feet of the betrayers of the socialists, while continuing a stubborn struggle on the front and creating the might of the Red Army. This step would regain the sympathy of the popular stratum, and it would willingly take up arms to save its land and freedom. Do not call this assembly a territorial assembly or a Constituent Assembly, but convene it. The nation is groaning. I have forwarded many affidavits to the Revvoyensovet of the Southern Front, including the following. A peasant of the Thirty-fourth Section, renamed the Leninskaya Volost. Family of twenty-one persons; four pair of oxen. Their own kommuna. For refusal to join a kommuna the commissar took away the oxen; and when the peasant complained, he was killed. I also forwarded a report from one Ermakov, chairman of a tribunal: what he said was terrifying. I repeat: the people are ready to throw themselves into the embrace of landowner servitude—just so their sufferings are less painful and obvious than they are now. Fifth, the purging of the Party must be carried out on the following principle. All who have become Communists since the October Revolution should be assigned to companies and sent to the front. Then you will see who is a real Communist and who is self-serving; who is simply a provocateur and who has filled up all the revkoms and special sections. Example: the Morozovsk Revkom, which slaughtered sixty-seven persons, and was then shot.

> Original signed by Citizen P. Mironov,
> commander of the Special Corps.[4]

Of course many of Mironov's proposals were unacceptable to the Soviet government and the TsK RKP(b) and unfeasible under the conditions obtaining in 1919. But they could scarcely be regarded as alleged "Don Constituent-Assemblyism and Left SRism," as Trotsky evaluated them.[5]

Mironov did not limit himself to reports on the Special Corps' lack of combat readiness. Upon assuming command of that corps, he strengthened it by building up its units and morale with mobilized Cossacks and refugees from the Don Region. He also addressed himself to the refugees and soldiers of his own corps, calling upon them to strengthen revolutionary discipline and combat pillaging, desertions, and anti-Semitic agitation.

The situation on the southern front had deteriorated to such an extent that the Special Corps, intended to deal with the insurgent Cossacks in the rear of the Red Army, had lost its former meaning—what had previously been the rear area was now the front. It was just at this time that the idea of using mobilized Cossacks and refugees from the Don Region to form a new Don Cossack Corps arose.

On June 3, 1919, S. Skalov, a member of the RVS of the Special Corps, sent the following telegram to Lenin:

> Dear Vladimir Ilich! Comrade Mironov needs your help in the rapid and strong organization of a new corps. Supply all technical equipment so that this corps can become a real battering ram in the experienced hands of Comrade Mironov. Then we can defeat Denikin's bands before the harvest, which this year will be especially good throughout Voronezh Province. Comrade Mironov is tremendously popular among the local inhabitants, and all the real fighting soldiers are thronging to him. I therefore urge you to participate most directly in our formation of a new corps. I am working with him on the forging of an iron corps. I am an old Petersburg worker whom you know very well and can fully trust.
>
> S. Skalov,
> member of the RVS of the Special Corps.[6]

The idea of forming a Don Cossack Corps was supported by the Cossack Section of the VTsIK and the RVS of the Southern Front. Saransk, a town which at the time was far in the rear of the southern front, was selected as the formation center for the corps. Under the conditions then obtaining, it hardly seemed a good choice.

In early July, Mironov was summoned to the Cossack Section of the VTsIK in Moscow. He gave that section an extensive report on the situation in the Don Region and the attitude of the laboring Cossacks toward the Soviet regime. On July 8, Mironov and

Makarov, chairman of the Cossack Section of the VTsIK, were received by Lenin. In the course of their long talk, Mironov repeated the gist of his report to the VTsIK and promised that by August 15 he would complete the formation of a Cossack Corps of three divisions. With this corps he would attack Denikin. For his part, Lenin promised Mironov all possible assistance.

Mironov also gave Lenin a brief written report on the situation in the Don Region. In this report he noted that the question of conscripting Don Cossacks into the Red Army had been decided in the affirmative by the supreme commander in March 1919, and that by the time Mironov had been ordered to form a Cossack division the order had been revoked for reasons unknown to him—something he regarded as a "terrible mistake." Mironov then set forth for Lenin his ideas on the political situation in the Don Region. In particular, he wrote:

What General Kaledin did not succeed in doing, General Krasnov did (and, in recent days, General Denikin has done the same to an even greater extent). Once returned home, the combat Cossacks—deprived of active communication with political centers, deprived of political education, and ultimately falling (thanks to their mental backwardness) entirely under the influence of their fathers and grandfathers, as well as of counter-revolutionary clergy and officers—inadvertently went over to the camp of the enemies of the people. Oh, we are all guilty of a great deal in this matter. The Don Region was abandoned, left to its own devices, so that later it could choke on its own blood. It should be noted that at that time (March-April) the border areas of the Don Region were beginning to undergo violence on the part of provocateurs, huge numbers of whom had got into the ranks of the Red Guards. Villages were burned, churches were shelled by artillery during services, etc. People like General Mamontov and Colonel Zastegayev were overjoyed: the Revolution itself had put the reins of a Cossack uprising into the hands of these Tsarist gendarmes. Someday, impartial history will illuminate this terrible drama of the combat Cossacks. Hundreds of Cossacks were shot by evil cliques; thousands are languishing in prisons and mines. The Don Region is still politically ignorant and backward. The Revolution has changed things so profoundly that the Cossack's limited mind is powerless to understand current events, powerless to realize the scope of the proletarian revolution encompassing half the world. He does not understand the requisitioning of livestock and grain surpluses taking place in the Don Region today, due to the famine in the nation. On the basis of the foregoing, being deeply convinced that the Cossacks are not so counter-revolutionary as they are thought to be, and as people try to portray them, and that through practicality and skillful political work they can again be brought into the camp of fighters for proletarian interests, I suggested these measures to the Republic Revvoyensovet when I was leaving for the western front on March 15.[7]

According to Makarov, commissar of the Cossack Section of the VTsIK, when Lenin had read Mironov's proposals on Party policy in the Cossack areas, he said: "It's too bad that I wasn't informed of this in time." And of Mironov himself he said: "We need people like him. We must use them skillfully." As for M. I. Kalinin, who was present at the meeting between Lenin and Mironov, he was (according to Makarov) generally sympathetic toward Mironov, but expressed apprehension that the latter might, from a criticism of unworthy individual Communists, move to an anti-Party position.[8]

On July 19 the Cossack Section of the VTsIK acknowledged Mironov's value and coopted him as a member of that section.[9] The section promised Mironov that it would render all possible aid in forming the Don Corps and would send to Saransk all the refugees from the Don Region who made contact with the Cossack Section.

With these encouraging parting words, Mironov went to Saransk. But upon his arrival he encountered many difficulties. First of all, he was then in the midst of active fighting. Many of the units in action required immediate reinforcements, weapons, and ammunition. This hampered work on forming the Don Corps. Also, it became clear that someone in the Republic RVS and the RVS of the Southern Front was obstructing the corps' formation. Rumors about Mironov were circulating and petty intrigues sprang up.

A letter has been preserved that was written by a senior Party member, V. Trifonov, to his friend A. Solets, also a senior Party member. In this letter, written July 3, 1919, Trifonov sharply criticizes the situation that had developed on the southern front by the summer of that year. He concludes by saying:

> They are trying to drag me into yet another adventure—the organization of a Cossack division under the command of that adventurist Mironov. When they lack organizational talents, they try to take things by cunning. It's a hopeless situation, since they have as few brains as organizational talents. My friend, I'm in such a mood right now that I could shoot all those blockheads or maybe shoot myself. The fate of a great Revolution is in the hands of those idiots. It's enough to drive you out of your mind.
>
> Well, so long, I embrace you. Valentin[10]

It is hard to understand why such a perceptive person as Valentin Trifonov, who had met Mironov the previous month, should call him an "adventurist." But one can easily imagine what was said about Mironov by those whom Trifonov, not without some justification, called "idiots" in his letter; and one can only regret that Trifonov, the old Bolshevik, who had only recently agreed to become commissar of the Expeditionary or Special Corps commanded by Mironov, should have refused to cooperate with the latter in forming a Don Cossack Corps. In his book, *The Gleam of the Campfire*, Yu. V. Trifonov rightly says: "Like Chapayev, he [Mironov] needed a Furmanov. But he had no Furmanov."[11]

The difficulties in forming the Don Corps were exacerbated by the extremely weak cadre of political workers sent to Saransk. We have already described, in the preceding chapter, those flagrant abuses and crimes committed in the spring of 1919 in the Khoper District, both by individual officials and by various agencies of the Soviet regime. V. Larin, onetime chairman of the Khoper Revkom, himself acknowledged that the inhabitants ascribed all these crimes to the revkom. Yet among the Cossacks in the Don Corps being formed in Saransk, the majority were from the Khoper District. These Cossacks had had personal contact and unpleasant experience with all kinds of tribunals, special sections, food-requisition detachments, village and stanitsa revkoms, and the district revkom.

The following two documents, written at a later time, shed light on the Cossacks' interaction with some political workers.

From a resolution of the Cossack Section of the VTsIK:

> . . . Taking into account the reports of comrades Makarov, Kuzyuberdin, Efremov, and others, the Cossack Section of the VTsIK has resolved: (a) to ask the TsKP(b) [sic] not to send again for work in areas in the Don Region where they have already been those comrades who according to local reports so badly compromised themselves that their reappearance in those areas could have a ruinous effect on the construction of the Soviet regime; (b) in view of the deceitful activity of certain political workers vis-à-vis the Cossack Section of the VTsIK —with a manifest tendency to discredit the latter in the eyes of the workers, peasants, and laboring revolutionary Cossacks—to regard the undermining and slanderous agitation against the Cossack Section of the VTsIK on the part of comrades Rogachev, Boldyrev, Zaitsev, and Larin, political workers in the corps, as criminal from the revolutionary point of view, and to institute proceedings against them in accordance with Decree No. 53 of the Presidium of the VTsIK dated August 8, 1919.[12]

From a letter written by E. Stasova, secretary of the TsK RKP(b), to I. T. Smilga, member of the RKP(b) and of the Republic RVS:

> Dear Ivan Tenisovich!
> At the last session of the Orgburo there were heated debates as to certain Cossack officers who had behaved one way or another . . . in their work in the Don Region. With respect to these officers there had been previous warnings, pointing out that in the past they had deliberately carried out a directive especially accurately, knowing that such behavior would inevitably provoke a sharp reaction, which in its turn would lead to an uprising. After we retreated from the Don Region, some members of the Cossack Section of the VTsIK warned

that Larin, Boldyrev, and Rogachev must not be allowed in the Don
Region in the future, since they had left a ghastly legacy behind them,
and that they could not be trusted in any case, especially in the Don
Region.[13]

But these two documents, like certain others that gave an equally
unflattering account of Larin, Boldyrev, Rogachev, and Zaitsev,
appeared later. Meantime, in July 1919 it was precisely these men
who were directing political work in the Don Corps in Saransk. It
is not surprising that the Cossacks were estranged from the corps'
political workers.

One could easily foresee that Mironov, who after July 10 came
to Saransk to direct the forming of the Don Corps, would also come
into inevitable conflict with the "Khoper Communists." Mironov
never confined himself to the military aspects of a situation; he
always tried to educate the soldiers of his units. Thus in Saransk,
as elsewhere, he had long talks with refugees from various districts
of the Don Region and held meetings and assemblies. It was only
in these days that he fully realized the results of the "decossackization" policy. Most important, he learned from these talks and
the letters he received that the mass terrorism on the Don in late
February and March 1919 had been carried out in accordance with
special instructions received by the Don revkoms from Moscow. He
was shaken by this. He could not put up with the policy of "decossackization," nor could he in good conscience work with the
"Khoper" political workers who had implemented that policy. For
their part, the latter denounced Mironov to Moscow and even demanded disbandment of the corps, or at least Mironov's removal
from its command. This caused the attempts at forming a corps to
grind to a halt.

Mironov decided to write Lenin. This letter has been preserved,
and is one of the very important documents of the era. Its main
theme is a defense of the working Cossacks. Unfortunately, it was
not until the autumn of 1919 that Lenin received it and read it.
Although in several respects Mironov criticized the Communist
Party and Communists in general, Lenin paid close attention to that

criticism, occasioned by the actions not only of certain pseudo-Communists but of certain very influential organizations—e.g., the Orgburo of the TsK and the Donburo of the RKP(b). In many places in the margins of this letter, notations have been made in Lenin's hand: "important," "very important," "this is good," etc.

Mironov's political position is also clear from his letter to Lenin. It refutes what Colonel P. Dmitriyev, Candidate of Historical Sciences, says of Mironov in an article entitled "P. K. Mironov, Commander of the 2nd Cavalry Army." He groups Mironov with those military specialists from the old army whom the Party brought into service in the Red Army:

> Under the supervision of the military commissars [Dmitriyev writes] they worked successfully in command staff positions and administrative positions. Some of them took the side of the laboring people without vacillating. For others, this transition was complex and painful. . . . Among the old military specialists of the civil war period, one of the most talented commanders—who at the same time was a complex and contradictory personality—was P. K. Mironov.[14]

We can by no means agree with this evaluation of Mironov's personality. Of his own accord, he set out on the path of revolutionary struggle in 1906 and 1917. On his own initiative he took part in making a workers' regime on the Don, as he understood it, and in the creation of Red Guard detachments, using revolutionary Cossacks and peasants.

Some of Mironov's relatives and comrades-in-arms are now calling him a "true Leninist," a Communist, a man who immediately after the October Revolution supported the program of the Bolshevik Party. But in many respects, this is an exaggeration in the other extreme. Prior to the October Revolution, Mironov sided with the Trudovik Party. He was not familiar with the work of Marx and Engels; he was not, nor could he have been, a *proletarian* revolutionary. But none of this in any way diminishes Mironov's merits as a revolutionary. He was a spokesman for, and defender of, the interests of the best element of the laboring revolutionary Cossackry (and to some extent of the middle peasantry in general). If the concept of "petty-bourgeois revolutionary" had not subsequently acquired an odious meaning, one might have called Mironov a representative of the cream of the petty-bourgeois revolutionaries, who in the course of the Revolution, by the logic of the struggle, adopted the position of the Bolshevik Party—the position of the proletariat. One might have called Mironov a peasant revolutionary, a representative of that element of the peasantry that supported the proletariat and without whose support the proletariat could never have triumphed in a country like Russia. Mironov knew the interests and needs of the laboring Cossackry better than many prominent proletarian revolutionaries. He was able to enlist the support of the laboring Cossacks; and in that sense his revolutionary activity took on especially great significance. Herein lies the chief interest in studying the life and activity of Mironov.

Mironov steadfastly fought for the victory of the "social" (as he called it) revolution. His vacillations, his protests, his frequently direct attacks on "false Communists" (in his letter to Lenin he often speaks simply of Communists, but he by no means has all Communists in mind) were provoked not by the "contradictory character" of the middle peasantry and the petty bourgeoisie but by those grave mistakes our Party made in early 1919 in dealing with the Cossackry as a whole and the laboring Cossackry in particular. When these mistakes were acknowledged and corrected, the main cause of Mironov's conflict with the Communist Party disappeared, and he himself applied for and achieved membership in the RKP(b). But as this happened six months after the events we are describing, we shall discuss it later. Meantime, let us return to Mironov's July 31 letter to Lenin. He opened by saying:

> Citizen Vladimir Ilich: On June 24 of this year I sent you from Anna Station an encoded telegram in which I said, inter alia: "I have stood, and still stand, not for the covert construction of social life in accordance with a narrow Party program, but for publicized construction—construction in which the people take a lively part."

After setting forth the content of his telegram, Mironov proceeds to cite instances of many totally unjustified acts of violence against laboring Cossacks on the Don and middle peasants in Saratov Province. He sharply condemns the directive on "decossackization" and the mass terrorism against the Cossacks that he had learned about in letters from the Don Region and from oral accounts given by refugees.

These oral accounts given by refugees from the Don Region did not much amaze me, since I had already seen in broad outline the Communists' policy toward the Cossacks, who were guilty only of being benighted and ignorant; guilty of having been, through a fatal mistake, the offspring of a free Russian peasantry which in the past had fled from the boyar yoke and cudgels to the free steppes along the Don; guilty in that under Peter I (the Great) its freedom was strangled, at the price of a stream of blood by the Russian people themselves; guilty in that, after the imposition of servitude, the Tsarist regime became somewhat attentive to the Cossacks and by means of a prolonged barracks regimen extirpated their human understanding and transformed them into the police guardians of Russian thought and Russian life; guilty in that the agents of the Soviet regime paid them even closer attention, and instead of words of love brought vengeance, fires, and ruin to the Don and the Urals. How can one justify this kind of behavior by scoundrels in the stanitsa of Veshenskaya—the same stanitsa which first realized the fatal mistake and, in January 1919, abandoned the Kalachevo-Bogucharsky Front? It was the above-mentioned behavior that provoked the general insurrection on the Don. If not fatal it was at any rate menacing and fraught with inexhaustible consequences for the course of the entire Revolution.

Mironov next cited cases of totally unjustified shootings, pillaging, and violence on the Don, when merely along the route of the 8th Army, the tribunals shot more than 8,000 persons "for the good of the social revolution." (Often the Cossacks were shot simply for demanding payment for requisitioned grain and horses.) Then Mironov exclaimed:

Vladimir Ilich, it is impossible—I don't have enough time and paper —to describe the horrors of "Communist construction" on the Don! . . . Need one have been astounded by the uprising on the Don? In *Pravda*, No. 236, in an article titled "On the Don," a certain Varov touched upon the events in the stanitsa of Veshenskaya, fearing he might offend the Communists. For him, these events assumed only a "discomforting aspect," and those Cossacks who rose up against violence and oppression were renamed "White Guard sympathizers." . . . Another Soviet correspondent—a certain A.V.—lumped all the savagery, violence, and horror into one general phrase: ". . . the not-always-tactful acts of the authorities." The petty, base soul of autocracy's hack writers has been translated into the hack writers for the Soviet regime. The people have no need for servants of the free word in lackey's livery. Perhaps, Vladimir Ilich, you will ask by what right I take the liberty of writing you. I cannot accept, I cannot assume that you should have taken a superficial view of all these horrors; that all this was done with your approval. I can no longer keep silent. I haven't the strength to tolerate the sufferings of the people in the name of something abstract and far-removed.

Mironov declared that success on the southern front depended not so much upon military actions as upon winning good will in the rear areas.

Only with such a successful strengthening of the rear area could the military line on the front have been impregnable. The strengthening of the rear area demanded a knowledge of its psychology, its special traits, its weak points, etc. . . . Unfortunately, the political leaders of the southern front did not possess such knowledge. . . . Our units advanced in good order, in no way provoking grumblings and indignation among those Cossacks who recounted and wrote so much about the "savagery" of the Bolsheviks. Consequently, the impression was most favorable. . . . And when our units had passed through . . . organizational work was begun by the political sections of armies, divisions, and brigades. But unfortunately, by virtue of technical limitations and purely bureaucratic organization, they did not manage to accomplish a single one of their great tasks. The rear area was put under the control of Communists who were perhaps very reliable but who knew nothing of the Cossacks' psychology or their special traits. They were regarded as a counter-revolutionary element, dangerous from top to bottom. And the slightest discontent due to one incident or another was suppressed by force of arms and not by force of words. Under such conditions there could be no question of strengthening the rear area. The volost and district revkoms, which had been put together hurriedly, were unfamiliar with their own functions, and looked upon the Cossacks from the viewpoint of "pacifiers." Then came the requisitions, the confiscations, the arrests, etc. The worst thing of all was that this was done without appropriate explanations—with no definite system. The bewildered Cossacks threw up their hands, gasped, expressed amazement, and finally concluded that the "Kommuniya" was no good because the Communists were "mighty" fierce. On the other hand the local soviets, made up of poor people and governing justly, were a good thing. Hence: "Long live the soviets and down with the Communists!" This was the cause of the whole conflagration. All this taken together not only stirred up the Cossacks against us but demoralized the southern armies. Rumors of the uprisings reached them. Some units even had to "pacify" insurgents. This unnerved the army. The army saw our mistakes, became indignant, and was shaken. . . . Such were the fruits of distrust and doubts on the part of the Communists, with no knowledge of the most elementary principles of life. . . . They did precisely what was needed to nourish the counter-revolutionary tendency among the Cossack masses on the Don. They did what General Krasnov had pointed out in his orders and proclamations, starting the fire of insurrection on the Don in April 1918, and what had seemed provocation in the mouths of the Krasnovite and Cadet bands. The annihilation of the Cossacks became an irreversible fact as soon as the Don became Soviet. It goes without saying that when such a policy is pursued by the Communists, there will never be peace and the counter-revolution will live. . . .

I do not believe that honest workers at factories and plants tolerate the fact of slaughtering honest people and shooting innocent workers like themselves in villages, even in the name of social justice. I do not believe it, since the workers have suffered more than anyone else from tyranny. It was tyranny that made them take to the barricades. And tyranny itself, whatever is invoked for its practice, will always be tyranny. I do not believe that the honest worker thirsts for blood and agrees that everything should be razed to the ground—even in the khutor, the stanitsa, or the village with which sometimes he has not yet broken not only his spiritual ties but his physical bonds. . . . The entire activity of the Communist Party, headed by you, is aimed at exterminating the Cossacks, at exterminating mankind in general. . . . In my telegram to you, Vladimir Ilich, I begged for a change of policy, for a revolutionary concession so as to alleviate the suffering of the people and by such a step to win over the popular masses to the side of the Soviet regime and the strengthening of the Revolution. . . . With such views, I repeat, I diverge from the Communists. Here is the root of the distrust toward me. And the Communists are right: I am not willing to support their policy of exterminating the Cossacks, and then the well-to-do peasants. I repeat: the Communists are right. I will not join in the madness that has just now revealed itself to my eyes. And with all the strength remaining to me, I will fight against the extermination of the Cossacks and the middle peasants. . . .

And now, Vladimir Ilich, judge what kind of person I am. I can no longer tolerate the violence, the anarcho-Communist trend that prevails in our republic and that has condemned a category of many millions of people—the Cossacks—to extermination. What I advocate is this: without infringing upon the peasants' ordinary, religious way of life, without violating their customs, we should lead them toward a better and radiant life by personal example and illustration, and not with the empty, pompous phrases of the half-baked Communists who are not yet dry behind the ears and who for the most part can't tell wheat from barley, although at meetings they teach the peasants with great aplomb how to farm. . . . I do not mean to say that all the laboring peasants have been broken away from the Soviet regime. No, they still believe in its benefits and do not want to go back to the landowners and capitalists. But, exhausted from vain searching for truth and justice, and wandering in the Communist gloaming, they appeal to us Soviet ideological workers: "Don't promise us pie in the sky. Give us bread in the hand."

Now I want to say a few words about myself. . . . I nonetheless want to go on being a dedicated worker for the people, a dedicated defender of its aspirations for land and freedom. Resorting to the last means, I reject all the slander of the Communists, with whom I have never agreed, with their narrow Party policy that is ruining the cause of the Revolution. That same diabolical plan that has come to light—the plan to exterminate the Cossacks—compels me to repeat at meetings the statement I made when I saw the outrages committed by the Communists: if things continue in this way, one will have to stop fighting the Krasnovites and start fighting the Communists.

And now, laying bare my innermost thoughts and views, I state:

1. I am a non-Party man.

2. I shall go along to the end with the Party of the Bolsheviks—if they follow a policy that does not get out of hand, either in words or in deeds—as I have gone along before.

3. I regard as inadmissible any interference by doubtful Communists in the sphere of education among the officers.

4. In the name of the Revolution and the sorely tried Cossacks, I demand that the policy of exterminating them be discontinued. It

follows that a policy toward the Cossacks must be proclaimed once and for all. Also, that all those scoundrels who artificially stirred up resentment among the population with a view to a pretext for extermination must be immediately arrested, brought to trial, and be subjected to revolutionary punishment for the death of innocent persons. The construction of the Revolution is unthinkable without a definite, open life of behavior [sic] toward the Cossacks. The social life of the Russian people, to which the Cossacks belong, must be constructed in accordance with its historical, domestic, and religious traditions and worldview, and the rest must be left to time. In the practice of the present struggle we are able to see and observe the confirmation of a given theory: for Marxism, the present is only a means, and only the future is the end. If such is the case, I refuse to take part in such construction, when the entire people and everything it has accumulated is expended on the goal of a remote, abstract future. Isn't present-day mankind an end? Doesn't it want to live? Is it so deprived of sensory organs that at the cost of its sufferings we want to build the happiness of some remote mankind? No, it is time to stop the experiment. The experiment of almost two years of suffering by the people should convince the Communists that the negation of the human personality is madness.

5. I am fighting against the evil being done by individual agents of the regime; i.e., for what Comrade Kalinin, chairman of the VTsIK, expressed in these exact words: "We must resolutely remove those commissars who have wreaked ruin and destruction in the countryside, and propose to the peasants that they elect those they find necessary and useful." But alas! Life is showing the contrary. I realize that the evil I am revealing is completely unacceptable to the Party, and that you, representing the regime, are also fighting it. But then why are all those people who strive to point out that evil and openly combat it persecuted to the point of being shot? It may be that after this letter the same thing will fall to my lot. But I make bold to assure you that what is subjected to persecution in my person is not my individual protest against the evil spreading over the Republic but a collective protest—the protest of tens of millions of people. . . .

6. By virtue of my deep-rooted revolutionary and social convictions I am unwilling to be an ally of Denikin, Kolchak, Petlyura, Grigoryev, or the other counter-revolutionaries. But I view with repugnance the violence committed by the pseudo-Communists against the laboring people. And by virtue of that I cannot be their ally, either.

7. With profound commiseration for the laboring people and the possible loss of their revolutionary gains, I feel that I can render real

aid at this critical moment in the struggle, given a clear and definite policy on the Cossack question and complete trust in me and my views —which, although non-Party, are vitally healthful. You can judge from this letter whether I am deserving of such trust.

Since in this letter I have reflected not my personal view of the situation that has developed but the view of many millions of laboring peasants and Cossacks, I have felt it necessary to send copies of this letter to my many loyal friends.

Saransk, July 31, 1919.

With sincere respect for you and devotion to your ideas, I remain,
Commander of the Don Corps,
Citizen Cossack of the Ust-Medveditsa Stanitsa,
Mironov[15]

But the situation with respect to forming the Don Corps had not improved even by early August. Relations with the political workers continued to deteriorate. Refugees from the southern front were no longer being sent to Saransk. Mironov proposed that captured deserters be sent to his corps but he was turned down. Next he proposed mobilizing the peasants in the region where the corps was being formed, but this too was prohibited.

On August 8, 1919, Mironov wrote to the political section of the 1st Don Cavalry Division requesting that he be "registered as a member of the Communist Party." He thought his joining the Party would improve relations in the corps. He stated that he fully supported the following slogans of the Party. "All power to the soviets of workers, peasants, Cossacks, and other deputies of the toilers, who must be the executors of the people's will and its leaders in creating a new life." "The abolition of private ownership of land and all means of production, with the people becoming the owner." "Long live the Russian Proletarian-Peasant Laboring Republic."

But under pressure from Rogachev, Larin, and Boldyrev, the divisional political section rejected Mironov's application, thus refusing to accept its own corps commander as a member of the Communist Party. Needless to say, this further aggravated relations between Mironov and the corps political workers. As early as August 5 V. Larin, a member of the Don Corps RVS, had sent a letter to G. Sokolnikov at the Southern Front RVS, demanding that steps be taken against Mironov. On August 12 S. Skalov, another member of the RVS of the Don Corps and a former supporter of Mironov's, proposed that formation of the Don Corps be discontinued, and that it be scattered among other units of the southern front. Although the Cossack Section of the VTsIK had been made responsible for controlling the corps' formation, its leading political workers bypassed the Cossack Section in their letters and denunciations of Mironov—sometimes even resorting to sending them through private channels.

In mid-August a young Communist named E. E. Efremov was named commissar of the Don Corps. Efremov had worked in the Grazhdanupr of the southern front but differed sharply from Syrtsov in his attitude toward the Cossacks. He willingly expressed a desire to work in the Don Corps, and soon established a good relationship with Mironov. But the general atmosphere in the corps continued to be increasingly tense.

At this time, meetings in the corps were held almost every day. At one such meeting Mironov received a note asking: "How should mankind live, and what is the social revolution?" At about that time Mironov had become familiar with the program of the Maximalist SR's. Having been deeply affected by the fate of the Don Cossacks, having learned from the press and from letters about the grave consequences of the policy of "decossackization" in the region of Uralsk, hearing around him the mutterings of the middle peasants who resented the requisitioning of foodstuffs, and knowing of the successes of Denikin's forces, Mironov had been pondering the same thing day and night: What is the social revolution? How can its successes be consolidated while avoiding extremes? How should the life of the Russian people—and primarily of the peasantry and the Cossackry—be built in the future? At the same time, he was plainly offended and aggrieved by the refusal of the Don Corps Communist cell to accept him as a member of the RKP(b). It is not surprising that the program of the Maximalists struck him as convincing and correct. In a private conversation at about that time he said, "I regarded myself as a non-Party man, and now it turns out that I belong to the Maximalist Party." Desirous of giving some kind of order to his thoughts and convictions, Mironov wrote for his own private purposes a special declaration under the heading of "Long Live the Russian Proletarian-Peasant LABOR REPUBLIC." He did not distribute this declaration among the Cossacks of his corps and made only a few copies of it. These copies were among his papers, and were seized and entered in the record of the "Mironov case," discussed in the next chapter. The declaration was anonymous and signed with the words, "The Worker-Peasant-Cossack Party," although no such party existed at the time. But Mironov never denied his authorship of it; nor did he deny that in his speeches and in certain appeals he had expressed many of the thoughts and theses in this manifesto. In that declaration, Mironov not only developed but expressed in more concise form many of the ideas he had already set forth in his letter to Lenin dated July 31, 1919. Later he publicly acknowledged that much of the thesis in the declaration had turned out to be wrong. Nonetheless this document is an important indication of how the many tragic events in the spring and summer of 1919 were perceived by a good part of the middle peasantry and the laboring Cossackry. Mironov noted:

Artificially stirring up the Cossacks, through tyranny and violence, to counter-revolution, not taking their ignorance into account, the Communist Party—or rather, some of its chiefs—has set itself the goal of exterminating the Cossacks. Is this not the very reason why rural Russia has come to hate the Communists? Is this not why there are so many deserters? Freedom of speech has ceased to exist throughout Russia. Capital punishment has been restored on a scale never practiced by the government of the overthrown Tsar. . . . Anti-profiteer detachments are taking the last pound of flour from toilers in all stanitsy. . . . The laboring peasants' hopes for land and freedom to the extent to which they have a right to them have not been fulfilled. . . .

The evil Russian reality that we are now living through asks us:

1. What does General Denikin want?
2. What do the Communists want?

3. On whose side is moral force?

4. On whose side is physical and technical force?

All these questions are frightful, but we must answer them. First, General Denikin is striving to restore the power of capital, the power of the landowner, the power of the bourgeoisie. It makes no difference whether there will be a constitutional Tsar or a bourgeois republic. In either case the Russian worker and soil-tilling peasant will have to give up for many years—both for himself and for his children—his dream of freedom, of a better lot, his dream of land and an untrammeled life, his dream of factories and plants. He will again become a slave of need, of hunger and cold; a slave of benightedness and ignorance. The proletariat and the peasantry will have to make restitution for all the losses suffered by the bourgeoisie during the Revolution, and many of them will have to pay with their own lives. We see that Denikin has one task—clear and definite.

Second, we do not see that the task of the Communists, who have taken all power into their hands, has been clear and definite. We do not understand that impudent monopoly over the power of the people by a handful of individuals who in their fanaticism have imagined themselves to be the builders of social life according to an unprecedented method: fire and the sword. . . . The agrarian policy has been manifested in the artificial establishment of so-called *kommuny* and Soviet farms with the use of hired labor. This policy is leading to the creation of a new class of Soviet hired laborers and peasants bound to the state. . . . By depriving the laboring peasants of the last remnants of live and dead stock and the land they won from the landowners, the Communists are blocking the opportunity for further progress; i.e., the advance of agriculture, which is the basis of the entire national economy.

No brotherhood.

No equality.

No justice.

No love.

And besides: no bread in the city, no salt in the country.

As under the Tsar, the administration of the country is not in the hands of freely elected soviets and their executive organs. Instead it is in the hands of some commissars. . . . Under cover of socialist phrases and words, the Communists are carrying out a policy of narrow Party interests and violating the class interests of the revolutionary toiling masses. As for the countryside, the Communists are concerned about it insofar as it is necessary to drain it of grain, livestock, money, and people by all measures and means. . . . They are not trying to put out the fire of civil war. . . . The Communists have reached a dead end. They themselves do not know what they want or where their utopian dreams will end up. . . .

Third, since the building of the Communist paradise is being effected by means of oppression that angers the laboring masses, moral force is on the side of Denikin. Because of the Communists' methods the Red Army is becoming demoralized, and its fighting efficiency is deteriorating. Desertion is simply the peasants' answer to the forcible building of the *kommuny*.

Fourth, physical force is on the side of Denikin. So that the Communists, deceiving the people and the Red Army men, should not paint a picture of the demoralization of the White armies, we can boldly affirm that with each advance Denikin gains hundreds of new troops. . . .

Consequently, the worst enemies of the social revolution are: on the right, General Denikin; and on the left—strange as it seems—the Communists.

Before the Russian people, not yet dazzled by the utopia of Communism—before the proletariat, the laboring peasantry, and the Cossackry—there now looms a tremendous question: What to do? . . . We answer: first of all, stop Denikin, and then defeat him. Denikin can be stopped only by the unification of the forces of the people. And that unification will take place only when the Communists have left the stage. . . . They will not want to leave the stage voluntarily. They will have to be ordered: Go away. And as soon as the Don Cossacks hear that the Russian people have thrown out the Communists, they will stop. And Denikin will have to make his first halt in spite of himself. He will be compelled by Red Army rifles to make his second halt, whereupon his undertaking will deteriorate as rapidly as Krasnov's career.

OUR PROGRAM IS AS FOLLOWS:

All power, all land, all factories and plants—to the toilers.

OUR TASK COMPRISES:

The elimination of all obstacles and barriers to creating favorable conditions for the peaceful (evolutionary) development and achievement of the ideal forms of human arrangements, the best forms of human existence. . . . We set as the goal of social revolution not what we would like to arrange but what is possible and what can be effected by revolutionary means.

The entire laboring people is now faced with the following tasks:

1. The complete destruction of the power of capital.
2. The dissolution of all institutions of the bourgeois system.

3. The organization of society on new labor principles—not by means of force but by means of prolonged, patient, and loving example.

Hence the POLITICAL PROGRAM of the "Russian Proletarian-Peasant Republic" is as follows:

1. All power belongs to the laboring people in the person of authentic SOVIETS of worker, peasant, and Cossack deputies of the toilers, which must be the executors of the people's will and their leaders in building a new life. Consequently it is essential immediately to restore, by all means and measures, both locally and at the center, the real power of the SOVIETS by means of re-electing soviets and calling an All-Russian Congress of Representatives of the Re-Elected Soviets.

2. Dissolution of the bureaucratic power, which has created an insurmountable barrier between the laboring masses and the regime; re-election of all executive organs of the Soviet regime; and review of all Soviet personnel staffs.

3. Dissolution of the Council of People's Commissars, transferring all its functions to the Central Executive Committee.

4. Granting broad powers to local soviets in the economic construction of the country.

5. Abolition of capital punishment. Down with capital punishment! When Kerensky tried to restore the death penalty for failure to obey military orders, the Communists shouted that he was a hangman. But now they themselves are using it at every step. Deserters—i.e., those who do not recognize the Communists—are shot by them hundreds at a time.

6. Dissolution of extraordinary commissions and revkoms.

7. Establishment of freedom of speech, of assembly, of the press, and of association for revolutionary parties.

8. Unswerving implementation of the socialization of land and fostering the unification [sic] of all means of production.

9. Socialization of factories and plants.

10. Review of taxation rates, with their establishment on a just basis.

11. With a view to combatting famine: dissolution of the requisitioning system, which has stirred up the countryside against the cities. Dissolution of all bureaucratic agencies for taking grain from the countryside. Combatting world imperialism to effect the exchange of products within the Soviet Republic through peasant and worker consumer-labor cooperatives on the basis of an all-Russian plan.

12. So long as the enemy threatens the Revolution the existence of the Red Army is vitally necessary. Therefore the workers and peasants must look upon the army as their offspring without which the

existence of the Revolution is impossible, as is, consequently, the toilers' power over the land.

13. It is advisable fully to unify all revolutionary forces in a general program for the most rapid realization of the social order.

14. To use all measures and means to stop the pitiless extermination of the Cossacks begun by the Communists, showing the laboring peasantry who is responsible and the hidden meaning of this diabolical plan. . . .[16]

It is not difficult to discern in Mironov's declaration the influence of the SR programs, and of the petty-bourgeois illusions of the Trudoviks. Likewise, many of the proposals in this declaration seem utopian and unfeasible under conditions of a bitter civil war. But at the same time one can see the influence on Mironov—an honest and sincere revolutionary—of the profoundly mistaken policy of "decossackization" carried out in the spring of 1919 on the Don and in the Urals, and of that violence against the middle peasantry committed by local organs of the regime in the name of the RKP(b) and criticized by Lenin. Thus in April 1919, Lenin said:

If there is dissatisfaction among them [the middle peasants], we say that that dissatisfaction was engendered from above, and we must find out how legitimate it is, given our shortage of personnel. You people here in the capital know how difficult it is to combat red tape and bureaucratism. . . . But what is going on in the villages? There, people who call themselves Party members are often scoundrels who use violence with no qualms whatsoever. And how often it is necessary to fight against inexperienced people when they confuse kulaks with middle peasants![17]

On August 18, 1919, Mironov learned from friends of his that the corps' political section had officially demanded of the Southern Front RVS the dissolution of the corps, accusing Mironov of "a plot like Grigoryev's" (*grigoryevshchina*).* At the same time he

* During the Red Army's successful advance into the Ukraine in January 1919, N. Grigoryev, ataman under Petlyura, went over to the Red Army with his troops. But in May 1919, he launched an insurrection in the rear of the Red Army and seized Kherson and Nikolayev. This disorganized the Red Army's rear area and helped Denikin to advance into the Ukraine. Grigor-

learned that Denikin's army, having repulsed an unsuccessful advance by the Red Army, had gone over to a new attack. A cavalry corps under the command of General Mamontov had broken through between the 8th and 9th armies and, after disorganizing the Red Army rear, had seized several cities, including Tambov and Kozlov. The headquarters of the southern front, located in Kozlov, had been rapidly evacuated to the north. An extremely alarming situation developed all along the southern front. Mironov neither could nor would wait any longer. Although his corps was not yet completely formed, he began to prepare for an attack on the southern front against Denikin. The Republic RVS was promptly informed that the corps was being prepared for an unauthorized attack. Alarmed by this information, I. Smilga, a member of the RVS and of the TsK RKP(b), called Mironov by direct line and ordered him not to send units without authorization. Smilga convinced Mironov to call upon him in Penza and work out a plan of action. Mironov agreed to come, but insisted on being accompanied by a bodyguard.[18]

Mironov immediately prepared to leave for Penza. But the stationmaster at Saransk categorically refused to provide railroad cars for the one hundred fifty Cossacks in Mironov's escort. And Mironov, afraid of arrest, refused to go without the escort.

Mironov then decided to act at his own risk and attack Denikin. On August 23, he sent the following telegram to 9th Army headquarters:

Please inform the Southern Front that, seeing the failure of the Revolution and overt sabotage against the forming of the corps, I can no longer remain idle, knowing from letters from the front that I am awaited there. With the forces available to me, I shall engage Denikin and the bourgeoisie in a hard-fought battle.[19]

---

yev's insurrection was provoked by mistakes of Soviet organs in the Ukraine in their national, agrarian, and food-procurement policies. The insurrection was put down in some ten weeks' time, and Grigoryev himself was murdered.

On August 24, the undermanned Don Corps left Saransk for the southern front, moving toward the position occupied by the 23rd Division, which Mironov had previously commanded and which was now under the command of his former deputy, A. Golikov. Before leaving Saransk, Mironov sent a telegram to I. Smilga, stating his intentions and warning that if the Communists reprimanded him by waging war against him, he would begin killing Communists.

Mironov's action was of course a violation of discipline. Basically, he was provoked by the RVS's decision to discontinue the formation of the corps; by the policy of "decossackization"; and by the conflict between the RVS and the political section of the Don Corps. It was an act of desperation, but it was by no means an anti-Soviet insurrection. Mironov had not the slightest intention of going over to Denikin's side. Viewed from the outside, however, his actions resembled mutiny; and they were so interpreted by many people at southern front headquarters and in the Republic RVS.

Without making any attempt to look into the reasons for Mironov's actions, I. Smilga quickly declared him a traitor. In an appeal "To the Troops of the Don Corps," Smilga ordered that Mironov be brought "to the headquarters of the Soviet forces, dead or alive." On August 28, Smilga issued a new order in which he stated, quite without grounds, that "Mironov, former commander of the 23rd Infantry Division and subsequently commander of the Don Corps, has entered into relations with Denikin and started an insurrection against the Soviet regime." In this order it was affirmed that "bandits under the leadership of Mironov are plundering the population and doing violence to peaceable citizens," and that "from an intercepted letter of Mironov's it is evident that he intended to flee to the army, start an insurrection there, and open up our front for Denikin."

Mironov had left Saransk with several thousand men, only half of whom had rifles. But some of the troops obeyed orders from Smilga and broke away. The rest of the corps went south with Mironov. They followed a route through the forests, avoiding populated places and confrontation with Red Army units that had been ordered to pursue Mironov.

Lenin learned of Mironov's action from the Republic RVS and at first believed Mironov was a traitor. On August 30, Lenin wrote a note to E. M. Sklyansky insisting on the immediate capture of "Sokolnikov's godson"—i.e., Mironov.[20] At the time, Lenin had little access to information about Mironov's action. It is strange, however, that the editors of Volume LI of Lenin's *Complete Collected Works* should have written, in a scholium to this note of Lenin's, that Mironov, "Sokolnikov's godson," started an anti-Soviet insurrection in the Saransk Region.

Fairly sizable forces were assigned by the RVS to "capture" Mironov. A. Golikov, commander of the 23rd Division, received orders to capture, disarm, and arrest the unit. Any resisters were to be shot on the spot. S. M. Budenny, commander of a cavalry corps, also received orders to detain Mironov. Here is how Budenny describes that episode in the first part of his memoirs: "Without having completely formed his corps, Mironov led his Cossacks out of Saransk, ostensibly to render assistance to the southern front but actually in order to go over to the Whites." At that time, Budenny writes, he received orders to move toward Novokhopersk to crush General Mamontov's cavalry corps, which had broken through into the rear of the Red Army. "But," wrote Budenny, "I did not want to let the traitor Mironov escape. Since we possessed information about Mironov, we routed our movement to Novokhopersk in such a way that we would encounter his corps in the zone of movement." The encounter actually took place on September 14, 1919. As Budenny tells it, when his units encountered Mironov, the latter drew up his detachment in formation. But a cavalry detachment under O. Gorodovikov galloped up to him, took him under escort, and brought him to Budenny. Mironov was indignant.

"What kind of arbitrary action is this, Comrade Budenny?" he shouted. "I drew up my corps so that we could have a meeting with your corps and call upon our troops to endeavor to save democracy."

"What kind of democracy were you intending to save? Bourgeois democracy? No, Mr. Mironov, it is too late. You are too late."

"What does that mean?"

"Stop pretending, Mironov. You know very well you have been disarmed as a traitor who has been outlawed."

It seems likely that this entire conversation was dreamed up many years later. It is a fact, however, that when Budenny's corps was encountered by Mironov's enfeebled and undermanned detachment, which by now numbered only about five hundred men, Mironov and his unit surrendered and laid down their arms *without the slightest resistance.*

After briefly interrogating several unit commanders of the Don Corps, Budenny ordered that Mironov be shot and that those unit commanders and commissars who had followed him be court-martialed. But before Budenny's order could be carried out, Trotsky, who happened to be with Budenny's corps at the time, ordered that Mironov and all his "accomplices" be sent to Balashov to be tried by a special court-martial.

Subsequently, the Cossack Section of the VTsIK also declared that Mironov's arbitrary departure from Saransk was an act that could be termed counter-revolutionary, and Mironov was expelled from the Cossack Section. But while it did not object to Mironov's being declared an enemy of Soviet Russia, the Cossack Section demanded the creation of a special commission to clarify all the circumstances of Mironov's action and the mistakes of the political workers in the corps.

THE BALASHOV
TRIAL

It was on September 14, 1919, that Philip Mironov and his detachment were surrounded and disarmed—or rather, voluntarily **VIII** laid down their arms. This took place in the rear of the 9th Army, which had its own investigative organs and its own revolutionary tribunals. But for the trial of Mironov and his "accomplices," Trotsky decided to set up a special investigative commission, which was subsequently transformed into a tribunal. On September 16, Trotsky sent the following telegram to E. Sklyansky in Moscow for the TsK:

The captured Mironovites have been taken to Balashov, where an investigative commission for this case is functioning. I am getting in touch with Smilga to see that the commission is converted into a tribunal and the case tried in Balashov. The reasons: (1) the large number of accused persons (430); (2) witnesses in the same area; (3) the trial must have great educative significance for the Cossacks; (4) the membership of the tribunal—the Kuban Cossack Poluyan; Anisimov, also from the Kuban; and Podospelov, chairman of the 9th Army Tribunal—is fully appropriate and authoritative. Properly handled, the Mironov case will serve to liquidate Don Constituent-Assemblyism and Left SRism. I propose that at the time of the trial Comrade Smilga come to Balashov to handle the case.[1]

Trotsky had taken an interest in the "Mironov case" even prior to Mironov's capture, having published several articles on Mironov and *"mironovshchina"* in the RVSR newspaper *En Route*. In one of these articles, which we have quoted from earlier, titled "Colonel Mironov" (Mironov was actually a *voiskovoi starshina*, or lieutenant colonel), Trotsky wrote:

The career of the former Colonel Mironov has come to a shameful and wretched end. He regarded himself—and was regarded by many others—as a great "revolutionary." . . . But what was the reason for Mironov's temporary adherence to the Revolution? Now it is completely clear: personal ambition, careerism, the urge to climb upward on the backs of the toiling masses. . . . The goal of the Revolution is to establish the full and stable dominion of the toilers. General Krasnov was the representative and chief of the exploiters on the Don. Therefore the struggle of the Soviet forces was aimed against Krasnov. The purpose of that struggle was to rouse up the most impoverished of the Cossacks, the most oppressed strata; to organize and unite them; and with their aid to put down the Cossack kulaks and nobility and make possible a more just and happier life on the Don. Mironov understood none of this, and had no deep feelings about it. He felt that if Krasnov were defeated and Colonel Mironov became the appointed ataman on the Don, all problems would thereby be solved. He viewed the people's revolution as a replacement of the people at the top; i.e., he saw the uprising and struggle of the toilers as merely a means to the furtherance of his own political career. When he began to realize that the victory of the Soviet forces would lead not to his own power but to power for the local poor, he became indignant and embittered. The longer this continued, the more he began to agitate against the Soviet regime.

Trotsky went on to acknowledge that in the spring of 1919 "certain Soviet authorities and the worst Red Army units" had committed "injustices and even acts of cruelty against the local Cossack population." But according to him, those who committed all those cruelties had been harshly punished by the central

Soviet government. He called the talk of "decossackization" a vile rumor put out by Denikin. Mironov's protest against the policy of "decossackization" on the Don and in the Urals was depicted by him as an attempt "to accumulate a bit of political capital; to build popularity and glory for himself on the basis of mistakes made by individual workers." Trotsky concluded his article as follows:

Having finally become convinced that he would never be ataman, Mironov decided on a desperate move. Like the Ukrainian ataman Grigoryev, who resembled him like a brother, Mironov raised the banner of revolt against the Soviet regime. Grigoryev's end is common knowledge. After the first few engagements the forces he had deceived were dispersed and defeated, and either fled or went over to the army. Grigoryev himself was murdered. It is completely obvious that the same wretched end is in store for Mironov—but it will come more quickly.[2]

In this article, Trotsky even declared that he had no doubt but what "secret communications had already been set up between Mironov and Denikin. Shady go-betweens went from Denikin's camp to Mironov's, and vice versa, behind the backs of the Cossacks deceived by Mironov."

Even after the arrest of Mironov and his detachment, Trotsky published yet another article, "The Lessons of the Mironov Affair," in the same newspaper. In that article he states:

Mironov's criminal and stupid adventure is over. Its chief perpetrator has been caught, along with his helpers and deceived followers. The capture was effected without a single shot's having been fired. There were no dead or wounded on either side. This fact alone is the best proof of how shaky and lacking in confidence the insurgents felt themselves to be. Whereas Mironov had begun the struggle in an attempt to become the appointed Don ataman, most of his followers had no clear idea of where they were going or for what purpose. At the critical moment, therefore, they did not even have the strength to resist. At the first encounter with the Red Soviet cavalry, they surrendered as a body. Hurried along and disarmed, they have been put at the disposal of the Revolutionary Military Tribunal.[3]

Trotsky acknowledged that, after surrendering, Mironov's troops asked to be taken into the Red Army. But in his opinion this simply meant that "among the Cossacks, the line between Reds and Whites has not yet been drawn clearly enough."

There is no point in bothering to refute the trumped-up charges that Trotsky brought against Mironov in this new article—that he was a careerist, that he was trying to gain appointment as ataman on the Don, etc. Along with these manifestly libelous notions, however, Trotsky unexpectedly stated that "Colonel Mironov" represented the views and attitudes of the middle Cossacks:

There is the impoverished class of Cossacks, who right now, with all their souls, are longing to be with us. There are the Cossack upper strata, who are intransigently hostile toward the proletariat and the Soviet regime. And there is the broad intermediate stratum of the middle Cossacks, who are still very backward politically. . . . The Cossack with middle holdings of land watches the bitter struggle between the Whites and Reds, and does not know which to join. Usually he joins those who at a given moment seem to him a bit stronger. . . . Mironov reflects the confusion and tergiversation of the backward middle Cossacks. So long as our troops were victoriously advancing toward the south, Mironov led his division in the common ranks of our army. But when our front swayed and gave way, and Denikin threw us back hundreds of versts, Mironov went over to the opposition and continued on that path to the point of open revolt.

There is, of course, no doubt as to Mironov's affinity—not only in his thinking, but in his actions—with the attitudes and interests of the basic mass of the working Cossackry (i.e., the middle Cossacks). But there are also some deliberate exaggerations in those judgments of Trotsky's that we have quoted. It was not merely during the advance to the south that Mironov moved with the Red Army. In the autumn of 1918, his division, fighting some bloody battles, also retreated to the north under the onslaught of the White Cossack Don Army. And now, in the summer of 1919, Mironov had not "tergiversated" to the side of Denikin, who was "stronger," but had roused his corps to battle against Denikin. There was no doubt as to the political instability of the Cossacks and the middle peasantry. But in the spring and summer of 1919 the Cossacks' political behavior was definitely determined by the mistaken policy of "decossackization"—a reality and by no means the product of "vile rumors" put out by Denikin or Krasnov. And this policy drove a considerable part of the laboring Cossackry into Denikin's camp. But Mironov restrained himself, although he paused at the crossroads. His desperation is clearly evident in a personal letter to Foma Kuzmich and Ivan Nikolayevich Karpov, written shortly before Mironov left Saransk. Referring to the secret instructions he had learned about and the practice of "decossackization," Mironov wrote:

And so the cataract has fallen from our eyes. I don't know what to do. I cannot abide the thought that if we are now going to conquer the Don Region and see them begin to exterminate our poor, ignorant Cossacks, the latter will begin to burn their own villages and stanitsy, having been driven to it by the ferocity of the new Vandals. It is hardly likely that our hearts will not quake at the sight of this hellish scene, or that the curses uttered by those miserable people will pass us by. On the other hand, Denikin and the counter-revolution. This means that enslavement of the laboring people against which we have fought for a year, and which we must continue to fight to the end. And so you stand there like the legendary Russian hero at the crossroads: if you go to the right, you'll be killed; if you go to the left, your horse will perish; and if you go straight ahead, both you and your horse will perish. . . . What to do? What to do? . . . Ponder it yourselves, and ponder it together with loyal people. As for me, I shall probably escape to the 23rd Division.[4]

Thus we see that in the summer and autumn of 1919 the reality was much more complex than Trotsky's elementary sociological constructions.

But to get back to the Balashov trial. The investigation* of the case was brief—and not merely because in those times no investigation was very prolonged. Mironov and his comrades-in-arms

---

* I.e., the preliminary judicial investigation which, under the Russian system (and those of certain other European countries), is conducted by an examining magistrate.—Translator's note.

had nothing to conceal; and they told the investigative commission everything they knew and thought.

The open hearing of Mironov's case by the Extraordinary Revolutionary Tribunal began on October 5, 1919, and lasted for three days. Comrade Poluyan, chairman of the tribunal, opened the first session by reading the indictment:

Mironov, former commander of the Don Corps, and his unit commanders are on the defendants' bench. The gist of the case is as follows. On August 24, on orders from Mironov, his corps, consisting of several regiments, left Saransk and moved in the direction of the 23rd Division. This action by the Don Corps was preceded by the following circumstances. On August 22, without the authorization of —and even contrary to the wishes and will of—the corps RVS, Mironov held meetings at which he spoke against the Communist Party, accusing it of criminal acts having a harmful effect on the country, and stating he intended to go to the front. At these meetings he asked his unit commanders which of them wanted to go with him. Most of the unit commanders expressed a desire to go with him, and only a part of them refused to go and remained in Saransk.

The indictment next quoted from proclamations by Mironov, emphasizing that he mentioned in one of them the "necessity of overthrowing the Communist Party." The indictment also set forth the content of Mironov's conversations with Smilga directly before the former's departure from Saransk. The indictment contained no charge of possible contacts between Mironov and Denikin. At this point it stated:

What were Mironov's motives in going to the front? There is information in the investigative material indicating that he was going in order to save the front. It would appear that he had two goals: on one hand, to help the front; and on the other hand, to wage war against the Communist Party—to wage war on two fronts, so to speak. And this slogan runs like a red thread through all his statements.

The indictment said that during the movement of Mironov's corps there were several skirmishes with units of the Red Army, with a number of killed and wounded on both sides. In order to complicate operations against him, Mironov ordered that the telephone and telegraph lines be cut. "There is information to the effect that along the way Mironov arrested Communists and a number of peasants. True, he later released them." The indictment also outlined the circumstances surrounding the arrest of the Communists Bukatin and Lisin, whom Mironov declared to be hostages, and who managed to escape only after several days.

Those who drew up the indictment went on to say:

In order to liquidate Mironov's revolt the Soviet regime had to exert tremendous efforts. Literally tens of thousands of troops were mobilized. And since cavalry did not suffice, it was necessary to transfer infantry—to withdraw it from the front—and overload the railroads, which did manifest damage to our position on the front. On the other hand, as soon as Mironov's action became known to the Red Army units it undoubtedly introduced an element of nervousness into their mood, which our enemy could not fail to take advantage of. Thus what we have here is manifest treason.[5]

After the reading of the indictment Mironov stated:

I acknowledge my guilt with respect to all the charges presented, except for certain details. But I ask that my confession be heard during the trial. . . . I say this not in order to bribe the court but so that I can go to my death with the definite view that I have been exonerated [ochishchen], and only this compels me sincerely to repent and acknowledge my guilt.

In his own defense Mironov justified himself by noting that since 1917 he had supported the program of the Communist Party and combatted the counter-revolution:

I have always spoken out in defense of the Soviet regime, explaining the program of the Communist Party as I understood it, first in the regiment and then, on the Don, to the public. I wholeheartedly strove for all this—something that is known to the tribunal, and something that runs through all my speeches up until the twenty-second—that fateful incident in Saransk. There, after I had been outlawed, I began to make sharp [or morbid: boleznennye] statements against individual members of the Soviet government who by their actions had damaged the prestige of the Party and played into the hands of the counter-revolution.

Mironov gave a detailed account of his struggle against Krasnov in the summer and autumn of 1918, and of the oppressive atmosphere that developed in the Don Corps in Saransk. Mironov explained that the reason for his departure for the front was the news he had received about the fall of Tambov and Kozlov and his desire to stop the collapse of the front. He hoped that as a victor he would avoid condemnation.

Explaining his arrest of Bukatin and Lisin, Mironov said:

That was only a tactical maneuver, since I didn't want anyone to interfere with me en route. I at first announced that Bukatin and Lisin would be shot, but then I ordered that it not be done, since as a matter of principle I am opposed to the death penalty. I did not have a single one of the arrested Communists shot. . . .

He further noted that proclamations in which he called for the the downfall of the "autocracy of the commissars" were issued after reading the order declaring him to be an outlaw.

As the following excerpts of the hearing show, Mironov defended himself on many accounts:

Chairman: Did you say that the Communist Party had the aim of exterminating the Cossacks? That the Communist Party had sent political workers to the Don to punish and shoot Cossacks?

Mironov: Yes, I mentioned that in my letter to Comrade Lenin.

Chairman: Did you possess any documents establishing the fact of crimes and outrages committed on the Don?

Mironov: When I was called to the Don, I met with the former commander of the 9th Army, who told me that the uprisings on the Don should be attributed to the policy of our Communists. He informed me of many instances* of arrests, massacres, and shootings of Cossacks.

* *Fakty*, meaning either "instances," as here or "facts," as in the next sentence.—Translator's note.

Chairman: I am not asking you about facts, but whether you have documents establishing those facts.

Mironov: There were no such documents. . . .

Chairman: You say that you had in mind local Communists, Communists at the front, who had done damage there. But what can you say when you called Trotsky "Bronstein"?

Mironov: That is a special question. After the October Revolution, when I took up the cause of the Soviet regime, Krasnov was always calling me a traitor. But being in the Don Region, I constantly explained to the Cossacks the meaning of the new system, I talked about the Soviet regime—about the new form of government in which all the toilers would participate. The Cossacks listened to me and agreed with me, and willingly supported the Soviet regime. But when I saw the outrages and excesses committed by the Communists on the Don, I felt like a traitor toward the people I had told about the Soviet regime and had urged to serve it. I had the idea that Trotsky was the author of that policy on the Don, and it distressed me that the Center should take such an attitude toward the Cossack question. In calling Trotsky "Bronstein," I had no intention of stirring up ethnic strife.

Chairman: Did you ascribe that policy to Trotsky as a political leader or as a Jew?

Mironov: As a Jew. I acknowledge my mistake.

Chairman: You try to show that you were not against high-principled Communists. Yet, among other things, you have written that the cause of the Revolution's failure must be sought in crimes of the ruling Communist Party, which has provoked the general discontent of the broad masses, and that therefore only one course of action is left: to overthrow that Party. You so state in your order-proclamation to the Don Corps. How do you explain that?

Mironov: I did not directly state that the Center should be overthrown. As we drew near to the front, in many areas I heard the peasants say right out that they would not defend the Communists. Having observed such discontent, I considered it my duty to report this to Comrade Lenin, who was not informed as to the real feelings of the broad masses. And in sending him the telegram I hadn't the remotest idea of damaging the Revolution. I was merely giving Comrade Lenin my own view, pointing out the necessity of changing the policy and creating a stable Red Army front. Just how badly our chief lacked information on the real state of affairs was something I became convinced of when I asked whether my telegram had been received and it turned out that it hadn't even been decoded yet. At a time when I was expressing my deep distress—at that critical moment

Comrade Lenin had not even been informed of my telegram. I repeat that I had no idea of overthrowing the Center—merely undesirable elements.

Chairman: Did you realize that your actions could have a harmful effect on our situation at the front?

Mironov: I realized it, but I had no idea my action would be so taken to heart, and that I would be considered a traitor.

Smilga: When you went to the front with your unit, you were aware and knew that the Soviet regime would oppose it. And if you intended to defend the front, was it logical on your part to defend that Red front by setting up a front in the rear of the Soviet regime? As an officer, what were your thoughts about that?

Mironov: Of course I acted illogically, and I recognize my fault. But try to understand my psychological state—to understand the atmosphere I had been living in for seven months. I am deeply distressed that I disregarded your order and went to the front. But I assure you that there was no malicious intent, and that everything I did was in order to strengthen the Soviet regime. Take my telegram of June 24. Isn't it true that every word of it is imbued with a desire to point out the weak spots in the Soviet regime?

Chairman: In your telegram of June 24 to Lenin you wrote that it was essential to create a people's government. What did you mean by that?

Mironov: I meant that the representatives of the working peasantry would have close contact with the soviets, and would notify and inform the masses of what was being done there.

Chairman: Is it your opinion that the existing soviets do not reflect the voice of the people locally?

Mironov: Yes, that is my opinion.

Chairman: And even more so at the Center?

Mironov: I won't undertake to talk about the Center—only local areas.

Chairman: And so in your opinion a government of the people should replace the soviets?

Mironov: No, that is not my idea. A government of the people is necessary so that the voice of the people, with its needs, can be heard locally.

Chairman: In your opinion, is there a kind of gap between the Center and local areas?

Mironov: Yes, there is a partition. There is great discontent among the peasants. They maintain that cows, horses, and foodstuffs are being taken away from them, and they can't find the guilty party.[6]

Poluyan, the chairman of the tribunal, asked Mironov a few more questions, and then began to question the other defendants: K. Bulatkin, P. Karneyev, Ya. Fomin, V. Shishov, E. Dronov, M. Danilov, I. Igolkin, and others. The majority of them did not acknowledge any guilt: they had believed they were going off to fight for the Soviet regime. Some of the defendants maintained they did not know that Mironov had been outlawed and therefore followed his orders. Others simply pleaded their own ignorance and failure to understand the situation. One of the defendants, Grigoryev, confirmed (*podtverdil*) that the Communists Lisin and Bukatin actually planned to murder Mironov in Saransk. Grigoryev immediately sent Mironov a report about it. Poluyan asked Grigoryev: "Why didn't you run to Mironov as soon as you heard an attempt was to be made on his life?" "Anyone else would have done what I did," Grigoryev replied.[7]

But Lisin, questioned as a witness, stated he did not remember the subject of the conversation he had had in Saransk with Bukatin and Grigoryev. He confirmed that in the spring of 1919 he was chairman of the Ust-Medveditsa District Tribunal, and that more than six hundred persons were tried by the tribunal. He said, however, that the only ones shot were atamans, officers, and Cossacks who had voluntarily joined up with Krasnov's forces.[8] In his subsequent testimony, Lisin tried to defame Mironov in every way. He testified, for example, that Mironov had allegedly declared "that he would wipe Penza from the face of the earth— and along with it, all the local vampires, like Smilga, who were spilling innocent blood."[9] Mironov, however, said that he never made such a statement. Lisin also said that when he was under guard in the baggage train he heard that Mironov told the Cossacks marching with the train that the corps was going to the "Yid-European front." But Mironov refuted that lie, showing that at all times during the movement of the corps he was in advance of the units and was never with the baggage train.[10]

S. Skalov, a member of the corps RVS who was questioned by the tribunal as a witness, confirmed that before the corps' departure for the front, Mironov permitted him to address the Cossacks and attempt to refute Mironov's arguments about moving to the front. But the majority of Cossacks and unit commanders, rather than supporting Skalov, followed Mironov.

Also thoroughly questioned as witnesses by the tribunal were the political workers of the Don Corps—Larin, Kovalev, Boldyrev, and others—together with Stepanov and Makarov, representing the Cossack Section.

Written depositions from the witnesses Prazdnikov, Matveyenko, Izvarin, and certain others were read aloud at the session of the tribunal held on October 6, 1919. Then, at Mironov's request, his letter to Lenin was read aloud. Comrade Makarov, commissar of the Cossack Section of the VTsIK, who had been present when Mironov was received by Kalinin and Lenin, gave testimony that was extremely important. He stated:

When Mironov came to Moscow and went to see Kalinin and Lenin, I was there too. I must say that Mironov, who had been at a far remove from the Center, struck me as politically childish. Kalinin told him: "If representatives of the Soviet regime on the Don are making mistakes, we will bring representatives of the Cossack lower strata into the administration. The Revolution is a great and difficult task, but in the final analysis only the Soviet regime will emerge onto the high road." Mironov agreed with what Kalinin had said, and I thought that if he had agreed he would stand firm. When Lenin touched upon the subject of the revkoms, he (Lenin) said that insofar as possible the revkoms should be replaced by local soviets. Lenin mentioned Mironov's speech in the Ust-Medveditsa area in which he (Mironov) spoke out against the Communists. Mironov replied that he had in fact made a speech to some Cossacks in 1918, but that in it he had spoken out not against the Soviet regime and the highly principled Communists but against the pseudo-Communists.[11]

I. T. Smilga served as prosecutor at the trial. In his speech he said the following, *inter alia*: "I accuse former Cossack Colonel Mironov and all his accomplices with having instigated an armed mutiny against the Soviet regime at a time when that regime was at war against Denikin, and when they (the defendants) occupied responsible positions in our Red Army." Having told of his conversations with Mironov on the direct line, of his prohibiting the departure from Saransk, and of his warning that Mironov would be outlawed and that strong forces would move against him, Smilga went on to say that Mironov did not heed his warning or orders, and that "from a military viewpoint, from the viewpoint of a commander who should set an example of discipline for his troops, there was no justification for Mironov."

Smilga went on to attack Mironov's personal character, and his arrogance in particular. He also had some sharp words on the other defendants, using the epithet "janissaries" for those unit commanders and Cossacks who were close to Mironov. And he went on to say:

Do we have the right to judge Mironov? Perhaps he is our direct class enemy, like those gentlemen from the National Center,* or those who throw bombs. Then he could say: "You can destroy me, but you cannot judge me. One does not judge one's class enemy." And he would be right. But this is a different case. The man sitting on the defendants' bench is by no means a Cadet. He is a man whose political activity dates from the October Revolution. He is one of the branches [sic] of the October coalition, and therefore we have the unquestionable right to judge him as a traitor to the Soviet regime. . . .

Whoever in revolutionary times plays games with the lives of his subordinates is not a leader but an adventurist. Mironov's entire undertaking was imbued with adventurism.

Smilga then proceeded to scoff at Mironov's policy of recruiting "Greens" and deserters. He called Mironov's protests against shootings and death penalties a "quasi-sentimental Tolstoyan melodrama." Mironov's references to the hardships and discontent of the peasants were labeled by Smilga "petty demagogy exploiting the ignorance of the masses," since the Communists had had nothing to do with the ruin of the country: the latter was the

---

* An organization of Cadets, moderates, and some conservatives that refused to recognize the Treaty of Brest-Litovsk and was in contact with Denikin.—Translator's note.

result of the four-year imperialist war and the actions of the counter-revolution. At the moment the Communists could not dispense with conscription into the Red Army and the compulsory surplus-appropriation system (*prodrazverstka*),* since without them it would be impossible to overcome the generals' counter-revolution. Smilga said nothing of those distortions of the Party line toward the middle peasantry which had been widely practiced locally, and which had often been criticized by Lenin as extremely damaging to the Soviet regime.

Likewise, Smilga said nothing of Mironov's contributions in battles on the southern front in 1918 and 1919. But he was unsparing in his insults, calling Mironov a "depraved political abortion." He explained the latter's tremendous popularity among the Don Cossacks by claiming Mironov had "bought that popularity with cheap demagogy—a cheap accommodation with the ignorant Cossacks, whom he sent home with their horses and saddles."

But Smilga did acknowledge in his speech the crimes committed by organs of the Soviet regime on the Don in the spring of 1919.

Now, about the atrocities on the Don. It is evident from the investigative material that those atrocities took place. But it is also evident that those chiefly responsible have already been shot. It should not be forgotten that all these incidents occurred under the conditions of a civil war, when passions are white-hot. Remember the French Revolution and the struggle between the Vendée and the Convention. . . .

Smilga concluded his speech by demanding execution by firing squad for Mironov and his accomplices.

Mironov's trial was organized as a show trial. That being the case, a defender—who represented all the defendants—took part in the proceedings along with the prosecutor. The defense counsel, Comrade Rybakov, spoke at the trial immediately after

---

* I.e., the requisitioning of farm products—in principle, only from those who had a surplus of them.—Translator's note.

I. T. Smilga. Rybakov asked for leniency toward the defendants. In his concluding address, he said:

. . . It is not from a historical viewpoint, not from the viewpoint of violating a political program, that we should view each of these men who have been accused of a crime. We must see them as simple people—experienced soldiers with little understanding of the political situation and little familiarity with the Party program. . . . History teaches us that great-hearted men cannot keep silent when they see flagrant injustices in their own country. We know that our great writer Tolstoy shouted: "I can no longer keep silent!" Likewise Mironov, incapable of witnessing with indifference the outrages being committed on the Don, cried out from the depths of his heart. And he was heard. And who knows whether a certain attitude toward the Cossacks on the part of the Center was not produced by that cry? We know that recently there has been a change in the Soviet regime's attitude toward the Cossacks. . . . All this means that Mironov was historically right when he cried out and declared that things couldn't go on like that. . . . Mironov shouted, and his shout awoke us to the need of treating one of the ulcers of Soviet Russia. That was the service he performed; and because of that service he should be pardoned. . . .[12]

After the speech by the prosecutor and the defense counsel's plea, the defendants were each afforded the opportunity of making a final statement. In his statement—in what he might well have thought was his last speech—Mironov said:

Citizen Judges! When I found myself in Cell No. 19, when the doors . . . of that stone cubicle clanged shut, I was suddenly at a loss as to what was going on. I had given all my life to the Revolution, and it had put me in prison. . . .
In that stone cell I meditated without hindrance—no doubt for the first time. There was no enemy around me. . . . And being in that stone cell, I was compelled to take up—perhaps for the first time—a book of more serious content [sic]. Smilga has told you that I was unfamiliar with Marx. That is true. But there, for the first time, I read a little book on the socialist movement in France. And quite unexpectedly I came across a definition characterizing people like myself. The thing is that in France there were socialists concerned with the idea of

justice who were seeking it everywhere, and these people were sincere
in the highest degree but lacking in scientific knowledge and methods.
And whereas Comrade Smilga said that I should have understood
and realized all the consequences of my action, I say with complete
sincerity that if I had had such political mentors as Comrade Smilga
and others I might have been a fine political leader, just as I was a
fine military one. People deprived of scientific knowledge who with
their hearts and feelings seek and strive for justice are called empirical
socialists. That's exactly what I am. It is my misfortune, and I ask the
Revolutionary Tribunal to bear it in mind. I say this in complete
sincerity. I shall not dwell on this, especially since a good deal is
already known to the judicial investigators. Rather, I shall say something about the revolutionary actions I performed in the course of
my life.

Mironov then recounted certain incidents in his struggle for
justice during those years when he was a rank-and-file Cossack and
a noncommissioned officer, and told of his participation in the
revolutionary movement on the Don in 1906 and in subsequent
years. In concluding his long speech, Mironov said:

I am guilty of committing a crime provoked by an entire chain of
circumstances. And I repent. . . . I declare that I am not against the
Soviet regime; that the circumstances were such that they made of
me not a man but a thing almost incapable of realizing its own
actions. I would ask the Revolutionary Tribunal not to attribute
special significance to my proclamations and declarations, since they
were written when I was in such a state that I was not a man but a
thing—when I was not in control of myself but circumstances were in
control of me. . . . It is painful for me to accept the epithet of traitor.
I was called that by the Whites; and now Soviet Russia is calling me
that, although I have always fought for her and defended only her
interests.

I won't talk about how I grew up—under what conditions I spent
my childhood. As one who wore second-hand clothes and was fed
from other people's kitchens, I early began to realize all the hardship
and oppression of poverty. Thus you see that I have spent all my life
wanting to help the people, to alleviate their sufferings. I myself came
of common stock, and understood the people's needs very well. From
the first days of the Revolution up to the present, I have never cut

myself off from the people. . . . I ask you to test me. Give me the opportunity to remain in the position of a revolutionary fighter and show that I can defend the Soviet regime. . . . Be lenient in the matter of my crime. . . . You can see that my life has been a cross. But if I have to carry it to Golgotha, I will carry it. And whether you want to believe me or not, I shall shout: "Long live the social revolution! Long live Communism!"[13]

But the Extraordinary Tribunal sentenced Mironov and ten of his closest comrades-in-arms and those Communists who had left Saransk with him to be shot. The remaining defendants were given varying terms of imprisonment.

The tribunal's decision also stated that the judgment was final and would enter into force immediately, and that the sentence would be carried out within twenty-four hours.

But the order was not carried out. After the sentencing on October 7, 1919, Smilga sent a telegram to the Politburo in Moscow requesting a pardon for Mironov and his followers. It seems likely that Smilga was influenced in this decision by speaking with the representatives of the Cossack Section of the VTsIK who had attended the trial, as well as with N. Krylenko, Procurator of the RSFSR, and with Trotsky. The majority of representatives of the Soviet public who attended the trial favored a lenient sentence, and this had to be taken into account. The Politburo of the TsK RKP(b), with Lenin participating, resolved: "Mironov and his accomplices not to be shot but brought to Moscow; Smilga to be instructed to submit suggestions on forms and conditions of mitigating the punishment."[14]

Twelve days after the end of the trial, Mironov—who by this time was in Moscow, staying at the Alhambra Hotel—described the day which (so he thought in Balashov at the time) was the last one of his life.

After the sentence was announced, they granted our request that we all share one cell so that we could spend our last day together. There, knowing that in a few hours you would be shot, that in a few hours you would cease to exist, you very respectfully observed those who, like yourself, were sentenced to death, and compared their state with your own. There a man told everything about himself, willy-nilly. No attempts to conceal the real state of your soul. Useless. Death, snub-nosed Death, looks you in the eye, freezes your soul and heart, paralyzes your will and mind. She has already embraced you with her bony arms but does not breathe on you right away. Instead she slowly, slowly squeezes you in her cold embrace, taking pleasure in your spiritual torments, and draws out the remnants of your struggling will.

And yet, despite her cold breath, despite the fact that there were only a few hours of life remaining, some of the condemned men, even under those conditions, were able to look her proudly in the eye. Others tried to show they were doing the same, summoning up their remaining spiritual forces. No one wanted to appear cowardly, and no one reached a state of hopeless desperation [sic] in the face of inevitable doom. One comrade, for example, tried to deceive both himself and the rest of us by jumping up from his place and beginning a kind of tap dance, beating his heels on the cement floor of the cell. But his face was immobile, his eyes were dim, and it was frightful for a living man to look into them. But this did not suffice for long. . . . The condemned man lay on the floor: he was overcome with fear. He had no more strength left for the struggle. And we no longer had the strength to look at him without the deep, complete desperation of pity. In his eyes we could read one puzzling question: "Why? Why?" Slowly, horribly, the last minutes of the condemned men dragged on. But even they were shortening the way to the inevitable. The dénouement was approaching, and the condemned men gave their best possessions to those comrades who had been sentenced merely to imprisonment. . . .

Above all, we tried to find forgetfulness in revolutionary and Cossack songs. With the words of the song, "Oh, Batyushka, the glorious, quiet Don," we took leave of those things we had loved more than life, and for which we were perishing. . . . But did our beloved Don hear us? Did it understand our love, our suffering for it? . . .

After the songs our spirits drooped again. Gradually the noise quieted down in the cell of the condemned men, and through the silence we seemed to hear the knocking sound made by the bones of snub-nosed Old Lady Death, who had crawled out from somewhere but always vanished as soon as one of us showed a sign of life. . . . With an incredible effort of the will our depressed spirits were again lifted up, although gradually; and again the cell of the condemned men came alive. One of the men was standing at one wall, a second at another, writing something. . . . As he prepared for death, he wanted to express his last thoughts for the edification of the living. How characteristic were these last inscriptions—the last words of a man going to the valley of death, "where there is neither grief, nor disease, nor lamentation but life eternal." Each man expressed his ideas in accordance with the scope of his mental outlook, his political maturity, and his self-awareness.

. . . That is what we went through while in the cell on death row. It was not the fear of death felt in the heat of battle, among the crackling of machine guns, the whistling of rifle bullets, and the gritting sound of shells, when a man plays with danger, since he knows his death is a matter of chance: one moment, and everything is over. But it is frightful for a human soul to realize the nearness of inevitable death, when there is no hope for chance, when you know that nothing in the world can keep you from the approaching grave, when the time remaining until that horrible moment grows less and less, until finally someone tells you: "The pit is ready for you."[15]

Smilga later wrote in his memoirs:

On the second day I and the entire membership of the court decided to request a pardon from the VTsIK. We had to hurry, since the time for executing the sentence was drawing near. But before raising that question we decided to ask the condemned men to pledge their word of honor that henceforth they would honorably serve the Soviet regime and the Revolution. The meeting with Mironov was held in the office of the Balashov Prison; that with the others in the cell. Mironov had aged visibly overnight. When I told him I would request a pardon, the old fellow broke down and wept. [Mironov was forty-seven years old in 1919, and Smilga was twenty-seven.] It was easier for the old soldier to take leave of life than to come back to it. When we approached the cell where the others were, they broke off singing some revolutionary song. When we went in, one of the prisoners shouted: "On your feet! Attention!" The others jumped up from the floor. When we told them the purpose of our visit, the joyful excitement was great. The cell rang with shouts of "Let's get Denikin! Long live the Soviet regime!" The men were glad of the chance to live and fight.[16]

On the evening of October 8 a session of the presidium of the VTsIK passed a resolution pardoning Mironov and his comrades-in-arms.[17] This decision was announced to the convicted men on

October 11. Immediately upon learning that he and his friends had been pardoned, Mironov submitted a request for membership in the Communist Party.

The revocation of the death sentence, however, did not mean the abrogation of all punishment. There is evidence that Lenin talked with some of the comrades who had returned from Balashov and asked them about Mironov. Apparently it was not until September 1919 that Lenin read Mironov's letter to him of July 31. On his personal order, Mironov and ten of his comrades-in-arms were brought to Moscow, still under guard. A commission headed by F. E. Dzerzhinsky was formed to look further into the "Mironov case." Dzerzhinsky, and later E. Stasova, met and talked with Mironov a number of times. Smilga, too, continued to concern himself with what would happen to Mironov, and gave consideration to the possibility of using him as a divisional commander. Dzerzhinsky and Stasova submitted their suggestions and conclusions to Lenin.

At a regular session of the Politburo held on October 23, 1919, Vladimir Ilich raised the question of what was to be done with Mironov and his associates. The discussion ended in the adoption of a resolution that exempted Mironov from all punishment and, further (by the vote of Lenin and Kamenev), made him a member of the Don Executive Committee; this second proviso, however, was ordered held in abeyance until N. Krestinsky had discussed Mironov with Trotsky. Krestinsky thereupon spoke on the direct line to Trotsky, who recommended that Mironov be assigned to an army command on the southeastern front. Subsequently, on October 26, the Politburo confirmed Mironov's appointment to the Don Executive Committee, but decided against giving him a command in the Red Army.

The Politburo's resolutions of October 23 and 26, the publication of Mironov's appeal to the Don Cossacks, his appointment to the Don Executive Committee, and an affirmative decision on the question of his acceptance into the Communist Party signified Mironov's full-fledged rehabilitation—and that of his comrades as well. Shortly thereafter, K. Bulatkin was appointed commander of a division, Ya. Fomin took command of a regiment, and M. Danilov went back to the army as a commissar again. And all the rest of Mironov's comrades-in-arms were given responsible posts. This meant rehabilitation in the juridical sense of the word.[18]

A year before the events described above, Mironov had married a second time, having previously been separated from his first family by the front lines. In October 1919 his second wife, N. V. Suyetenkova, was in Nizhny Novgorod. Late in October, therefore, when he had secured the necessary documents, Mironov set out for Nizhny Novgorod to join his wife on a vacation before assuming his post on the Don Executive Committee. En route, however, he came down with typhus and was hospitalized for more than a month. It was not until early December that he returned to Moscow. Immediately after his return he had his second meeting with Lenin—a meeting also attended by Dzerzhinsky and Stepanov, chairman of the Cossack Section of the VTsIK. They talked chiefly about the new Party policy in the Cossack regions and Mironov's work on the Don Executive Committee.

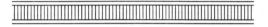

THE LIBERATION
OF THE DON REGION

While Mironov and his comrades were languishing in Balashov Prison awaiting trial, fighting continued on the southern front. The Red Army had failed to destroy General Mamontov's corps operating behind its lines. In September 1919, Denikin ordered his armies to initiate a general attack. By October 13, Denikin's forces had taken Orel and advanced toward Tula, which was not only an important center of arms production for the Red Army but the last large city on the road to Moscow. For Soviet Russia a genuinely critical situation had developed—the most critical in the entire civil war.

Denikin's victories over numerically superior units of the Red Army were due primarily to his large units of cavalry—at that time the most mobile and maneuverable of forces. These units—chiefly Cossack regiments and divisions—constituted Denikin's principal shock troops.

It was becoming more and more obvious that in addition to military measures it was essential to carry out several political acts aimed at alienating Cossacks from Denikin, creating a split among the Cossacks, and winning the working Cossacks over to the side of the Soviet regime and the Communist Party. Furthermore, the battle plan adopted by S. S. Kamenev, Supreme Commander of the Red Army, called for vigorous actions by the 9th and 10th armies in the Don and Kuban regions—i.e., on the flank and in the rear of Denikin's army—with the simultaneous checking of the enemy in the regions of Orel and Voronezh. It was intended to deprive Denikin, in this way, of his chief sources of troops and matériel, and thereby to compel his rapid retreat. But the success or failure of this plan depended not so much upon military efforts as upon the political mood of the Don and Kuban Cossacks.

Despite the importance of gaining the political loyalty of the Cossacks, the Donburo, headed by Syrtsov, went on pursuing its old, ruinous policy of "decossackization." Syrtsov maintained that the Soviet regime's defeat on the Don was the fault of the Red Army, which allegedly had not given the revkoms sufficient help in putting down the counter-revolutionary Cossacks.

By contrast, the Cossack Section of the VTsIK showed much more leniency in a special "Report on the Procedure for Governing Cossack Regions." In particular, the report called both for increasing Cossack participation in local government and for increasing representation in regional and national bodies. The Cossack Section was to have a direct part in the mobilization and formation of Cossack units. The Cossack Section strongly objected to the policy of terrorism and advocated the broadest kind of amnesty for those Cossacks—especially the working Cossacks—who had supported the Soviet regime against General Kaledin and General Dutov and who had begun to rise up against the Red Army only because of mass terrorism in the spring of 1919. The Cossack Section also protested against any resettlement of Cossacks to central Russia, and against the large-scale resettlement of peasants from central Russia in the Cossack regions. The Cossack Section warned that even the decree equalizing the rights of the Cossack population with the entire laboring population of the RSFSR was untimely, since it might be taken as a law on decossackization. In general, it was the opinion of the Cossack Section that all serious administrative and economic measures in the Cossack regions should be implemented only after careful study and the gathering of substantial statistical data, with the participation of regional committees.

But the Donburo and Syrtsov were supported by A. G. Beloborodov, a member of the TsK RKP(b) and of the 9th Army's RVS, who in several letters to the TsK insisted on the harshest policy toward the Don Cossacks.

These demands of Syrtsov and Beloborodov were not supported by the Republic RVS. On September 16, Trotsky drafted some notes titled "Guiding Principles for Our Policy on the Don in the Near Future."[1] As is evident from their content, these notes served as the basis for the new discussion of the Cossack problem by the TsK RKP(b) in late September 1919.

On September 30, 1919, an article titled "Theses on the Work on the Don" appeared in the newspaper then being published, *Izvestiya of the Central Committee of the Russian Communist Party (Bolsheviks)*. This article differed from previous directives and instructions on Cossack problems, and, a fortiori, from the documents and proposals of the Donburo. In these new theses the TsK noted that "the propertied counter-revolutionary upper strata of the Cossacks and the closely allied stanitsa kulaks are characterized by extreme class stubbornness." As for the working Cossacks, the theses stated that "until recently they have been held fast in the clutches of the Cossack social hierarchy and prejudices as to the commonalty of interests of all Cossacks."

The following were then proclaimed, in the theses of the TsK, as the fundamental principles of the Party's policy toward the Don Cossacks:

1. We shall explain to the Cossacks in words, and show them by deeds, that our policy is not one of vengeance for the past. . . .
2. . . . We will take under our firm protection and armed defense

those elements of the Cossackry who in fact come to meet us halfway. To those elements who take a wait-and-see attitude, we will afford an opportunity to orient themselves and get the lay of the land, meantime keeping a sharp eye on them. We shall pitilessly exterminate all those elements who directly or indirectly support the enemy or cause difficulties for the Red Army. . . .

3. We shall keep strict check to see that the advancing Red Army does not engage in pillage, violence, etc. . . . At the same time we demand of the local inhabitants everything necessary to the Red Army. . . .

6. A careful organization of communications and intelligence work is essential.

7. The idea that we will not force anyone to join a *kommuna* must be clearly and persistently publicized and put into practice. . . .[2]

The theses, partially quoted here, were adopted on September 30, 1919—that is, before the trial of Mironov and his comrades. It is therefore not surprising that in the introductory part of the theses there should have been frequent mention of "Mironov's revolt," of "Mironov's uprising," etc. It was precisely because Mironov's tremendous popularity disquieted those who drew up the "theses" that his name was so often repeated in the first part of that document. However, from the very first day of the trial it became evident that the greater part of the charges leveled against Mironov were not confirmed; and the charge of secret contacts with Denikin was not even included in the indictment brought against Mironov and his comrades-in-arms. Mironov's statement at the trial made a strong impression, not only on all those attending the trial but also on the members of the Extraordinary Tribunal. It might have been assumed that the tribunal would not give him a harsh sentence. On this score, there was an interesting exchange of opinions between Smilga and Trotsky, who was attentively following the course of the trial. On October 7, Trotsky asked Smilga on the direct wire:

Encoded. To Smilga in Balashov. The report on Mironov's trial suggests that things are tending in the direction of a lenient sentence. In view of Mironov's behavior, I daresay such a decision would be advisable. The slowness of our advance on the Don demands intensified political pressure on the Cossacks with a view to dividing them. Mironov could be used for this mission if he were called to Moscow after the sentencing and pardoned by the TsIK with the understanding that he would go behind the lines and raise up an insurrection there. Communicate your thoughts on this matter.[3]

In this case Trotsky had thought up a very doubtful scenario: first to sentence Mironov and his comrades to be shot; then to pardon them, with certain stipulations.

On October 10, after the VTsIK had already passed its resolution pardoning Mironov, Trotsky sent Smilga another phoned telegram:

First: I am bringing the subject up for discussion by the Politburo of the TsEKA. We are giving full quote autonomy unquote. Our forces are leaving the Don Region. The Cossacks as a whole are deserting Denikin. Appropriate guarantees must be created. Mironov and his comrades could act as go-betweens, for which purpose they should go deep into the Don Region. Give me your ideas on this in writing, at the same time as you send Mironov here. Do not release him from custody right away, but send him to Moscow under a lenient but vigilant guard. The question of what is to be done with him will be settled here in connection with the question mentioned above.[4]

Mironov, of course, knew nothing of Trotsky's plans. But even without any prompting from Trotsky or Smilga, Mironov, once he was released, immediately joined in the effort to alienate the working Cossackry from Denikin and the entire generals' counterrevolution by publishing appeals to the Don Cossacks.

About the Red Army's retreat in September and early October of 1919, A. I. Egorov, commanding the southern front, later wrote that the situation on the southern front "was assuming the dimensions of a strategic catastrophe. The forces on the front and in the immediate rear were under direct threat."[5]

But the White armies were incapable of carrying out the final drive to Moscow. Faced with being overrun, Soviet Russia became a military camp: all its resources were mobilized for this decisive battle. And only a few days after Denikin's forces had taken Orel, there was a reversal on the southern front in favor of the Red Army. On October 20, S. M. Budenny's cavalry corps, operating jointly with the 8th Army, defeated the cavalry units of General Mamontov and General Shkuro in hard fighting. Kromy was liberated, then Voronezh, and although the White armies still put up stubborn resistance, they could not stop the Red Army's counter-attack. On November 17 the Red Army liberated Kursk. Units of the southern front and the southwestern front began a rapid advance toward the south, entering the Don Region and the Donets Basin.

When the Red Army entered the Don, it sent out proclamations stating that land would not be taken away and that the Reds would overlook any previous criminal participation in other political movements. But this did not settle the question of setting up Soviet regime organs in this area. As early as September 1919 the Donburo had been reorganized into the Don Committee of the RKP(b). A temporary Don Executive Committee (Donispolkom) consisting of comrades Medvedev, Syrtsov, and Kopyatkevich was also set up in Saratov.[6] In late October, by decision of the Politburo, Mironov was made a member of this Donispolkom.

The Donispolkom's first sessions were, however, held in the absence of Mironov, who was ill, and then subsequently in Moscow. The questions discussed at these sessions included those of organizing the sections of the Donispolkom, foodstuffs, publishing the newspaper *The Soviet Don*, and choosing the day when they would move to the Don. Also discussed was the question of the Cossack congress being convened in Moscow by the Cossack Section of the VTsIK. The stanitsa of Uryupinsk, already liberated by the Red Army in early December, was chosen as the temporary seat of the Committee.[7]

Meantime the Red Army was rapidly advancing toward the south. In late December 1919 and early January 1920, after heavy fighting, the cities of Tsaritsyn, Taganrog, and Novocherkassk were captured. By January Rostov-on-Don fell and soon the Red Army reached the Sea of Azov and cut the front of Denikin's army.

The Donispolkom moved to Rostov in the liberated Don Region and set to work consolidating the Soviet regime. Mironov soon arrived in Rostov, taking up the post of chief of the Donispolkom's Agrarian Section.

Agrarian problems were central to Soviet policy on the Don: the attitude of the working Cossacks toward the Soviet regime depended on a correct solution to those problems. There was a tremendous amount of work to be done in liquidating the vestiges of feudalism in the region, equalizing the rights of the Cossacks and those of the indigenous peasants in the matter of land use, conveying to peasants and Cossacks the lands of officers and landowners who had fled from the Don Region, and organizing state farms to replace the large-scale capitalist horse-breeding farms. Mironov took an active part in all this work.

In January 1920, Mironov was accepted into the ranks of the RKP(b). For him this was a very important step. It indicated the party's acknowledgment that it had made a mistake in promoting the "decossackization" so repugnant to Mironov.

Restoring peaceful life in the Don Region was a difficult matter. The region was almost depopulated. Many Cossacks had been killed in battle and some were fighting in the Red Army. Numerous families had withdrawn to the Caucasus and the Crimea with the remnants of Denikin's army. They had feared a resumption of "decossackization."

In January 1920 an attempt was made by the Whites to unite, if only formally, the Don, Terek, and Kuban regions under a single regime—the Supreme Circle—which, when convened, approved the following proclamation:

We, the Supreme Circle of the Don, the Kuban, and the Terek, having taken all steps to ensure that there is no repetition of the mistakes and crimes that caused the recent catastrophe on the front, have

deemed it necessary for the welfare of the people, and success in the
struggle against the Bolsheviks, to establish—and we have established,
in complete agreement with the Supreme Commander of the Armed
Forces in the South of Russia—a common regime for all of South
Russia and unity of command for all armies so that, through the
joint efforts of the Cossacks, the troops of the volunteer army, and
the Caucasian mountaineers, we can crush the enemy and develop our
successes.[8]

The White military forces in the Northern Caucasus were still
very considerable. On January 15 and 16 the Whites inflicted several serious defeats on the Red Army, which had to retreat in
many directions. But there was no real unity in the White camp.
The conflicts between Denikin's volunteer army and the Cossacks
were sharply aggravated. Soon the Red Army, having regrouped,
renewed the attack. The 1st Cavalry Army and other cavalry units
of the Red Army smashed the Don and Kuban cavalry corps. By
early spring, most of the Northern Caucasus had been liberated
from the Whites. Some of the volunteer and Cossack units still fit
for combat were evacuated to the Crimea. General Denikin re-
linquished his title of Supreme Commander of Armed Forces in
the South of Russia and transferred his authority to General
Wrangel, based in the Crimea. Tens of thousands of Cossacks who
could not be evacuated to the Crimea, together with those who
were ill or wounded, were taken prisoner by the advancing Red
Army. Some of the Cossacks—like Grigory Melekhov, hero of
And Quiet Flows the Don—joined the Red Army and soon took
part in the war against an aggressive Poland. The other Cossacks
were disarmed and sent home.

Organs of the Soviet regime were set up in the Don Region at
this time, where the Red Army had passed through rather quickly.
In its liberated areas the villages and stanitsy were not burning,
and there was nothing resembling the mass terrorism of the spring
of 1919. But errors in management occurred, especially in implementing the surplus-appropriation system. The Don Foodstuffs
Committee had taken all the grain from the storage bins of the

poor farmers (this was simple to do); but the kulaks' grain—in pits—had not been touched. Also, they had collected seed grain and shipped it to another district.

Difficulties were encountered in consolidating the Soviet regime in Mironov's home territory—the Ust-Medveditsa District. There were few people capable of working in the district and stanitsa agencies of the Soviet regime. The Party organizations had very small memberships. As of January 14, 1920, there were only seventy Party members in the Ust-Medveditsa District, along with about two hundred candidate members and about two hundred Komsomol members.[9]

The chief concern of the district and stanitsa organs of the regime was to implement the surplus-appropriation system, organize propaganda, and distribute documents of the Soviet regime. Publication of the newspaper *The Red Word* (*Krasnoye slovo*)* was begun in the district. Representatives of the district Cossackry took part in the First All-Russian Congress of Working Cossacks, held in Moscow between February 29 and March 6, 1920. The agenda included questions as to Soviet construction in Cossack areas, the foodstuffs policy, the organization of the national economy, etc. The resolutions emphasized that the Cossackry was not a separate people or nation but an integral part of the Russian people, and that the Cossack areas were an integral part of Soviet Russia. The congress came out for the participation of the working Cossacks in all organs of the Soviet regime on the same basis as all laborers and peasants, and called upon the Cossacks to strengthen the alliance between the workers and peasants and concentrate all efforts on overcoming the economic ruin in the country.

On March 1, 1920, Lenin spoke at the congress. He talked about Soviet Russia's international position and internal conditions in the country. He did not, however, touch upon the specifics of the Cossacks' problems and those of the Cossack

* Also translatable as "Witticism."—Translator's note.

areas, or the recent history of the Soviet regime's relations with the Cossacks. Painting a bleak picture of the country's economic condition, Lenin called upon the peasants and Cossacks to make a grain loan to the workers so that they could restore industry and commodity production required by the entire population.

On March 25, the SNK RSFSR issued a new decree on the construction of the Soviet regime in Cossack areas. This decree confirmed the Cossack exemption from compulsory military service. It thereby proclaimed the abolition of the Cossackry as a special military caste. The decree also proclaimed equalization of rights between the Cossacks and all other citizens of Cossack regions. At the same time the decree noted that the land allotment (*pai*) of the working Cossacks would be preserved, and that the Soviet regime would not encroach upon the Cossacks' customs and way of life.

At that time freedom of local trade was permitted in the Don Region, which made it easier for the weak Soviet regime organs to manage the food supply for the local population. For the Cossacks it stimulated the output of agricultural production. But given the commodity shortage then existing in the country, even limited freedom of trade made for difficulties. Prices of foodstuffs rose, and the situation of the poorest strata of Cossacks and peasants was very trying. The district Party organization favored revoking all freedom of trade and taking voting rights away from all former POW's who had previously fought against the Red Army.

In the spring of 1920, the secretary of the Party's Ust-Medveditsa District Committee was V. Dombrovsky, an unstable and hot-tempered man who could not work with the Cossacks. This made for numerous frictions in the district. The Fifth District Congress of Soviets, which Mironov attended, was held in the district in early June 1920. A number of disagreements arose between Mironov and the district leadership, and he spoke out in criticism of those "narrow-minded Communists" who were failing to enlist the sympathies of working Cossacks. A considerable part of the district congress supported this criticism by Mironov.

In July 1920, A. Skobinenko, an unprincipled and politically weak man, became secretary of the Party's District Committee. Under him, Party work in the district was badly mismanaged. On October 19, the Party District Committee removed Skobinenko because of the breakdown in Party work, and decided to bring him before a Party court for fomenting quarrels and creating an unhealthy situation in the organization, and for lack of discipline and "un-Communistic acts." This Party court was convened on December 5, 1920. It was decided to institute Party and administrative proceedings against Skobinenko, and to hand his case on to the Don RKP(b). Skobinenko was temporarily recalled from the district. (We dwell on this trifling local incident only because Skobinenko will soon reappear—although in a totally different role—in the pages of our historical sketch.)

In the spring and summer of 1920, Mironov spent most of his time in Rostov-on-Don, working in the Regional Executive Committee (*Oblspolkom*). Here, in midsummer, he was visited by one of the authors of this book, S. P. Starikov. They had a long, friendly conversation. Mironov obviously felt encumbered by his "peacetime" work. At the time, the war with the White Poles was still going on, and Mironov wanted desperately to go to the front. He was also alarmed by the actions of Wrangel, who clearly wanted to break through into the Don Region and the Kuban so as once again to stir up the Cossacks against the Soviet regime. They talked about the White Guard landing that had been made, under the command of General Ulagai, on the Black Sea littoral in the Northern Caucasus.

As before, Mironov's popularity among the Don Cossacks was very great. They continued to keep close track of what he said and did. For example, N. A. Sokolov, who was appointed military commissar of a brigade in the 23rd Infantry Division, found to his surprise that the soldiers in the brigade not only remembered their former divisional commander quite well, but were well informed as to his work in the Donispolkom and his joining the Party.[10]

Meantime, there were still a good many Don Cossacks in

Wrangel's forces. After Denikin's defeat, large numbers of Cossacks sought refuge in the mountains of the Caucasus. Mironov repeatedly issued appeals to these Cossacks, inviting them to give their allegiance now to the Soviet regime. These appeals were distributed in the form of leaflets, and more than a few Cossacks and peasants, after reading them or hearing them read, did in fact come back to their own farms, villages, and stanitsy.

MIRONOV'S COMMAND
OF THE 2ND
CAVALRY ARMY

The year 1919, with all its terrible, contradictory, and tragic events, now belonged to the past. Everything seemed to herald a quick

X   end to the civil war and the beginning of peaceful reconstruction. True, in the Crimea several tens of thousands of White Guards under the command of General Wrangel were still holding the line. But this army, although it consisted of crack units, did not by itself represent a great danger to Soviet Russia. It was no secret to the Soviet government, however, that Poland, then under the presidency of Jozef Pilsudski, was preparing war against Russia. The nations of the Entente were intensively arming the Polish Army, together with Wrangel's forces, in preparation for a new campaign. By spring, Poland had put about 500,000 men under arms. It was assumed that the Polish Army—whose first echelon comprised up to 150,000 troops—would, after launching an attack from the west, be able to link up with Wrangel's army in the Ukraine for a new drive on Moscow. The Soviet government was unsuccessful in preventing this new war by diplo-

matic means, or even by making considerable territorial concessions to Poland. In April 1920, the Polish Army attacked Soviet
Russia.

At that time the Red Army did not have substantial forces on
the western front. The basic armies were in the Northern Caucasus,
where they had just defeated Denikin, in Siberia, where they had
crushed Kolchak, and in the northwest, where they had recently
routed Yudenich. Taking advantage of their numerical superiority,
the Polish forces began a rapid advance. On May 6, the Poles
captured Kiev, but they couldn't move any farther east. Large
units of the Red Army were transferred to the western front, where
heavy fighting developed. By June the Poles were in retreat.
Kiev was recaptured on June 12, and Minsk on July 11. But the
Polish government sabotaged the peace talks that had been proposed. New divisions were created, utilizing huge deliveries of
arms and equipment from France and the U.S. The hopes placed
in Wrangel, whose forces were winning victories over the Red
Army at the time, bolstered the Poles' perseverance.

As early as June 6, in accordance with the general plan of the
Entente, Wrangel's forces opened their attack from the Crimea.
White Guard units defeated units of the Red Army positioned in
the southern regions of the Ukraine and took a considerable
amount of territory in northern Taurida. By the end of June
Wrangel's advance had been stopped, but it was soon renewed, and
again the Red Army had to retreat.

Meantime, by August the Red Army's advance toward Warsaw
ended unsuccessfully. On August 17 the Polish Army on the
western front counterattacked. The exhausted units of the Red
Army began retreating, suffering great losses. Simultaneously, stiff
battles were waged on the Wrangel front. The attacking White
Guard forces once more succeeded in pressing the Soviet units
back in several directions. The 2nd Cavalry Army was surrounded
and for several days fought behind enemy lines. The Red cavalry
managed to break out of the encirclement only with great effort
and heavy losses. These battles brought to light not only the

merits of the new army but its weaknesses: poor staff work, reconnaissance, and communications, as well as shortcomings in the direction of troops.

By fall the failures of the Red Army on both the Polish and the Wrangel fronts had put Soviet Russia into an extremely precarious situation. A real threat of a prolonged war had arisen, while the internal situation in the country grew increasingly complex. Workers and peasants alike were weary of wartime hardships, food shortages, and mobilizations. Economic conditions worsened. Under these circumstances the prospect of yet one more wartime winter seemed unbearable. The TsK RKP(b), and Lenin personally, posed before the nation's military leaders a task of the greatest importance: to decisively defeat the new campaign of the Entente and end the war before the oncoming winter.

In this critical time it was decided to use Mironov in a military capacity once again. Late in the previous August, the RVS of the Southwestern Front (A. Egorov and Stalin) had asked Moscow to send Mironov to the front as commander of the 2nd Cavalry Army. Trotsky agreed with the proposal, and on August 30 the Republic RVS, "taking into account Mironov's great military experience in commanding large units, and his knowledge of the strong and weak aspects of the enemy's utilization of cavalry," appointed him commander of the 2nd Cavalry Army.[1]

By September 6 Mironov had taken command of his new unit, which at the time was in the front's reserve. It had 2,760 "sabers" (cavalry troops), 130 machine guns, and 19 field pieces. The front's inspection commission noted in its findings that "the regiments are badly shrunk and familiar only with the simplest formations. The officers have a poor knowledge of regulations and are not trained theoretically."[2]

Mironov at once initiated intensive military and political training. In addition to the reinforcements planned previously, the army was rapidly beefed up with volunteer Cossacks from the Don Region attracted by the opportunity to fight under Mironov. In a little more than three weeks, the 2nd Cavalry Army had been transformed: it had acquired 6,299 sabers, 303 machine guns, and 34 field pieces.

On September 20 the formal establishment of an independent southern front finally took place. M. V. Frunze was named commander of the front, and S. I. Gusev, a very senior Party official, was appointed a member of the front's RVS. Among those named as members of the 2nd Cavalry Army's RVS were A. Makoshin and D. Poluyan. The latter, less than a year before, had been chairman of the Extraordinary Tribunal that had sentenced Mironov to be shot, and Mironov was vexed and offended by this appointment.

After investigating the state of the 2nd Cavalry Army, a special commission of the southern front's RVS arrived at the following conclusion:

> Since the arrival of Mironov, a tremendous amount of organizational work has been done in the 2nd Cavalry Army. Under the vigilant attention of both the political workers and the officers, . . . the 2nd Cavalry Army has been completely transformed and converted into a unit that is orderly, organized, and welded together with conscious discipline.[3]

This was confirmed in a telegram to Supreme Commander S. Kamenev from Gusev.

Meantime, on September 14, Wrangel's forces resumed their offensive against the Red Army. But whereas in the summer of 1920 Wrangel had tried to break through to the Don and the Kuban, now he had regrouped his forces and, seeing the Red Army failures on the western front, decided to drive to the north and west and link up with the Polish Army. At the same time he could deprive Soviet Russia of the grain regions of the Ukraine. After hard fighting, Wrangel's forces pushed back units of the 13th Army and reached the Dnieper. They took Mariupol, Volnovakha, and the large railroad center of Sinelnikovo.

On October 3, General Wrangel issued a directive on a new regrouping of his forces to prepare for the decisive phase of his offensive: an advance across the Dnieper and into the right-bank area of the Ukraine.

Wrangel's preparations for his new offensive had not escaped the attention of the southern front command. Late in the day of October 6 the 2nd Cavalry Army was ordered to occupy a sector between the flanks of the 6th and 13th armies on the right bank of the Dnieper and defend it stubbornly. On October 8, before Mironov could carry out this order, Wrangel's army began its offensive. A shock force consisting of three infantry divisions and three cavalry divisions was ferried across to the right bank at previously prepared crossing points. The White cavalry units were commanded by Wrangel's best generals, Barbovich and Babiyev. Wrangel was counting on breaking through the Red Army front on the right bank, simultaneously liquidating the Kakhovka bridgehead on the left bank (which was of vital importance to Soviet forces), and thus opening up the way for his farther advance to the north and west.

At this time the 2nd Cavalry Army was directly in the path of the enemy's chief thrust. The stability of the entire front depended on its capacity to hold the line. Yet in terms of troop strength and firepower it was markedly inferior to Wrangel's attacking forces.

Frunze, commanding the southern front, decided to organize vigorous offensive actions on the left-bank area of the Ukraine so as to decoy a maximum of Wrangel's units in that direction, thereby depriving Barbovich and Babiyev of security in their rear. As for Mironov, Frunze assigned him the task of stopping the advance of the White divisions by any means, preventing them from turning the flank of the 6th Army, and thus preventing the withdrawal of the Red Army from the Kakhovka bridgehead.[4]

On October 8, 9, and 10 a cavalry division of the 2nd Cavalry Army was holding back the advance of Wrangel's units in the region of Tomakovka.

Between October 11 and 14, a rugged battle was fought in the right-bank area of the Ukraine between Barbovich and Babiyev's shock force on the White side, and the 2nd Cavalry Army plus a few infantry units under Mironov's command, together with the left-flank units of the 6th Army, on the Red.[5] The Whites' operation was successful at first, and they managed to take Nikopol. From the statements of an officer captured by Mironov's forces it was learned that Wrangel was planning to ferry still another corps across to the right bank of the Dnieper—a corps under the command of General Pisarev.

After several days of indecisive combat Mironov ordered the units of the 21st Cavalry Division, which had pulled back, to stop their withdrawal, put themselves in order, and go over to the attack. Mironov himself, with his covering platoon deployed in a half-moon formation (*lava*),* attacked with the first wave. "This was necessary," he writes in his reminiscences, "since it was a rule of Mironov's that in order to demand of soldiers that they sacrifice themselves or carry out a certain order, he had to sacrifice himself or set an example—all the more so since this was the first time he was in a combat situation with the troops of this army and they did not know this side of him." The Whites directed artillery fire against the Red cavalry. Mironov's horse was wounded under him, and the 21st Division's advance was halted briefly. Soon, however, the Whites faltered and began to fall back. By nightfall on October 13 it had become plain that the initiative had been definitively snatched from the hands of Wrangel's forces. In the battle of the 13th the Whites suffered great losses. Mironov's units captured many field pieces, armored vehicles, and other matériel. General Babiyev, one of the most talented White cavalry commanders, was killed.

Night interrupted the fighting, but it was renewed the next day—the day of the Whites' final defeat on the right bank of the Dnieper. Mironov has left us a vivid description of that decisive battle:

---

* *Lava* is a Cossack term meaning an enveloping action by a cavalry unit in this formation.—Translator's note.

The day of October 14 should figure as a red-letter day in the history of the 2nd Cavalry Army and in that of the revolutionary struggle. . . . With the army deployed in battle formation, the commander inspected his troops. He made a short speech exuding confidence, convincing the soldiers they should scorn death, and ordered the red banners unfurled.

. . . At about ten o'clock the first artillery salvo thundered out. Soon the rifle fire began to crackle and the machine guns chattered, alternating with the infrequent artillery volleys. At 1220 hours the 21st Cavalry Division, whose advance units crossed the railroad line, reached the northwestern heights near the village of Marinskoye and engaged the enemy. The latter opened up with murderous artillery and machine-gun fire. The army's front, extending for more than ten versts, was spread out before one's eyes. Not only was each of our own units visible, but much that the enemy was doing did not escape observation. . . .

By 1100 the separate cavalry brigade of the 2nd Cavalry Army had reached the Buzuluk Bridge. But under heavy fire it was compelled to hurry and to begin the attack on the village of Grushevka with flying columns. . . . The village of Grushevka was being held by enemy infantry units with many machine guns and field pieces. . . . A slight disarray on the right flank . . . Uncertain conditions in the center . . . Aides-de-camp came galloping up with orders to make a vigorous, resolute attack so as to make it impossible for the enemy not only to maneuver (which he was already beginning to do) but even to get his bearings. The time had come for rapidity, purposefulness, and decisiveness. It was sheer hell, what with the thunder of the artillery and the clatter of machine guns and rifles. The enemy's cavalry units, in their indecision, rushed to the east of Marinskoye, then galloped to the south of the village, then (still uncertain) showed up toward the north in order to offer resistance to the 21st Cavalry Division, which was pressing hard. The stubbornness of the enemy's infantry in Grushevka seemed to inspire his cavalry, which tried to go over to a counterattack and for a time created confusion on our army's right flank. . . .

The commander turned to the commanding officer of the 2nd Cavalry Division, who was nearby. "Comrade Rozhkov," he said, "throw in one of your reserve brigades to strengthen the army's left flank. But in order to make an impression, and reduce losses from gunfire, move it out in a *lava* formation, squadron after squadron, over a distance of 200 to 300 paces."

Before the eyes of those looking on, there now flashed an unforgettable *tableau vivant*. Over a distance of 200 to 300 paces, eight squadrons went at full gallop toward where merciless death was reaping a bountiful harvest. From behind the heights where they had been concealed up to that time, living targets presented themselves to the enemy every five minutes. It seemed they would never stop coming. The enemy tried to stop this flow of Red cavalry with artillery fire. But no sooner had he fired one volley at his target than a new target would appear. Hence his furious artillery fire was nervous and virtually ineffective. . . . And the first squadrons were coming closer and closer to the living defenders of the trenches, who were beginning to lose confidence under the influence of this scene they were witnessing. . . . Comrade Rozhkov, the divisional commander, joined in the attack with the last squadron. . . . The 16th Cavalry Division, expected momentarily, had not yet arrived. But finally the 6th Army's cavalry appeared, coming straight out of the west. The brigade commander, Comrade Sablin, had been informed in time of the planned attack by the 2nd Cavalry Army on October 14. While continuing to observe the picturesque battle, the commander dictated a report to southern front headquarters. The report's conclusion was laconic: "We have hopes of throwing the enemy back to the left bank of the Dnieper. The battle is continuing." Fighting continued all along the front. But so long as we had not taken Grushevka, where the enemy's infantry was dug in with a large number of machine guns, it could not be thought that the enemy's cavalry would abandon the village of Marinskoye. By 1725 flying columns from the separate cavalry brigade of the 2nd Cavalry Army and from one brigade of the 2nd Division were driving the enemy out of Grushevka. . . . One more effort, one more bit of pressure . . . The enemy abandoned Marinskoye, because Grushevka had been taken.

Such was one of the military events ["pages"] of the Russian Revolution—an event that took place on October 14 in the bottomlands of the Dnieper; an event anxiously awaited by the worker-peasant regime; an event being monitored, with equal tenseness, by Kharkov, Kiev, Moscow, the Kremlin, and Lenin.[6]

The enemy was crushed all along the front. The White Army remnants rushed to the river crossings, escaping to the Dnieper's left bank. Units of the 2nd Cavalry Army and left-flank units of the 6th Army captured tremendous amounts of matériel and several thousand prisoners. As Mironov said later, beginning on October 15 the 2nd Cavalry Army replenished its military supplies almost exclusively from captured matériel.

Among the White forces crushed on the right bank of the Dnieper were Barbovich's corps, the Markov and Kornilov divisions, General Babiyev's cavalry, and the 6th and 7th infantry divisions. In an order dated September 17, Frunze evaluated the Nikopol (Trans-Dnieper) operation as follows: "The enemy's advance to the right bank of the Dnieper in the region of Aleksandrovka and Nikopol ended in the defeat of his 1st Corps and the destruction of his best cavalry. This marked the turning point in the campaign and the beginning of Wrangel's defeat."[7]

Eight years later, Wrangel himself wrote in his memoirs:

. . . I was awakened in the middle of the night. General Dratsenko reported that, having encountered strong enemy forces on the right bank of the Dnieper, having suffered heavy losses, and not wanting to subject the army to destruction, he had been compelled to order a withdrawal back to the left bank. . . . The entire operation was doomed; and the assault on the Kakhovka bridgehead on October 2 [Wrangel gives dates according to the Old Style] was beaten off. . . . At nine o'clock in the morning I received a short telegram: "General Babiyev was killed by an artillery shell on the evening of September 30." Everything became clear. With the death of their beloved leader, the spirit went out of the cavalry. They lost their élan and their belief in their own strength. The situation was beyond retrieving by General Naumenko, who took command and was wounded almost immediately. Regiments panicked. Units headed back toward the river crossings at a trot. Encouraged, the enemy went over to the attack. The panic grew greater in the ranks of the disorganized cavalry. It was no longer possible to restore order: everyone was rushing toward the river crossings. Retreating cavalry and infantry units became entangled with one another at road bottlenecks and in the bottomlands. Shaken by all he had seen, the bewildered General Dratsenko ordered his entire army to withdraw to the left bank of the Dnieper. An operation that had been correctly conceived, thoroughly prepared, and developed according to plan ended in failure. . . .

On October 1 . . . I called in generals Shatilov and Kutepov for a conference. I proposed we discuss all aspects of the question as to whether we should accept battle beyond the Crimean defile or leave northern Taurida and withdraw behind the isthmus. Having taken the totality of conditions into account, we reached a unanimous decision to accept battle in northern Taurida. This was our last gamble. Any other decision would have predetermined the inevitable end.[8]

In the second half of October, fierce battles were fought in northern Taurida. The command of the southern front was striving to defeat Wrangel's army in this particular area, not allowing it to withdraw to the Crimea and build itself up there. The Red Army's decisive attack was set for October 28. The 2nd Cavalry Army was ordered to cross the Dnieper several days before the general offensive and establish on the left bank a solid bridgehead for organizing the next blows against the enemy. The crossing of the Dnieper presented a complex military and engineering problem which, moreover, had to be solved in an extremely short time. The 2nd Cavalry Army coped with that task brilliantly. When the army's basic units had already been ferried to the left bank, Wrangel's forces made a great effort to prevent the establishment of a bridgehead and annihilate the 2nd Cavalry Army, throwing its remnants back across to the right bank. Fierce battles were fought here on October 26, 27, and 28. General Wrangel sent in his best corps, the 1st Army Corps, to oppose Mironov's units. But Mironov's troops beat off all the attacks made by that corps and secured the bridgehead.

The other armies of the southern front (including the 1st Cavalry Army, recently thrown against Wrangel), which went over to the attack on October 28, were able to deal several crushing blows to Wrangel's units. The plan worked out by Frunze's staff called for cutting off Wrangel's escape route to the Crimea and completely destroying his army in northern Taurida. But this did not prove successful, and the greater part of Wrangel's forces managed to break through into the Crimea. In the third part of his memoirs, Budenny blames this temporary failure on several commanders, including Mironov, while at the same time whitewashing all the actions of the 1st Cavalry Army. But from operations documents it is clear that on October 30 and 31 the 2nd Cavalry Army beat off fierce attacks by General Govorov's Don Corps and several other units, which took Mironov's army to be the 1st Cavalry Army.

In the battles of October 30 and 31 the 2nd Cavalry Army not only defended itself but prevented the crushing of the 6th Army's left flank. From Wrangel's memoirs it is obvious that it was through the battle formations of the 1st Cavalry Army that Wrangel's main forces fought their way into the Crimea—thanks chiefly to their superiority in equipment—in armored vehicles and tanks that cavalry units could not stand up to. Also, Wrangel's intelligence service had in its possession the campaign plan worked out by Frunze's staff.

After withdrawing to the Crimea, Wrangel had counted on holding out for the entire winter behind the Perekop defenses. But the Red Army had received orders to take the defenses on the Isthmus of Perekop by storm as quickly as possible, and liberate the Crimea. Preparations for the new offensive took several days. The Perekop-Chongar operation was launched on the night of November 8. The 51st Infantry Division, commanded by V. K. Blyukher, was assigned to make a head-on assault on the Perekop ramparts. At the same time, units of the 52nd Division, crossing the dried-up bottom of Lake Sivash at night, took Litovsky Peninsula, which was poorly defended. On the night of November 10-11, units of the 30th Division under I. K. Gryazno captured the Chongar positions. On the day of November 10, A. I. Kork's 6th Army, to which these divisions belonged, took the Ushun positions. This decided the fate of General Wrangel's army.

But even after the fall of the Perekop defenses, the White Army continued to offer stubborn resistance. On November 11 it even tried to go over to the attack. However, fresh Red infantry divisions and units of the 2nd and 1st cavalry armies (together with "Old Man" Makhno's* "partisan" forces—which had fought

---

* "Old Man" (Nestor) Makhno was a partisan leader who at various times opposed both the Reds and the Whites.—Translator's note.

earlier in Crimean battles and were placed temporarily under Mironov's command) were put into the field on that same day.

By evening, units of the 2nd Cavalry Army and Makhno's army had taken the station of Voinka. The next day, the 2nd Cavalry Army took the station of Dzhankoi and captured many prisoners, field pieces, and munitions. (It would not be inappropriate to note here that in this rapid thrust toward the southern Crimea, the 1st Cavalry Army lagged a full day's march behind the 2nd Cavalry Army.) On the evening of that same day, after heavy fighting, the 2nd Cavalry Army captured the station of Kurman-Kemelchek. As Mironov wrote:

The flight of the defeated, crushed enemy was a spectacle that defied description: abandoned field pieces, caissons, machine guns, rifles, telegraph and telephone equipment, hundreds of bags of flour, groats, sugar. Cases of tea, tobacco, soap, and other products marked the road of retreat over dozens of versts; and that road led to Simferopol. It was there that Baron Wrangel's forces suffered their final defeat. And we can proudly say that the last orders given on the Crimea were spoken by the artillery of the 2nd Cavalry Army. The last joyous rays of the sun witnessed the last volley from the Red artillery on November 12, 1920.

On November 13, Wrangel announced that his army was disbanded, and told everyone to escape as best he could.

The further pursuit of the Whites involved almost no fighting. On November 14 the 2nd Cavalry Army entered Simferopol and stopped there. Meantime, units of the 1st Cavalry Army were rapidly occupying cities along the Crimean littoral: Sevastopol, Evpatoriya, Feodosiya, and others.

Mironov concluded his memoirs in the following words:

The 2nd Cavalry Army stopped at the line it had reached, since it made no sense to wear out the horses chasing after the shadow of Wrangel and his defeated bands. . . . The 2nd Cavalry Army does not claim the chief credit for the defeat of Wrangel. But it likes to speak the truth—and that for history in the future, so that our generation should know the truth. . . . Thus ended that inglorious phase of the

Russian counter-revolution associated with the name of Baron Wrangel. And so, whatever anyone says, November 12 was the last day of fighting in the Crimea. On November 13 the Crimean Peninsula received, in the greatest silence, the Red troops moving in to occupy the cities of Evpatoriya, Sevastopol, Pot, Feodosiya, and Kerch. On November 11, 12, 13, and 14 the 2nd Cavalry Army alone seized 25,000 prisoners, more than 60 field pieces, up to 100 machine guns, several tens of thousands of shells, 32 aircraft, 63 motor vehicles, millions of poods of foodstuffs, and various kinds of matériel. Such was the original estimate of the matériel that passed through the hands of the 2nd Cavalry Army. But since it left all this, and was replaced by other units which also made estimates of the same matériel, the amount of that matériel so calculated is by now colossal. It is appropriate to note that the 2nd Cavalry Army began operations on the right bank of the Dnieper using munitions from its own reserve, but that from then until the final liquidation of Wrangel it lived off the Whites, constantly replenishing its supplies of ordnance, shells, cartridges, and uniforms for soldiers from the enemy's baggage trains. I have written a lot in this memoir, but I have lived through even more.

Mironov, Commander of the 2nd Cavalry Army.[9]

About two hundred soldiers, unit commanders, and political workers of the 2nd Cavalry Army were awarded the Order of the Red Banner for their feats in these battles. Mironov, as the army's commander, was first awarded the Honorary Revolutionary Weapon—a saber with a gilded hilt upon which a red banner was embossed—and then the Order of the Red Banner.[10]

THE LAST MONTHS
IN THE LIFE
OF PHILIP MIRONOV

XI Certain sub-units of Makhno's "partisan army" had taken part in the offensive against Wrangel. But Makhno himself, with a large detachment, was sequestered in the Gulyai Pole region in the southern Ukraine. The alliance between him and the Red Army was only temporary. Those detachments of Makhno's army in the Crimea were only nominally subordinate to the command of the southern front. In many areas they pillaged and committed other excesses. On November 23, 1920, Frunze sent Makhno an ultimatum demanding that he disband his "partisan" units. Makhno countered by announcing military conscription in the regions he controlled. In response to this action, Frunze declared Makhno and his forces to be enemies of the Soviet regime, and ordered the commanders of all units of the Red Army who had contact with units of Makhno's army "to disarm them, and destroy those who offer resistance." Mironov passed on this order to the units of the 2nd Cavalry Army, but at the same time he ordered his army to avoid any engagements

unless provoked. Psychologically, it was considerably more difficult for Mironov to carry out vigorous military actions against
Makhno's troops, who had recently been allies of the Red Army,
than against Wrangel's army.

At this time the 2nd Cavalry Army was reorganized into the
2nd Cavalry Corps. The 2nd, 16th, and 21st cavalry divisions
were included in the corps, and it was decided that the separate
cavalry brigade would be absorbed into the divisions to bring
them up to strength. In the RVSR's order on this subject it was
stated that Mironov would temporarily be named commander of
the corps.

But at the beginning of December there was no one to whom
Mironov could hand over the corps, and he remained in command
when the corps was transferred to the southern Ukraine to combat
Makhno's detachments, which had been using partisan war tactics.
Thus, on December 18, the 2nd Cavalry Corps was ordered to
"pursue Makhno relentlessly, wherever he is bound . . . to seize
Makhno and destroy his detachment."[1]

As early as December 13, Comrade Efunk, military commissar
of the corps, sent the following telegram to Frunze:

According to a telegram from the RVSR dated December 4 Comrade Mironov, the former commander, is being recalled from the
corps in accordance with his personal wishes. . . . In view of the
situation that has developed, it compels me [sic] to make the present
report to the RVS: the vagueness of the situation is affecting Comrade
Mironov and having a strong effect on his work. In a personal conversation, Mironov expressed his desire to remain with the corps. As a
military commissar I must point out that Mironov's prestige and
popularity among the units of the corps are rather great that I have
yet seen [sic] in my experience as a divisional military commissar. His
policy toward Makhno's revolt, which in my opinion at first suffered
from a certain softness and a perhaps not entirely correct evaluation of
what had taken place, has, after today's personal conversation, changed
in the direction of a correct evaluation of the events corresponding to
the operational orders issued to the units of the corps. It would be
desirable to leave Comrade Mironov in command of the 2nd Cavalry

Corps, which would undoubtedly guarantee to the Republic the creation of a completely regular cavalry corps. Provided only that his recall is made necessary by a critical need [*sic*].

Frunze forwarded this telegram to Supreme Commander Kamenev under cover of the following telegram:

In forwarding the following telegram from the military commissar of the corps, I report for my part that in view of the lack of a deputy, the continuing vagueness as to the status of Comrade Mironov is having a very harmful effect on the entire work of the cavalry corps.[2]

In late December, on the basis of an order from the supreme commander, the 2nd Cavalry Corps was put at the disposal of the commander of the Caucasian front. Units of the corps were ordered to move to the region of Likhaya Station, where they would be operationally subordinated to the commander of the forces of the Don Region.[3] Mironov nonetheless continued as commander of the 2nd Cavalry Corps until January. He was then appointed Chief Inspector of Cavalry in the Red Army, a post later occupied by Budenny. In light of subsequent tragic events, it is difficult to say whether this new assignment was genuine. Any historian is inevitably faced with the question: Was not this appointment merely a convenient pretext for removing Mironov from the direct command of a large military force with a view to facilitating his arrest—which, in all likelihood, was already being planned by certain high authorities?

However that may be, Mironov turned over his corps to N. D. Tomin in late January, and on January 30, 1921, departed from Usmanskaya Station for Moscow. He was provided with a special train consisting of two cars: a Pullman and a heated cattle car. Mironov, his wife (N. V. Mironova-Suyetenkova), two aides-de-camp, and a cook traveled in the first car. Mironov took along no bodyguard, although it was customary to do so in those still-dangerous times. Grand welcomes were arranged for him at almost every large station. He was honored as a hero of the recent battle against Wrangel, and as a celebrated commander. At

Rostov-on-Don, after one such welcome, I. T. Smilga got on the train. He and Mironov had a long talk, laughing as they remembered the trial in Balashov at which Mironov was a defendant and Smilga the prosecutor.

From Rostov, however, Mironov went to Tsaritsyn, and from there to the stanitsa of Ust-Medveditsa (now the municipality of Serafimovich). He wanted to visit his family—his first wife and his children—who during the civil war had endured much as relatives of Mironov, so hated by the Whites. Late in the evening of February 6, Mironov reached home by sleigh.

In that winter of 1920-21 the situation on the Don had been very trying. The 1920 harvest had been poor, and there was little grain. Pressure on the peasants and Cossacks to provide grain had been stepped up in December, but by mid-January only 35 percent of the surplus-appropriation quota had been fulfilled. Needless to say, the food-requisition detachments had to use force, for the most part, rather than persuasion, which in turn only aggravated resentment of the Soviet regime's foodstuffs policy. During that winter, in many parts of the Don Region, an actual famine set in. Also, many farms had no grain for spring sowing. The same situation obtained in most parts of the Kuban. In the midst of all this, Mironov returned to his native stanitsa.

It is not surprising that increasingly loud mutterings came from the Cossacks on the Don and in the Kuban and also from the middle peasants in all the grain-growing provinces of Soviet Russia in that trying winter of 1920-21. The surplus-appropriation system, an integral part of so-called War Communism, had come into sharp conflict with the interests of the mass peasantry. Soviet Russia was beset by the most serious political crisis in its history. According to Lenin, the danger arising from the discontent of the country's many millions of inhabitants was in many respects worse than the danger from Kolchak and Denikin.

Clearly, the serious political and economic crisis affecting the whole country had also affected the Don Region, including the

Ust-Medveditsa District, to which Mironov came in early February. In certain respects the situation on the Don was especially bad, since the Bolsheviks did not yet have a strong influence in the Cossack stanitsy. In many Soviet organizations in Rostov, Novocherkassk, and Taganrog, and in various districts and stanitsy, it was necessary to use either soviet and Party workers who had been compromised by their roles in implementing the policy of "decossackization" or former administrators and officials from the previous Voisko governments. Moreover, the foodstuffs-procurement agencies assumed that the Don and Kuban regions had more substantial grain surpluses than the other regions of European Russia. When confiscating grain, the food-requisition detachments did not even make exceptions for those Cossacks who for the previous eighteen months or two years had been fighting in the Red Army and had just returned to their native villages and stanitsy after having been discharged. In the winter of 1920-21, dozens of small detachments and several large ones, sometimes comprising as many as a thousand Cossacks, were operating in the Don Region.

It would be an oversimplification to say that the new uprisings taking place in the Don Region were exclusively anti-Soviet and counter-revolutionary, although the Cossack detachments that started the uprisings were subsequently joined by many actual counter-revolutionary elements, and by remnants of the White Cossack units defeated a year before. The majority of the "partisan" detachments operating in the Don Region were led, more often than not, by men who had recently been commanding officers in the Red Army. And some of them, ever since the first months of the civil war, had fought bravely for the Soviet regime in Mironov's divisions, in units of the 1st Cavalry Army, and in other units of the Red Army. The majority of these people were provoked into armed action against the Communists by excesses in the appropriation of foodstuffs—by the brutal, illegitimate actions of the food-requisition detachments. Thus in condemning the uprisings that occurred on the Don, one must not forget the words of Lenin, who later said repeatedly that in the winter of 1920-21 the peasants had good grounds for dissatisfaction with the policy of War Communism, which had been continued too long.

Shortly before Mironov came to the Don Region, an uprising was started by the garrison in the settlement of Mikhailovka, led by I. Vakulin, formerly a regimental commander in the famous "Mironov" 23rd Division. Vakulin and his deputy, Popov, were the first men in Mironov's division to be awarded the Order of the Red Banner—at that time a rare award that testified to great services. The majority of the soldiers in the Mikhailovka garrison had also served previously in the 23rd Division.

Taking advantage of his past service with Mironov, and of Mironov's popularity among the Don Cossacks, Vakulin began to spread rumors and distribute appeals to the effect that Mironov supported the uprising; that he would soon come to the Don to head the uprising; that the 2nd Cavalry Army, under Mironov's command, would join the insurgents. This lie was largely believed by the rank-and-file Cossacks whom Vakulin had deceived and also by individual Party and soviet workers—especially by some of the political workers in the Don Corps with whom Mironov had come into sharp conflict in 1919. Among the Party and soviet workers in the Don Region, some with grudges against Mironov spread rumors about him and called him an "adventurist."

And so, just when the atmosphere was extremely tense, Mironov decided not to go directly to Moscow from Rostov but to pay a brief visit to his native Ust-Medveditsa District. At precisely the same time, units of the 2nd Cavalry Corps, which now had a new commander, were ordered to the Don Region to combat the insurgent movement gaining headway there.

Burov, chairman of the Don Cheka, was extremely frightened by the insurrections breaking out first in one area and then in another, and by the counter-revolutionary groups surfacing in various parts of the region. Seeing ripples of anti-Soviet and anti-Bolshevik feeling spreading among large segments of the Cossack

and non-Cossack population, and confused by the false denunciations and just plain slander that came his way, he believed the
calumny being spread about Mironov. Learning of Mironov's
arrival in Rostov-on-Don, and of the latter's intention to visit the
Ust-Medveditsa District, Burov ordered one of his deputies to
follow Mironov to observe his movements and personal contacts.
One cannot rule out the possibility that Burov, in issuing such instructions, was in his turn following the instructions or advice of a
more highly placed official. Both in the headquarters of the North
Caucasus District and in the Republic RVS, there were people ill-
disposed toward Mironov. Mironov was too important a figure
(he had already been appointed to a very high post in Moscow)
for Burov to deal with him merely through the Don Cheka. It is
more than likely that Burov cleared his actions with someone. But
on the basis of available materials it is as yet impossible to ascertain with whom Burov consulted, or upon whose instructions he
acted.

In all fairness, it should be noted that in those days of February
1920, which were so fateful for him, Mironov could not have
surmised the danger that was threatening him, which explains why
he acted imprudently and sometimes even rashly. It seemed to
him that after defeating Wrangel no one would doubt his devotion
to the Soviet regime and the Communist Party.

When Mironov reached Ust-Medveditsa, the news of his
arrival spread rapidly through the whole stanitsa. In honor of
his arrival the revkom arranged a meeting at which Mironov spoke.
Mironov called upon the people of the stanitsa not to be taken in by
any provocations, not to support the uprising, but to bend every
effort to strengthen the Soviet regime locally and to heal the wounds
inflicted by the war. He also stated that he had joined the Communist Party only because he was convinced of the fairness of that
Party, which alone reflected the interests of the people and would
lead them along the right path. At the same time he criticized
several perversions and distortions on the part of local workers,
and promised that in the future he would help to correct those
mistakes.

On February 7 there was a meeting of the members of the stanitsa Party organization. The agenda included one main question: the choice of delegates to the Fifth District Party Conference, to be held within the next few days in the settlement of Mikhailovka. Mironov was invited to the meeting and his name was placed in nomination as a delegate. Mironov asked the members to withdraw his name because he had to be in Moscow soon. Moreover, since he had not been working in the stanitsa, he could not represent it at the district conference. But his arguments were brushed aside, and he was elected anyway. Mironov valued highly this trust placed in him by the people from his own stanitsa and decided to delay his departure for Moscow in order to take part in the conference.

The next day at home he received friends and acquaintances who had served with him in the 23rd Division: Golenov, Voropayev, Elanskov, and a Cossack whom he knew only vaguely, V Kochukov. They were accompanied by a man Mironov had never met: Skobinenko, an inhabitant of the Raspolinskaya Stanitsa and a worker in the district food-procurement section in Mikhailovka. Skobinenko* was also a secret informant of the Don Cheka. He was an unprincipled and contemptible man, who had served as deputy chairman of the Don Cheka. He not only initiated a conversation about the troubles in the Ust-Medveditsa District but actually transformed the discussion into a conference over which he himself presided. Although Mironov did not know Skobinenko, he participated in the impromptu conference and sharply criticized the policy of district and regional authorities in the Don Region. Mironov predicted that unless policy in the Don Region changed, there would be new and even more dangerous uprisings in the region by spring. It was agreed that those who had taken part in the conference would regularly inform Mironov, in Moscow, of affairs on the Don, sending him encoded letters. Mironov did not place much trust in the district workers in Mikhailovka, and wanted to have a separate channel for in-

* See Chapter IX, page 195.

formation on Don affairs so that he could, if necessary, defend the interests of the Don Cossacks in those higher Moscow institutions to which he would now have rather free access. He asked those present to set up similar information groups in other stanitsy as well. Needless to say, there was nothing criminal in this attempt to set up an information group independent of local authorities and based on personal trust. But in carrying on a confidential conversation among friends in the presence of Skobinenko, a stranger, Mironov made a serious mistake.

The Don Cheka immediately received an informer's report from Skobinenko in which the nature and purpose of the evening conference at Mironov's home were represented as an incitement to insurrection and the creation of a secret anti-Soviet organization. In his informer's report, Skobinenko wrote exactly what the leaders of the Don Cheka expected and wanted to hear from him.

The opening session of the District Party Conference in Mikhailovka was held on February 10, 1921, and Mironov was elected an honorary member of the presidium. On the third day of the conference he made a long speech calling the delegates' attention to the difficult political and economic situation in the Don Region and the Ust-Medveditsa District, and to the food shortage, the result of two wars. Mironov criticized the actions of local authorities and the War Communism policy as a whole. He declared that as the civil war was over, the surplus-appropriation system should be replaced by a direct agricultural tax (tax in kind), and that the Cossacks and peasants should be allowed to sell, at their own discretion, the surpluses of agricultural products they had left. He called for the opening of bazaars and markets in the district and the region. He leveled especially sharp criticism at Lisin and Bukatin, agents of the Don Cheka in the Ust-Medveditsa District, and at Ermakov, chairman of the revolutionary tribunal, who had terrorized the inhabitants, frequently carrying out illegal repressions, shootings, and requisitions, and thereby stirring up the Cossacks against the Soviet regime.

At the same time, Mironov condemned Vakulin and the other

insurgents. He expressed regret that his former comrades of the 23rd Division should have staged such an uprising. He went on to say that the insurgent commanders and soldiers of the Mikhailovka garrison obviously had incorrectly understood the situation and could find no other way to overcome the tyranny created by the Mikhailovka district leaders. He added that upon reaching Moscow he would ask the government to appoint a special commission to investigate the illegal actions of the Mikhailovka district leaders.

At that time the question of replacing the surplus-appropriation system by a tax in kind had been raised by many soviet, Party, and food-procurement workers. Lenin himself had written a "Rough Draft of Theses on the Peasants." In that document—the first one in which he lays the groundwork for the New Economic Policy—Lenin says:

1. To satisfy the desire of the non-Party peasantry in the matter of replacing the surplus-appropriation system (in the sense of confiscating surpluses) with a grain tax.

2. To reduce the amount of that tax relative to last year's surplus appropriations.

3. To approve the principle that the amount of the tax should conform to the diligence of the farmer, in the sense of decreasing the percentage of the tax as the diligence of the farmer increases.

4. To expand the farmer's freedom of utilization of his surpluses above the tax in local economic turnover, provided payment of the tax is prompt and complete.[4]

A few days after Lenin had jotted down these notes, *Pravda* published an article by P. Sorokin, Foodstuffs Commissar of Moscow Province, and M. Rogov, Chief of the Moscow Provincial Agricultural Section, titled "Surplus-Appropriation System or Tax?" in which the authors defended the advantages of the tax in kind over the surplus-appropriation system. This article had been read and discussed by the editors of *Pravda* and by the members of the TsK and the Politburo.[5] But the workers in far-removed areas as yet knew nothing of these ideas and proposals entertained by Lenin and other Party leaders for abolishing the surplus-appropriation system and expanding—or, more accurately, permitting—local trade.

Mironov's speech, therefore, fell like an exploding bombshell on the Mikhailovka District Party Conference. The next speaker after Mironov was E. E. Efremov, former commissar of the Don Corps, who had previously been on good terms with Mironov. But as deputy chairman of the Mikhailovka District Executive Committee of Soviets he sharply criticized Mironov's desideratum for facilitating private trade, declaring that this proposal diverged completely from Party policy. Mironov, hot-tempered and impetuous, jumped to his feet and called Efremov "childish." At this point the presidium cut the discussion short and suspended the conference. Mironov and several delegates walked out of the hall in protest.

At the conclusion of the conference, A. Krzhevitsky was re-elected secretary of the District Committee. He had come to the Ust-Medveditsa District in January 1921. He was a locksmith from a working-class family, and had had only elementary schooling. A Party member since 1919, he had never met Mironov before, and knew little of the Cossacks' problems. It is not surprising that he complied with the demands of the Don Cheka agents, who at this time were secretly keeping an eye on Mironov.

After the conference, Mironov went to Mikhailovka, where he was staying with his wife. He began packing his things for Moscow. But at midnight, on orders from Krzhevitsky, martial law was declared in the settlement. Patrols roamed the streets. All movement of trains was stopped on the Povorino-Tsaritsyn section of the railroad line. Krzhevitsky called a skeleton conference of specially chosen persons at District Committee headquarters that excluded the majority of members of the District Committee's bureau—among them Efremov. Citing reports from the Cheka informers Skobinenko and P. K. Ignatov (who were also invited to that nocturnal conference), Krzhevitsky announced that Mironov was planning an armed uprising in the district. It was immediately decided to arrest him. The order for his arrest was issued to V. Simonenko, chief of staff of the district militia. Under Simonenko's direction, Mironov's house was surrounded by a local force, and Simonenko presented him with the arrest order. But Mironov refused to let himself be taken into custody, saying that as commander of the 2nd Cavalry Army (Corps) en route to Moscow on orders from the Revvoyensovet, he was not subject to arrest by the local authorities. He suggested waiting until morning, when he could get in touch with Moscow and clear up the misunderstanding. Leaving a guard posted around Mironov's house, Simonenko went to Krzhevitsky and reported all this. But the latter confirmed his order for the arrest, and gave instructions to use force if Mironov did not voluntarily surrender his weapon. Mironov then gave up his weapon and submitted to arrest.

Under heavy guard, Mironov was sent to Sebryakovo Station. From there he was taken, again under heavy guard and no longer in his own railroad car, to Moscow. Arrested along with him were his wife and his former colleague, S. P. Starikov. At that time Starikov had begun work as a member of the Cossack Section of the VTsIK. After finding an apartment in Moscow, Starikov had come to Mikhailovka for his wife. At Sebryakovo Station, Starikov had, on the eve of the District Party Conference, chanced to meet Mironov, and the latter had suggested that Starikov go to Moscow with him. Starikov agreed; and together with his wife, he had been waiting in Mikhailovka for the end of the conference.

But whereas, after his arrest, Mironov was sent to Moscow, Starikov was taken to Tsaritsyn, where he spent two months in prison. He was then released without any charges having been brought against him.

Starikov was a member of the Cossack Section of the VTsIK, and the local officials lacked the authority to arrest him—or to arrest Mironov, for that matter. Nor did the local officials have the authority to stop the movement of trains on the Povorino-Tsaritsyn section of the railroad line. There is no doubt that the power behind Krzhevitsky was Myshatsky, deputy chairman of the Don Cheka, who issued the orders for all these actions. But the authority of Myshatsky and Burov was confined to the territory of the Don Region. The fact that Mironov after his arrest was sent to Moscow instead of Rostov indicates that some highly placed Party officials in the capital were in on the plans to arrest Mironov.

In Moscow, Mironov was first confined in a solitary cell in the Lubyanka, and then transferred to a general cell in the Butyrskaya Prison. His wife was incarcerated in the same prison. Organs of the VChK launched an investigation into the "Mironov case" in which the main "proofs" were the denunciations by A. Skobinenko, P. Ignatov, and certain other Don Cheka informants.

It is worth noting that in Rostov on February 21, 1921, Burov, chairman of the Don Cheka, reported on the case to the plenum of the Donispolkom. Greatly exaggerating the situation in the region, Burov reported that the Don Cheka "possessed information" on the preparation in the Don Region of a great uprising in which units of the 2nd Cavalry Corps were allegedly to take part. He stated that "Mironov is playing a far-from-minor role" in all this.[6] But Burov did not mention that Mironov had already been arrested. Apparently, his report was calculated to prepare public opinion in the Don Region and the leaders of the Donispolkom for the news of Mironov's arrest. It was not until March 1 at a skeleton conference of the Donispolkom's presidium that Burov declared: "We have ascertained the active participation of reactionary officers, up to and including generals, in the preparation of a large-scale uprising, and have ascertained the involvement therein of Mironov, who has now been arrested."[7]

It may be supposed that Trotsky knew of Mironov's arrest, since the latter was going to Moscow to take up duties under the Republic RVS. Lenin knew nothing of it, as is evident from his note to E. M. Sklyansky, deputy chairman of the RVSR: "Comrade Sklyansky! Where is Mironov? How are things going with him?" Instead of replying, Sklyansky forwarded to Lenin a telegram from two military leaders of the Northern Caucasus front:

February 17. According to a report from Paukov, military commissar of the Ust-Medveditsa District, based on information in his possession for the accuracy of which he vouches, Mironov, former commander of the 2nd Cavalry Corps, who had come on leave of absence to the Ust-

Medveditsa District, was preparing an organized uprising against the Soviet regime. Local inhabitants, local military units, and (allegedly) units of the 21st Cavalry Division were to take part in the uprising. On February 13 the district military commissar, keeping his action secret from the local inhabitants and Voisko units, arrested Mironov and sent him in an individual railroad car to Moscow, together with an indictment. Allegedly, certain representatives of the ispolkom took part in the plot. The Don Cheka is now arresting the plotters. All those arrested are to be brought to Mikhailovka no later than February 18. Pugachev, chief of staff. Pechersky, military commissar.[8]

It is not known how Lenin reacted to the telegram from Pugachev and Pechersky. Probably he asked Dzerzhinsky or Menzhinsky to look more closely into the case of Mironov. But during those weeks Dzerzhinsky was in Petrograd in connection with the Kronstadt Rebellion. After his return to Moscow the VChK instructed the Don Cheka to send Mironov and all the other participants in the "plot" to Moscow. Apparently it had not been immediately reported to Dzerzhinsky that Mironov was already in Moscow and had been there for a considerable time. The Don Cheka transferred to Moscow those former colleagues of Mironov's who had taken part in the conference of February 8: Golenov, Voropayev, Kochukov, and Elanskov. Mironov's son-in-law, Chernushkin, was also taken to Moscow.

Yet even after Mironov's "accomplices" had been brought to Moscow, the investigators could not obtain any convincing evidence that a "plot" had existed. In mid-March, protesting against his incarceration, Mironov declared a hunger strike.

Mironov was not denied the opportunity to make notes and to read. He kept very close track of all events in the country—especially the course of the Tenth Congress of the RKP(b), then being held, and Lenin's speeches and articles, together with those of Kalinin and other Party leaders.

Mironov wrote a letter to Kalinin, Trotsky, Kamenev, and Lenin that did not reach any of its addressees in time. It is not known whether they read it later. But the text was preserved in archives with which S. P. Starikov was able to familiarize himself. The following are only a few excerpts from Philip Kuzmich Mironov's last letter.

> Dear Citizen and Comrade Mikhail Ivanovich!*
> A letter from the Central Committee to all members of the Party (*Pravda*, No. 64) says:
>> ... the task of all Party organizations consists in penetrating more deeply into the rural areas and stepping up work among the peasants. The Party has decided, at whatever cost, to abolish bureaucratism and isolation from the masses. . . .
>
> This letter ends with the exclamation: "To the masses! . . . That is the chief slogan of the Tenth Congress."
> During four years of revolutionary struggle I never isolated myself from the broad masses. Whether I lagged behind them or got ahead of them, I do not know. But, sitting in Butyrskaya Prison with a heavy heart and a devastated soul, I feel that I am sitting† and suffering for that slogan. For the moment I shall quote only one passage from Comrade Lenin's report to the Tenth Congress on the tax in kind (*Pravda*, No. 57): "But at the same time it is an undoubted fact— and we need not conceal it in agitation and propaganda—that we have gone further than was theoretically and politically necessary." I have quoted this excerpt by way of asking myself and others: Who, in the final analysis, has proven to have been isolated from the masses? And who, as it turns out, has gotten ahead of the game? But however I may have resolved that question for myself, I can neither catch up with nor wait for the Communist Party to catch up with me, so as to be in its ranks in the new front proclaimed by the Party congress, in the struggle for a better future for mankind, since I am in prison. . . .
> This appeal comes to you from the man who, on October 13 and 14, snatched the prospect of victory from the hands of Wrangel; who on those same days snatched up General Shkuro's black banner with the wolf's head (the emblem of the predatory capitalist) and the legend "For a Unified and Indivisible Russia," and handed it to you as a pledge of loyalty to the social revolution among political leaders and leaders of the Red Army. . . . That weary and exhausted man appeals to you in the name of social justice. . . .

---

* Kalinin, the principal addressee. The others named above were sent copies of the letter.—Translator's note.

† One meaning of the Russian verb "to sit" is "to go to (or serve time in) prison."—Translator's note.

And if you, Mikhail Ivanovich, do not respond by April 15, 1921, I will commit suicide in prison by starvation.

If I felt the least bit guilty, I would consider it shameful to go on living, and to send you this letter. I am too proud to make deals with my conscience.

The entirety of my tormented, eighteen-year revolutionary struggle testifies to my constant thirsting for justice, my deep love for the toilers, my altruism, and the fairness of those means of struggle I have employed so that I might see equality and brotherhood among people.

A monstrous charge has been brought against me: "organizing an uprising on the Don against the Soviet regime." The ground for this absurdity was the fact that the bandit Vakulin, who started an uprising in the Ust-Medveditsa District, referred in his proclamations to me, as one who was popular on the Don—claiming that I would support him with the 2nd Cavalry Army. In like manner, he claimed support from Comrade Budenny.

Vakulin started his uprising on December 18, 1920. At the time I was crushing Makhno's bands in the Ukraine, and learned of his (Vakulin's) uprising from operational summaries. In addition to the uprising in the above-mentioned district, similar ones broke out simultaneously in other districts—apparently under the influence of Antonov's uprising in Voronezh Province. . . .

I have always seen the success of the social revolution in the slogan, "To the Masses"—about which I had the honor of writing on July 30, 1919, in a letter quoted during my trial, on October 7, 1919. I also wrote about something taken up, very belatedly (*Pravda*, No. 65), by Comrade Kurayev in his article, "Our Policy": "We must also make appropriate changes in our procedures and methods of working among the peasants, and in our approach to them. . . . The old procedures and methods of working may be more harmful than the propaganda of enemies."

Life has cruelly proven that to us. At no time in the struggle in the interests of the social revolution have I let fall from my hands that slogan, "To the Masses"—something that is confirmed by the broad trust that the masses placed in me up until the last minute before my arrest. . . . And I make bold to declare that the strength of my prestige among the broad toiling masses of the Cossackry and peasantry on the Don is based on conviction and not on violence, whose overt enemy I have always been. Hence I am not capable of urging the popular masses on to new sacrifices; and I know the price of insurrection from the Ukraine.

This is the confession of a man about to die. . . .

I shall now discuss what brought me to Butyrskaya Prison. . . . I shall tell briefly what happened on February 8 in Ust-Medveditsa Stanitsa, where I spent only two days, and for that "pleasure" ended up in prison.

Comrade Stukachev, chairman of the troika* for the restoration of the Soviet regime in the district, suggested to me by phoned telegram (there is a transcript of the conversation in the file) that I hold several meetings in the stanitsy of the district at which I would disclaim Vakulin's inflammatory use of my name. On the evening of February 8, after the meeting, I was visited by five persons, three of whom I knew well, one slightly, and one not at all. Affected by Vakulin's inflammatory proclamations, by the fact that people were beginning to starve to death in the stanitsy and villages, by the hundreds of letters and complaints (which I wanted to show you when I reached Moscow) accompanied by tears and touching scenes, and especially by the declaration from the delegates of the company of soldiers doing local guard duty, who complained of hunger and cold (they were dressed like beggars)—seeing all this as kindling for an uprising, I decided that not only the inhabitants but the Red Army men must have lost faith in the local authorities if, when they heard of my arrival, these people came to seek help even without knowing me. I promised such help in the name of the chairman of the Republic Revvoyensovet, if I reached Moscow.

But my trip was delayed. . . .

Taking into account the insurrections that had broken out in the Don Region four different times, the Antonov uprising, and the general low muttering of the broad farming masses whose sound reached me easily, since these masses and their representatives had always come to me trustingly, if only for moral support, which they got in the form of sound advice—having nothing criminal in mind and not admitting even the thought that what was concealed in the depths of my soul might make for a crime—I frankly expressed my innermost, tormenting thoughts about an impending counter-revolution from within—a counter-revolution much more dangerous than that of Denikin, Wrangel, and the entire bourgeois world. One could hardly devise a better test of my political loyalty, my fidelity to the proletarian revolution (whose tasks I understand very well indeed).

---

* Any special commission consisting of three persons, and not necessarily (as the English loan word has come to signify since the Stalin era) a drumhead court of three members.—Translator's note.

But . . . A Judas was sitting there: even to speak of his provocatory ways is repellent.

I began with what had been torturing and tormenting me, and ended by saying that if the policy of the ruling Party did not meet the demands of life, which could not be done without making concessions, by spring there might be uprisings that would lead the country to anarchy. . . . I repeat that I did this in order to point up the seriousness of the current moment and what had to be done to prevent any attempt at an uprising.

After an exchange of opinions emphasizing the danger to the Soviet regime, I proposed the following plan as a person who was going to take up a post under the supreme commander. The five of them would constitute a basic cell; and, provided certain requirements (from the brochure *The Republic of the Soviets*) were met, they would then organize ancillary cells, with these aims:

1. The cells could combat in an organized manner—through Communist cells, Party and non-Party gatherings and conferences—those White Guard and other harmful elements who were hangers-on of the Communist Party and the Soviet regime.

2. In the event of uprisings, the onset of anarchy, and the cutting-off of communications with the executive organs, the cells would constitute strongholds for the defense of the Soviet regime locally.

3. If Polish and Rumanian troops, together with a Wrangel still showing signs of life [*nedobityi Wrangel*], should begin to threaten Moscow at the urging of the Entente, all the cells with all the volunteers would, when I issued the call, go into action to save the central Soviet regime. (Incidentally, I emphasized that this last task was not a likely possibility.)

Nor was this refuted by the informer at the interrogation and the confrontation. It was just that I could not give an accurate definition of those cells. But there was no doubt as to their spiritual content [*dukhovnoye soderzhaniye*]. . . .

Since a struggle against the local evil in the person of a certain food-requisition agent and others could not accomplish the purpose, it was decided the cell would secretly send me information on abuses so that I could act through prominent members of the VTsIK.

Such was the basic reason for the code we set up among us.

All this has brought me to the torments of prison.

Is there anywhere even the slightest indication of an organized uprising on the Don against the Soviet regime?

If I am guilty, I am guilty only in that, as a Communist, I should not have organized that cell outside the Party. But I repeat, because of the threatening reality I saw nothing criminal in that. If I am guilty, I am guilty of violating Party discipline. (And the "Workers' Opposition"?) *. . .

I do not want to admit even the thought that the Soviet regime would guillotine one of its best soldiers—"the valiant commander of the 2nd Cavalry Army" (RVS Order of the Day for December 4, 1920)—on the basis of a false, unfounded informer's report. I do not want to believe that vile slander will prove to be stronger than the evident fact of my political and military services to the socialist revolution and the Soviet regime—than my honesty and sincerity toward it.

I refuse to believe that vile slander will eclipse the resplendent image of the Order of the Red Banner, that symbol of the world proletarian revolution, which I bear with unconcealed pride. I refuse to believe that the poisonous breath of slander will tarnish the gilded hilt of my honorary weapon; that the hands of my gold watch will stop moving when I am strangled by a traitor, to the accompaniment of his satanic laughter. . . .

I went to believe that I will lead Red regiments to victory in Bucharest, Budapest, etc.—as I said on that ill-starred February 8 to the ill-starred (for me) group of five people, among whom there were provocateurs.

But what is the source of that hope?

First of all, my innocence before the Soviet regime. Next, that which has caused me to suffer and has constantly been pounding on my head—something recognized both by the Tenth Party Congress and by yourself.

. . . Prison conditions are having a ruinous effect on my health, weakened by many years of exhausting struggle. I am slowly wasting away. . . .

The sufferings and tears of hungry, defrauded people compelled me to raise this question [of food] at the District Party Conference on February 12 and examine it thoroughly, with a view to taking whatever measures were necessary against the impending famine and the tyrannous treatment of hungry people. Also, with a view to acquiring seed grain for the spring sowing so as to avoid a repetition of what had happened in the fall, when fields were left fallow because of a lack of

---

* An opposition group that arose within the Party in 1920 challenging current policy on a number of basic issues. They were labeled "anarcho-syndicalists" and censured by the Tenth Party Congress.—Translator's note.

seed grain. My proposal provoked hot rejoinders from short-sighted politicians, who were quick to accuse me of favoring free trade (i.e., virtually of being a counter-revolutionary), which compelled me to protest against this unfair interpretation of my thinking. I believe that was recorded in the minutes of the session for a routine informer's report on my seditious ideas.

Whether I was lagging behind or moving too far out in front, life has shown us that the central regime, too, took the same view of things on March 23, 1921, with its decree on free exchange, sale, and purchase. And now I am to be brought to trial for just that foresight. The Soviet regime has replaced the policy ["front"] of compulsion with a policy of persuasion—a front on which I was so strong. But so far, I am not destined to serve in the ranks of troops on that vital front. . . .

Is it really true that that bright page of the Crimean campaign, inscribed in the history of the Revolution by the 2nd Cavalry Army, is to be darkened by a few words: "Mironov, commander of the 2nd Cavalry Army, starved to death in the Butyrskaya Prison, slandered by provocateurs . . ."?

But that shameful page—which would bring joy to my defeated enemies, generals Krasnov and Wrangel, and to the Chairman of the Voisko Circle, Kharlamov—will not be written.

> March 30, 1921. Butyrskaya Prison.
> I continue to have deep faith in justice.
> Communist P. K. Mironov,
> former commander of the 2nd Cavalry Army.[9]

It may be confidently asserted that this letter hastened Mironov's end. That person or group of persons, still unidentified, who in early February were backing up the Don Cheka, were apparently the first to see the letter, and were frightened by its great force. Everything was done, therefore, to ensure that the letter did not reach those to whom it was addressed—Kalinin and Lenin, above all. As for Mironov, it was decided to deal with him as quickly as possible.

On April 2, 1921, the exercise period was canceled for all prisoners, but Mironov was taken out for exercise. He was walking alone through the courtyard of Butyrskaya Prison, around which was a brick wall. Suddenly a shot rang out, fired by one of the guards, and Mironov fell—cut down by a shot in the back.

The murder was not preceded by any trial or any decision by the presidium of the VChK. It is possible that such a decision was formalized after Mironov had been murdered. But no formalized decision of the VChK is to be found in the "Mironov file," which S. P. Starikov was able to consult. There are only records of the interrogation of Mironov, of the interrogation of the informer, A. Skobinenko, and certain other informers, of confrontations, and the written depositions of certain witnesses. The whole nature of this "case" makes it plain that it had only just been instituted, that nothing of a serious nature had been proved, and that the charges had not yet been clearly formulated. But on one of the documents there is a brief notation by an investigator to the effect that Mironov had been shot. Apparently this notation was made on the day of the murder.

It may be supposed that Kalinin later read Mironov's last letter.

Soon after Mironov's murder his wife, N. V. Mironova-Suyetenkova, was released. Three years later, in 1924, she was summoned to the People's Commissariat for Military and Naval Affairs for purposes of giving her a pension. At the offices of the presidium of the TsIK SSSR she was received by Kalinin, who had a long talk with her—without, however, touching upon the circumstances of Mironov's death. Afterward she was provided, at Kalinin's instructions, with sanitarium treatment at a mineral waters spa in the Caucasus.

In the 1920s, a number of memoirs about the civil war contained several reminiscences of Mironov. Certain authors cited interesting facts and details from the eventful life of P. K. Mironov; e.g., I. T. Smilga, in the book *Military Sketches.*

In the thirties Mironov's name ceased to be mentioned in Soviet publications. If a few words about him were written here and there, he was referred to only as a "traitor." When publication of the *History of the Civil War* was resumed after the Twentieth Party Congress, nothing was said about the military contributions of Mironov and the units he commanded. But the memory of Mironov lived on in the Don Region, among his friends and comrades-in-arms.

In 1956, after having been petitioned by Mironov's relatives and his friends who had served with him, the CC CPSU and the USSR Supreme Soviet instructed investigative organs of the USSR to review the "Mironov case."

As a result of four years of extensive and thorough work, the group of investigators ascertained the absence of a corpus delicti in the actions for which Mironov was incriminated in early February 1921, which had served as grounds for his arrest and then for the violence done, without any trial. We shall not dwell in detail here on that investigation. We shall merely quote a few excerpts from the decision of the Military Collegium of the USSR Supreme Court, which at its session (with Colonel Tserlinsky presiding, and colonels Aksenov and Pisarev serving as the two other members) of November 15, 1960, considered the finding of the USSR General Procurator "in the case of P. K. Mironov, former commander of the 2nd Cavalry Army, born 1872, arrested on February 13, 1921, who on April 2, 1921, pursuant to a decree from the presidium of the VChK, was subjected to capital punishment by shooting."

The final decision of the Military Collegium of the Supreme Court states:

As can be seen from the materials of the case, the grounds for arresting Mironov, and actually the only evidence for charging him with treasonous activity, was the denunciation by A. T. Skobinenko, a secret agent for the Don Cheka in the Ust-Medveditsa District, in which it is stated that Mironov, on February 8, 1921, while stopping at the stanitsa of Ust-Medveditsa, played host at his apartment to a gathering of people devoted to him and created an anti-Soviet cell of adventurists whose task was to prepare an armed uprising against the Soviet regime. However, the affirmations contained in this denunciation, not having been confirmed in the course of the preliminary investigation, do not correspond to reality, and are completely refuted by the materials of the subsequent inquiry into the case.

The document then examines the meeting on February 8, 1921, at Mironov's apartment, which Skobinenko himself presided over and directed.

At this meeting it was decided that after Mironov had gone to Moscow, Voropayev and others who had taken part in the conference would inform him of the state of affairs in the district, and that he would report to the Soviet government and the Party TsK on all perversions and violations of socialist legality. When interrogated as to the substance of this part of the indictment, Mironov did not acknowledge that he was guilty. Mironov categorically denied the statements in Skobinenko's denunciation as to the anti-Soviet trend of this conference, and affirmed that all those participating in the conference declared their loyalty to the Soviet regime and talked only about ways of strengthening it locally. Voropayev, Kochukov, Golenov, and Elanskov, also arrested in connection with this case, likewise did not acknowledge any guilt. Owing to the fact that the investigative organs possessed no proof of the guilt of Voropayev, Kochukov, Golenov, and Elanskov, proceedings against them were dropped by decree of the presidium of the VChK dated November 15, 1921, and they were all released from custody.

Of all the above-mentioned "accomplices" of Mironov, only Elanskov was still alive in 1960. The Military Collegium, in its decision, quoted long excerpts from his new interrogation which fully confirm Mironov's innocence. The Collegium then cited facts about Mironov's revolutionary and military activity.

A. T. Skobinenko, the chief "witness for the prosecution" in the Mironov case, was expelled from the Party in the early twenties; and in 1934 he was sentenced to ten years' imprisonment for the theft of socialist property. Shortly after serving his prison term, he died. Thus it was impossible to re-interrogate this man, whom the Military Collegium of the USSR Supreme Court characterized in its decision as a "careerist." Likewise, after careful investigation, the Collegium found untenable all the additional charges brought against Mironov in 1921; for example, the charge in connection with his speech at the District Party Conference on February 12, 1921, and others. The concluding part of the decision we have quoted from states:

The Military Collegium of the USSR Supreme Court rules: The decree of the presidium of the VChK, dated April 2, 1921, concerning

P. K. Mironov, is revoked; and owing to the lack of a corpus delicti in his actions, the proceedings against him are dropped.

This decision was handed down almost forty years after the tragic death of P. K. Mironov. During that time many of Mironov's military contributions were ascribed to other military leaders in the Red Army. Hence it is not surprising that in certain circles the decision to rehabilitate Mironov—first made by the highest judicial authorities, and then by the highest Party authorities— instigated dismay and bitterness. As early as 1961, twenty-five former unit commanders and political workers of the erstwhile 1st Cavalry Army sent the CC CPSU a collective statement seeking to discredit the decision of the Military Collegium of the USSR Supreme Court and demanding a new review of the Mironov case. Although the CC CPSU rejected that request, certain historians and writers with patronage in high places continue, even today, to publish articles and novels containing numerous slanderous fabrications about Mironov.[10]

January–October 1973

ABBREVIATIONS
NOTES
GLOSSARY
INDEX

LIST OF ABBREVIATIONS AND ACRONYMS

General

Cadet	Constitutional Democrat.
CC	Central Committee. In this book, used only in combination with *CPSU, q.v.* See also *TsK*.
Cheka	Extraordinary Commission (for Combatting Counter-Revolution and Sabotage). Also used colloquially to designate any of the various political police agencies that succeeded the *VChK, q.v.*
ChK	See *Cheka*.
CPSU	Communist Party of the Soviet Union.
DIK	Don Executive Committee.
Don ChK	The Don Cheka. See *Cheka*.
Donispolkom	Don Executive Committee.
Grazhdanupr	Civilian Administration.
Ispolkom	Executive Committee.
Kombed	Committee of the Village Poor.
Komsomol	Young Communists' League.
MVD	Ministry of Internal Affairs.
Narkomprod	People's Commissariat of Foodstuffs.
Narkomzem	People's Commissariat of Agriculture.
N.S.	New Style (Gregorian calendar).

Obispolkom	Regional Executive Committee.
Okrispolkom	District Executive Committee.
Orgburo	Organizational Bureau.
O.S.	Old Style (Julian calendar).
Politburo	Political Bureau.
Posevkom	Commission for the Development and Improvement of Seeds.
Prodrazverstka	Surplus-appropriation system.
Raikom	Raion Committee.
RAPP	Russian Association of Proletarian Writers.
Revkom	Revolutionary Committee.
Revvoyensovet	Revolutionary Military Council.
RKP(b)	Russian Communist Party (Bolsheviks).
RVS	Revolutionary Military Council.
RVSR	Revolutionary Military Council of the Republic.
SKVO	Northern Caucasus Military District.
SNK	Council of People's Commissars.
Sovnarkhoz	Council of the National Economy.
Sovnarkom	Council of People's Commissars.
SR	Social Revolutionary (Party).
STO	Council for Labor and Defense.
TsIK	Central Executive Committee.
TsK	Central Committee.
UMO	Ust-Medveditsa District.
VChK	All-Russian Extraordinary Commission (for Combatting Counter-Revolution and Sabotage). See *Cheka*.
VRK	Military Revolutionary Committee.
VSNKh	Supreme Council of the National Economy.
VTsIK	All-Union Central Executive Committee.

Bibliographical
(used chiefly in notes)

Arkh.	Archive.
ch.	part.
d.	file.
ed. khr.	storage unit.
f.	fund.
GAOR	State Archives of the October Revolution.
l.	sheet.

op.	list of contents.
otd.	section.
PSS	Complete Collected Works.
TsGAKA	Central State Archives of the Red Army.
TsGAOR SSSR	Central State (Historical) Archives of the MVD, USSR. *See* GAOR.
TsGASA	Central State Archives of the Soviet Army.
TsGVIA	Central State Archives of Military History.
TsPA	Central Party Archives.
VFPAPO	Great Russian Branch, Party Archives of the Pskov Oblast.
VIZh	Journal of Military History.

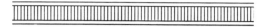

NOTES

Introduction

1. Several pages were devoted to him in Yuri V. Trifonov's book *The Gleam of the Campfire* (Moscow, 1966). The combat experiences of the 2nd Cavalry Army are discussed in V. V. Dushenkin's military-historical sketch, *The 2nd Cavalry Army* (Moscow, 1968). Brief items on Mironov may be found in the *Historical Encyclopedia*, in Vol. III (Book II) of the *History of the CPSU,* in the books of L. I. Berz and K. A. Khmelevsky, *The Heroic Years: The October Revolution and the Civil War on the Don* (Rostov-on-Don, 1964), and D. S. Babichev, *The Laboring Don Cossacks in the Struggle for the Power of the Soviets* (Rostov-on-Don, 1969), and in certain other publications.
2. TsGAKA, f. 246, op. 6, d. 1, ll. 195–200.

Chapter I

1. L. I. Berz and K. A. Khmelevsky, *Geroicheskiye gody. Oktyabr'-skaya revolyutsiya i grazhdanskaya voina na Donu* (Rostov, 1964), p. 3. D. S. Babichev, *Donskoye trudovoye kazachestvo v bor'be za vlast' Sovetov* (Rostov, 1969), pp. 5–6.
2. Kushnarenko-Kushnarev, *Polozheniye s.-kh. promysla v oblasti Voiska Donskogo* (1913), p. 35.

3. TsGVIA, f. 330, op. 92, d. 120, ll. 2–47.
4. In 1922 some districts of the Don were incorporated into Tsaritsyn Province.
5. D. S. Babichev, *Donskoye trudovoye kazachestvo* . . . , pp. 17, 23.
6. Article by S. Syrtsov, *"Vandeya Rossiiskoi kontrrevolyutsii."* Rostov Oblast Archives, f. 12, op. 26, d. 673.
7. F. G. Biryukov, *"Esli opirat'sya na printsipy istorizma,"* *Russkaya literatura,* 1971, No. 2, p. 76.
8. V. I. Lenin, PSS, XIII, p. 385.
9. *Ibid.,* p. 373. Cf. also pp. 207 and 198.

Chapter II

1. From a report from the acting head of the Gendarme Administration of the Don Region to the Department of Police on the disturbances among the Cossacks of the exempted regiments in the Taganrog and Ust-Medveditsa districts.

July 6, 1906. Secret. . . . On June 18, 1906, at the stanitsa of Ust-Medveditsa, an assembly was convened at which it was resolved: in the event of mobilization not to release for service the Cossacks of the second and third categories, since they would be required not to perform regular service but to protect the property of landlords. At the same time a deputation consisting of Junior Captain Mironov and the Cossack Konovalov was sent to Petersburg to request that the Cossacks of the second and third categories be put on inactive duty. (Rostov Oblast Archives, f. 8, op. I, d. 76, ll. 3–7–18.)

The Main Administration of Cossack Voiska:

August 13, 1906. #268. According to information received by the Ministry of Internal Affairs, Junior Captain Mironov, arrested for participation in an illegal assembly at the stanitsa of Ust-Medveditsa of the Don Voisko on June 18, when released from detention on July 14 on orders from the appointed voisko ataman, returned to the said stanitsa where he was greeted by a crowd of local inhabitants, and made a speech to them in which he thanked them for his release, stated it was necessary for the State Duma to be convened immediately, and expressed his readiness to divest himself of his uniform and decorations for the opportunity to stand up for the people. At the conclusion of his speech, the crowd carried him on their hands, and sang revolutionary songs. (TsGVIA, f. 4, 5, otd. 1906 g., d. 127, l. 17.)

From a report of the Department of Police:

. . . Meetings at which speeches of revolutionary content were made were also held, without hindrance, at the stanitsa of Ust-Medveditsa.

The speakers included the student Ageyev, Junior Captain Mironov, Lieutenant Sdobnov, and Deacon Burykin, who is still carrying out criminal agitation among the population. This resulted in great disorders, which had as their consequence, inter alia, the fact that at a stanitsa assembly held on June 18 on orders from the military commanders, the Cossacks resolutely refused to perform internal service, used threats to compel the ataman attending the assembly to leave, and signed a resolution containing a request to the Duma to put the mobilized regiments on inactive duty. On July 9, at the same stanitsa, there were new disorders the proximate cause of which was the appointed ataman's order to arrest the aforementioned agitators. The Cossacks of the stanitsa, convening an assembly on that same day, summoned the district ataman and demanded that he release the arrested persons. Brigadier General Filenkov, having no opportunity to calm the Cossacks by exhortation, and fearing their violence, sent a telegram to the appointed ataman requesting that he meet the demands of the Cossacks. . . . Owing to the passiveness of the district ataman, illegal assemblies at the stanitsa of Ust-Medveditsa continued thereafter. Colonel Popov, sent there with a squadron of Cossacks by order of the appointed ataman, did not arrest the ringleaders of the anti-government movement, among whom were the aforementioned Ageyev, Mironov, Sdobnov, and Burykin. As a result of the criminal activities of these and other agitators remaining at large, there were disorders in the settlement of Mikhailovka in the Ust-Medveditsa District in late July. On August 20 there was a meeting at the stanitsa of Ust-Medveditsa in the presence of the stanitsa ataman Sinyutin and the entire stanitsa administration. . . . The speakers called for disobedience to local authorities and the government. (TsGAOR, f. 102, *Osoby* otd., d. #700, ch. 33-1906 g., ll. 43-54.)

From a letter from the Main Administration of Cossack Voiska:

September 30, 1906. #22182. Secret. To the Voisko Appointed Ataman of the Don Voisko.

Pursuant to a report to the Minister of War on the case of the antigovernment activity of Junior Captain Mironov, attached to the Don Cossack regiments and now on inactive duty, His Excellency has ordered that in view of such activity on the part of this subaltern officer it would hardly be permissible for him to continue to be attached to the Don Cossack regiments, from which he might be transferred to service with one of the active regiments, where he might exert a harmful influence on the lower ranks; and he has deigned to order that Your Excellency be informed that Junior Captain Mironov should be discharged under administrative procedure in the event that his antigovernment activity is confirmed upon completion of his trial.

I have the honor of informing Your Excellency of this order from the Minister of War.

Major General Shcherbakov-Nerodovich, Chief of the Main Administration.
Colonel Kryuger, Section Chief of the General Staff. (TsGVIA, f. 4, 4, [*sic*] otd. 1906 g., d. 158, l. 5.)

Chapter III

1. TsGASA, f. 246, op. 6, d. I, ll. 81–85.
2. *Istoricheskii zhurnal*, 1940, No. 2, p. 131.
3. *Ust'-Medveditskaya gazeta*, 1917, No. 2 (April 9).
4. V. I. Lenin, PSS, XIII, p. 401.
5. *Ibid.*, p. 402.
6. Lenin, XIV, p. 24.
7. *Vol'nyi Don*, 1917, No. 58.
8. *Vol'nyi Don*, 1917, No. 93 (July 28).
9. *Vol'nyi Don*, 1917, No. 100 (August 5).
10. *Izvestiya TsIK i Petrogradskogo Soveta*, 1917, No. 197.
11. *Vol'nyi Don*, 1917, No. 110.
12. *Vol'nyi Don*, 1917, No. 121.
13. [Footnote missing in Russian original.]
14. *Ust'-Medveditskaya gazeta*, 1917, Nos. 53, 54.
15. V. I. Lenin, PSS, XXXIV, pp. 219–220.
16. TsGASA, f. 246, op. 6, d. 1/6, l. 9.
17. *Vol'nyi Don*, 1917, No. 156.
18. *Voprosy istorii*, 1973, No. 3, pp. 201–04.
19. TsGASA, f. 246, op. 6, d. 1, ll. 75–76.
20. Quoted from photocopies of leaflets printed in mid-December 1917 (5,000 copies) and distributed among the Cossacks on the Rumanian Front.
21. TsGVIA, f. 2126, op. 1, d. 318, l. 360.
22. TsGASA, f. 246, op. 6, d. 1, ll. 81–116.

Chapter IV

1. *Arkhiv russkoi revolyutsii* (Berlin, 1922), Bk. V, p. 145.
2. *Bor'ba za vlast' Sovetov na Donu. Sbornik dokumentov* (Rostov, 1957), pp. 236–37.
3. *Vol'nyi Don*, December 7, 1917.
4. The collection *Proletarskaya revolyutsiya na Donu*, No. 4 (Moscow/ Leningrad, 1924), pp. 207–08.
5. *Proletarskaya revolyutsiya na Donu*, No. 4 (Moscow/Leningrad, 1924), pp. 192–93.

6. *Sotsial-Demokrat*, 1917, No. 219 (November 28).
7. *Proletarskaya revolyutsiya na Donu*, No. 4 (Moscow/Leningrad, 1924), p. 195.
8. Rostov Oblast Party Archives, f. 12, op. 25, d. 45, l. 13.
9. *Ibid.*, pp. 218–19.
10. *Vol'nyi Don*, 1918, No. 30 (February 8/21).
11. V. I. Lenin, PSS, L, p. 46.
12. V. I. Lenin, *Sochineniya*, 4th edn., XXIX, p. 256.
13. *Bor'ba za vlast' Sovetov na Donu*, p. 286.
14. *Ibid.*, p. 315.
15. TsGASA, f. 192, op. 1, d. 10, ll. 8–9.
16. TsGASA, f. 246, op. 6, d. 1, ll. 195–224.
17. *Bor'ba za vlast' Sovetov na Donu*, p. 293.
18. Mikhail Sholokhov, *Tikhii Don*, Bk. II, Part V.
19. S. Piontkovsky, *Grazhdanskaya voina v Rossii. Khrestomatiya* (Moscow, 1927), pp. 404–05.
20. *Donskoi Krai*, August 17 (30), 1918.

Chapter V

1. TsGASA, f. 246, op. 6, d. 1, ll. 195–224.
2. A leaflet of 1918.
3. *Ibid.*, d. 810, l. 78.
4. TsGASA, f. SKVO, 25896, op. 3, d. 726, l. 150.
5. *Donskoi Krai*, 1918, No. 97 (August 17/30).
6. TsGASA, f. 1304, op. 1, d. 486, l. 249.
7. TsGASA, f. 1304, op. 1, d. 486, l. 235.
8. TsGASA, f. 1304, op. 1, d. 487, l. 194.
9. I. Stalin, *Sochineniya*, IV, pp. 123–24.
10. TsGASA, f. 1304, op. 1, d. 484, l. 143.
11. TsGASA, f. 1304, op. 1, ed. khr. 486, l. 107.
12. TsGAOR, f. 1258, op. 1, d. 142, l. 3.
13. TsGAOR, f. 1304, op. 1, d. 151, ll. 1–99.
14. V. V. Dushenkin, *Vtoraya konnaya* (Moscow, 1968), p. 102.
15. TsGASA, f. 1304, op. 1, d. 146, l. 8.
16. Lenin, PSS, L, p. 221.
17. S. Piontkovsky, *Khrestomatiya*, pp. 430–31.
18. [L. Trotsky], *Sochineniya* (Moscow, 1926), XVII, Part I, p. 337.
19. TsGASA, f. 1304, op. 1, d. 383, ll. 35–36.
20. *Yuzhnyi front [mai 1918–mart 1919 g.]. Bor'ba sovetskogo naroda s interventami i belogvardeitsami na yuge Rossii. Sbornik dokumentov* (Rostov-on-Don, 1962), p. 276.

21. TsGASA, f. 1304, op. 1, d. 195, l. 121 ob.
22. *Arkhiv russkoi revolyutsii* (Berlin, 1922), Bk. V, p. 305.
23. A. Denikin, *Ocherki russkoi smuty*, II, pp. 72–73.
24. TsGASA, f. 192, op. 1, d. 19, ll. 29–30.
25. TsPA, f. 17, op. 6, d. 81, l. 19.
26. TsGAKA, f. 60/100, op. 1, d. 10, l. 125.
27. TsGAKA, f. 60/100, op. 1, d. 10, l. 126.
28. TsGAKA, f. 60/100, op. 1, d. 10, p. 126.
29. TsGAKA, f. 60/100, op. 1, d. 10, l. 123.
30. TsGAKA, f. 192, op. 1, d. 12, ll. 119–120.

Chapter VI

1. *Izvestiya VTsIK*, No. 111/375, June 2, 1918.
2. . . . The glorious laboring Cossackry has not been able to preserve its sovereign rights. The Tsarist system has again been instituted on the Don. Villages and stanitsy have been emptied of people. The grain stands unharvested. The laboring Cossack clans are impoverished and perishing.

   In order to set limits to the deceit and crafty designs of the insurgent Krasnov and his allies and implement the decrees of the central government on a new and free workers' administration of the Don land, the Council of People's Commissars has resolved:

   To create a Campaign Circle (*Pokhodnyi Krug*) of the Soviet Don Voisko, a voisko government with complete authority on the Don and consisting of representatives of the toiling Don population which with weapons in hand is defending the legal authority of the soviets against the rebellious bands.

   The Campaign Circle of the Soviet Don Voisko will consist of representatives of the Don Soviet regiments and those villages and stanitsy liberated from the rule of the officers and landlords.

   Pending restoration of a legally elected Soviet authority throughout the territory of the Don Voisko, the Campaign Circle of the Don Soviet Voisko will have all the rights and privileges of voisko soviets enumerated in the decree of the People's Commissars dated June 1, 1918.

   The most immediate task of the Campaign Circle is to restore the Soviet socialist system on the Don land and clear the territory of the Don Voisko of all counter-revolutionary forces. To this end the Campaign Circle has the right:

   1. To call up the entire laboring population for service with the Soviet armed forces.

2. To direct the organization of the Don armed Soviet forces.

3. To coordinate the actions of these forces throughout the Don front.

A special commission named by the presidium of the VTsIK will be responsible for laying down the procedure for elections and norms of representation, and for convening the Campaign Circle. (TsGAOR, f. 1235, op. 35, d. 23–25, l. 57.)

3. Rostov Oblast Party Archives, f. 12, op. 12, d. 191, str. 1.

4. 1. We, the members of the Cossack Section of the VTsIK, fully support the policy aimed at rendering harmless, isolating, or expelling from the Soviet Union the counter-revolutionary leaders of the Cossacks and of all other bourgeois hiding in Cossack regions.

2. We insist on the immediate and unconditional involvement of poor and middle Cossacks in active participation in the building of Soviet rule in the Cossack regions.

3. Taking into account past mistakes in the Cossack regions, we have arrived at the firm conclusion that the Soviet regime's position there can be strengthened only by a firm administrative policy carried out by the revolutionary Cossackry jointly with the other inhabitants of the Cossack regions, and a cautious economic policy that does not sharply encroach upon the life interests of the uneducated middle Cossack or peasant. By all legal means, we shall convince all our comrades that in the Cossack regions, as in all frontier regions of Russia, once they have been captured by our forces, an opportunity must be provided to get used to the Soviet rule and to feel that the Soviet regime is not their enemy but the real defender of the laboring masses.

4. We welcome the Soviet regime, which intends to transfer to the laboring Cossacks and peasants those free lands formerly owned by the counter-revolutionary upper strata and landlords.

5. We shall insist that the VTsIK grant amnesty and the restoration of citizens' rights to all laboring elements of the Cossackry who misguidedly followed the bourgeoisie against the Soviet regime. (TsPA, f. 17, op. 4, d. 21, l. 165.)

5. In order to keep the Cossack population sympathetic to the Soviet regime, it is essential:

1. To take into account its historical, ethnic, and religious way of life. Time and skillful political workers will dispel the ignorance and fanaticism of the Cossacks, inculcated by the age-old barracks training of the old police system, which has penetrated the entire organism of the Cossack.

2. In the revolutionary period of the struggle against the bourgeoisie, until such time as the counter-revolution is extirpated on the Don, the entire situation imperatively demands that the idea of Communism be implanted in the minds of the Cossacks and the native peasant population by means of lectures, talks, brochures, etc. But in no case must it be implanted and inculcated by means of force, as is now being augured by all the moves being made, and the means being employed, by the "windfall Communists."

3. At the present moment there is no point in keeping account of either livestock or dead stock. It is better to announce fixed prices, and on that basis to demand deliveries of foodstuffs from the population, imposing that demand on all the inhabitants of a given settlement, and taking its degree of prosperity into account.

4. To enable the population, under the leadership of experienced political workers, to build its life itself, making sure that no counter-revolutionary elements get into power; and to that end:

5. It would be better to create district (*okrug*) congresses to elect district soviets, with full power exercised by the executive organ of such congresses and not by persons appointed haphazardly. These congresses should be attended by important political workers from the Center. One cannot avoid calling attention to the ignorance of the Cossacks, who have not yet known any enlightened political workers and have been entirely in the hands of reactionary officers, clergy, etc. (TsGASA, f. 1304, op. 4, d. 46, l. 10.)

6. From the personal archives of S. P. Starikov.
7. The journal *Russkaya literatura*, 1971, No. 2, p. 81, article by F. G. Biryukov.
8. V. I. Lenin, PSS, V, p. 7.
9. *Ezhenedel'nik ChK*, No. 1, September 22, 1918, p. 11.
10. V. I. Lenin, *Sochineniya*, 3rd edn., XXIII, p. 294.
11. *Ibid.*, pp. 315–17.
12. TsPA, f. 17, op. 4, d. 21, l. 213.
13. V. I. Lenin, PSS, XXXVIII, p. 146.
14. *Ibid.*, pp. 78–79.
15. Rostov Oblast Archives, f. 12, op. 25, d. 51, l. 11.
16. An order of the RVS dated February 5, 1919 (No. 171), contains the following requirement on this point:

With a view to the immediate execution of measures to combat the counter-revolution, the Revvoyensovet of the Southern Front . . . orders the creation of temporary regimental military field tribunals on the following bases: [First], a military field tribunal will be temporarily set up for each regiment, and will accompany the regiment as it advances. Second, the tribunal will function in areas through which the unit moves and where it is positioned at a given moment, being the organ for reprisals against all counter-revolutionary elements not carried on the army rolls at the given moment. Third, the tribunal will consist of the regimental political commissar, who will serve as chairman, together with two members and one candidate from the regimental Party organization elected by the presidium of the cell and approved by the political commissar. Witnesses may be questioned if the tribunal finds it necessary. . . . Five, judgments of the tribunal may not be appealed. Six, materials on all cases handled by the tribunal must be forwarded to the appropriate district revkom through the divisional political section. This order will enter into force upon notice by telegram. (TsGAKA, f. 1304, op. 1, d. 350, l. 42–43.)

17. M. Sholokhov, *Tikhii Don*, Bk. III (Moscow, 1957), pp. 166–67.
18. *Ibid.*, pp. 233–34.
19. Yu. Trifonov, *Otblesk kostra* (Moscow, 1966), pp. 163–64.
20. TsGAOR, f. 1235, op. 82, d. 15, ch. 1, ll. 172–73.
21. TsPA, f. 17, op. 4, d. 21, l. 1.
22. One of the first proclamations of the Veshenskaya uprising to the soldiers of the Red Army stated:

Brothers in the Red Army—you who were forcibly mobilized by the Communists, or who joined the Red Army out of poverty and hunger—we have a brotherly word to say to you.

We are those same working Cossacks who only a short time ago were sitting at the same dinner table with many of you. Only a short time ago our skinny horses were carrying you to battle against the bourgeois. Do you know why we have raised the banner of revolt against the Communists?

We rose up because after you came Communists and extraordinary commissions, the so-called Cheka, who began to arrest and shoot our and your brother Cossacks and peasants, who were completely innocent. They began to plunder and rape, calling us prisoners of war, beating us with whips and rifle butts. . . .

We, the working Cossacks and peasants, have promised to drive the Communist tyrants out of our native Don lands. We will drive them out. . . . In our part of the country, the glow of the people's uprising is showing brighter and brighter in the sky with each passing day.

But at the same time we pledge that there will not be a single shooting, not a single act of violence committed against you, our brothers. And not even against your chiefs, the Communist commissars, if they surrender voluntarily.

We, the working Cossacks, left the Cossack front, extended to you

the brotherly hand of peace, and dispersed to our homes, having understood the great danger into which we were being led by our atamans,
who had organized punitive detachments behind our backs.

But you must realize, comrades, that much worse things are being
done by your chiefs. They are doing a horrible thing. They have a
"Cheka" that is more evil. Their anti-profiteering detachments and mass
shootings are more terrible.

Do you know that the Communists have put out a secret circular
letter on the extermination of the Don Cossacks and peasants down to
a man? Could anyone think up a more evil deed—to wipe from the
face of the earth the population of an entire region!

Do you know about the letter in which the Communist Reshetkov
asks the Communist Kostenko to send him a detachment of hangmen,
since eight hangmen couldn't handle all the shootings?

If you know this, make haste to leave the front, make haste to go
off to your homes. Because the laboring, toil-hardened Don Cossack
people, both Cossacks and peasants, have firmly decided to drive your
Communist chiefs out of the free Cossack steppes.

Down with the kommuna and the shootings!

Long live the power of the people!

Forward for the cause of the people!

The District Council of the Upper Don District
(TsGASA, f. 24/394, op. 2, d. 608, l. 35.)

Another appeal from the Meshkovsky Regiment to the soldiers
of the Red Army said:

Comrade Soldiers!

The civil war between us has now been going on for two years. At
first it flamed up from the fire set by the bourgeois and the Tsar's followers. But now it is continuing. And we laboring Cossacks will tell
you why.

Comrades, in December of last year, we Cossacks made a decision
after we learned of our deception by our own leaders, and of the unjust
and inhuman crimes of a punitive detachment which had appeared,
sent by no one knows whom. We decided:

1. Immediately to leave the entire front and go to our own homes;

2. To allow Soviet troops into the territories of our own stanitsy to
pursue the counter-revolutionaries;

3. To turn over all weapons in the hands of Cossacks; and

4. To help the Soviet troops in every possible way.

And what, comrades, did we get by way of gratitude for our concessions? Hundreds of corpses—those of our brothers, who had been
shot. The confiscation of all property and livestock almost to a head.
And different acts of violence against peaceable inhabitants.

Comrades! All this was done by people lacking human hearts—

people given authority in "extraordinary commissions and anti-profiteering detachments."

Now tell us, comrades, what is the difference between the punitive
detachments and the anti-profiteering detachments?

From our viewpoint, none.

The foregoing reasons prompted us to rise up and continue the civil
war. . . .

Comrades, let us destroy these murderers and marauders, but without destroying the Soviet regime, which has been achieved at such great
cost to us.

Comrades, let there be brotherhood and equality among us, with a
full sense of humanity!

Down with the murderers and marauders who have put on the masks
of Communists!

Down with the civil war!

Long live brotherhood and equality!

Long live the working Cossackry and peasantry!

Long live the Soviet regime!

23. In a telegram to the Don Ataman and the chairman of the Voisko
Circle, Lieutenant General Ivanov wrote:

I am happy to share with you some joyous news I have received from
the insurgent Cossacks in the Upper Don District. A brave flier,
Junior Lieutenant Tararin, has just flown back from that district. I had
sent him there on April 26, along with Squadron Commander Bogatyrev, who has remained there. The insurrection is in full swing, and
the rebels have as many as 25,000 troops. They have ordnance and
machine guns, and have seized ammunition from the Reds. Their spirit
is magnificent. They have decided to die rather than submit to the
Jewish commissars, who in their cruelty have spared neither women
nor children. The news of the arrival of our pilots spread quickly along
the whole front held by the insurgents, and has inspired them for a
long time to come. (TsGAOR, f. 1258, op. 1, d. 240, l. 9.)

24. The new six-volume *History of the CPSU* has the following to say
about this discussion in the TsK:

The change in the Soviet regime's policy toward the Cossacks was
of tremendous importance in the struggle against Denikin and Kolchak.
As early as the spring of 1919 it had become clear to the Central Committee that in this matter *mistakes had been made.* Life had shown that
the directive on relations with the Cossacks that the Orgburo of the
TsK had promulgated in late January 1919 in a circular letter was
incorrect. The instructions to prosecute all Cossacks who had been
active participants in anti-Soviet actions hampered the isolation of the
counter-revolutionary upper strata from the laboring Cossackry and
its rallying around the Soviet regime. The directive should have been

corrected. On March 16 the Central Committee again considered the question of the Cossackry. A report was given by G. Ya. Sokolnikov, a member of the Revvoyensovet of the Southern Front. Taking into account the fact that some of the Don, Orenburg, and other Cossacks had helped the Soviet regime rather than oppose it, the TsK decided to discontinue the use against the Cossacks of those measures stipulated in the January circular letter, and to carry out a policy of stratification among them. The purpose of this decision was to win over new strata of the Cossackry to the Soviet side. But local Party, soviet, and military authorities on the Don—and primarily the members of the Don Revkom—were in no hurry to implement the instructions of the Central Committee. They adhered to the old line of "decossackization," and thereby did serious damage to the Republic. [Emphasis ours—authors.] *Istoriya KPSS*, III, Book V (Moscow, 1968), pp. 357–58. This new discussion of how to deal with the Cossacks was held without Ya. M. Sverdlov, who had died on March 16, 1919, after a brief illness.

25. TsPA, f. 17, op. 4, d. 21, l. 7.
26. TsGASA, f. 1304, op. 1, d. 631, l. 83.
27. TsPA, f. 17, op. 6, d. 81, l. 19-6 [*sic*].
28. TsGASA, f. 60/100, op. 1, d. 26, l. 252.
29. M. Sholokhov, *Tikhii Don*, Book III (Moscow, 1957), p. 390.
30. TsPA, f. 17, op. 5, d. 81, ll. 1–8.
31. TsPA, f. 17, op. 4, d. 20, l. 163.
32. TsPA, f. 17, op. 6, d. 83. Cf. also *Russkaya literatura,* 1971, No. 2, p. 82.
33. TsPA, f. 17, op. 4, d. 21, l. 13.
34. In its Order No. 27 the Revkom of the Kotelnikovsky Raion of the Don Region abolished the name "stanitsa" and prescribed the designation "volost," in accordance with which the Kotelnikovsky Raion was divided into volosts. In various parts of the region the authorities have prohibited the wearing of stripes on uniform trousers, and have abolished the word "Cossack." In the 9th Army Rogachev has, without good reason, requisitioned horses and carts from the laboring Cossacks. In many areas of the region local fairs, customary among the peasants, have been prohibited. Austrian prisoners of war have been named commissars in the stanitsy. We call attention to the necessity of being especially cautious in the matter of destroying such ethnic trifles, which have absolutely no significance in general policy but which at the same time set the population on edge. Hold the course firmly in basic questions, and be compromising and indulgent as regards those archaic vestiges to which the population is accustomed. Answer by telegraph. Lenin, chairman of the Sovnarkom. (V. I. Lenin, PSS, L, p. 387.)

35. TsPA, f. 17, op. 6, d. 85, ll. 1–4.
36. V. I. Lenin, PSS, XXXIX, p. 206.

Chapter VII

1. TsGAKA, f. 33987, op. 2, d. 32, l. 169.
2. TsGAOR, f. 1235, op. 82, d. 15, ll. 370–74.
3. TsGASA, f. 100, op. 3, d. 70, ll. 237–38.
4. From the archives of S. P. Starikov.
5. TsGAOR, f. 1235, op. 83, d. 1, l. 44.
6. TsGAOR, f. 130, op. 3, d. 133, l. 515.
7. TsGAOR, f. 1235, op. 82, d. 15, ch. 2, ll. 394–97.
8. *Ibid.*, ll. 397–98.
9. TsGAOR, f. 1235, op. 82, d. 4, l. 62.
10. Yu. V. Trifonov, *Otblesk kostra* (Moscow, 1966), p. 152.
11. *Ibid.*, p. 154.
12. TsGAOR, f. 1235, op. 82, d. 15, l. 415.
13. TsGASA, f. 246, op. 6, d. 1, l. 249. One cannot help noting the insincerity of E. D. Stasova, who was trying somehow to justify the profoundly mistaken directive on "decossackization." What kind of directive is it whose "especially accurate" implementation inevitably leads to insurrection?
14. "VIZh," 1962, No. 10, pp. 90–91.
15. TsGASA, f. 1304, op. 4, d. 46, ll. 7–17.
16. *Ugolovno-arkhivnoye delo No. N-217*, II, pp. 48–51.
17. V. I. Lenin, *Sochineniya*, 3rd edn., XXIV, p. 215.
18. TsGASA, f. 430/4406, op. 1, d. 1, ll. 22–22 (verso).
19. TsGAOR, f. 1235, op. 82, d. 15, ch. 2, l. 17.
20. V. I. Lenin, PSS, LI, pp. 40, 483. Lenin gave Mironov this appellation because it was G. Sokolnikov who in June 1919 had demanded Mironov's return to the southern front.

Chapter VIII

1. TsGASA, f. 33987, op. 2, d. 32, l. 414.
2. The newspaper *V puti,* 1919, No. 94.
3. In the newspaper *V puti*, 1919, No. 95. Trotsky included the article later in his *Sobraniye sochinenii* (Moscow, 1926). Cf. Vol. XVII, Part II, pp. 215–18.
4. TsGAKA, f. 430/24406, op. 1, d. 1, ll. 18–19.
5. *Stenogramma sasedaniya Chrezvychainogo Tribunala*, pp. 56–60.
6. *Ibid.*, pp. 64–96.

7. *Ibid.*, p. 114.
8. *Ibid.*, p. 118.
9. *Ibid.*, p. 119.
10. *Ibid.*, p. 121.
11. *Ibid.*, pp. 150–51.
12. *Ibid.*, pp. 160–65.
13. *Ibid.*, pp. 165–69.
14. *Ugolovno-arkhivnoye delo No. N-217*, XII, l. 195.
15. TsGAKA, f. 246, op. 6, d. 1, ll. 195–200.
16. I. Smilga, *Voyennye ocherki* (Moscow, 1923).
17. *Ugolovno-arkhivnoye delo No. N-217*, I, l. 374 (verso).
18. Rehabilitation in the juridical sense means, first, restoring the reputation of an unjustly accused person; second, restoring his previous rights with repeal of a criminal sentence that has entered into legal force, and of all its defamatory consequences. It was precisely this that was stipulated in the resolutions of the Politburo.

Chapter IX

1. [L. Trotsky], *Sochineniya*, XVII, Part II, p. 299.
2. *Izvestiya TsK RKP(b)*, 1919, No. 6 (September 30).
3. TsGASA, f. 33987, op. 2, d. 32, l. 441.
4. TsGASA, f. 33987, op. 2, d. 32, l. 443.
5. A. I. Egorov, *Razgrom Denikina* (Moscow, 1931), p. 133.
6. TsGAOR, f. 1235, op. 83, d. 3, l. 94.
7. *Bor'ba za vlast' Sovetov na Donu*, pp. 494–95, 491.
8. *Arkhiv Russkoi revolyutsii*, XI, p. 147.
9. Data taken from the historical reference book *Organizatsiya Sovetskoi vlasti v UMO*, compiled by A. Karpov. Volgograd Defense Museum.
10. TsGASA, f. 199, op. 2, d. 139, l. 6.

Chapter X

1. "VIZh," 1972, No. 19, p. 93.
2. TsGASA, f. 101, op. 1, d. 418, l. 20.
3. TsGASA, f. 101, op. 1, d. 418, l. 141.
4. M. V. Frunze, *Sochineniya*, I, p. 369.
5. A detailed description of this battle is found in V. Dushenkin's book, *The 2nd Cavalry*, published in 1968. But an even more detailed and accurate description of it is given in Mironov's own manuscript. This manuscript, under the title of *The Defeat of*

Wrangel: The Historic Days of October 11–14, 1920, was written by Mironov in December-January 1920–21 in the Crimea shortly after the battles were fought, and found in the archives of S. P. Starikov. In giving a description of the battles of October 11–14, Mironov—not without reason—calls them "one of the most beautiful episodes in the struggle against the counter-revolution, when, for attempting to snatch the initiative from the hands of the Reds (which initiative, by the way, we did not yet have), Baron Wrangel also lost that which he already had."

6. Here and subsequently we quote Mironov's manuscript.
7. TsGASA, f. 246, op 3, d. 394, l. 17.
8. *"Beloye delo." Letopis' byloi bor'by*, Bk. VI (Berlin, 1928), pp. 200–21.
9. P. K. Mironov, *"Razgrom Vrangelya." Rukopis'*.
10. *"VIZh,"* 1972, No. 10, p. 93.

Chapter XI

1. TsGASA, f. 246, op. 3, d. 277, l. 20 (verso).
2. TsGASA, f. 6, op. 4, d. 482, l. 137.
3. TsGASA, f. 246, op. 3, d. 277, l. 26.
4. V. I. Lenin, PSS, XLII, p. 333. This "Rough Draft . . ." was first published in *Pravda* as late as June 26, 1930.
5. *Ibid.* On the basis of the Politburo's decision the article by P. Sorokin and M. Rogov was published in two issues of *Pravda*—that of February 17, 1921, and that of February 26, 1921.
6. GAOR, f. 97, op. 1, d. 48, ll. 43–45.
7. *Ibid.*, d. 6, ll. 1–2.
8. *Leninskii sbornik*, XX (1952), p. 17.
9. From the archives of S. P. Starikov.
10. The most recent example known to us is A. Balakayev's novel, *Oka Gorodovikov (Volga*, 1972, Nos. 11 and 12, and 1973, No. 1), which mentions Mironov's action at Saransk. Balakayev does not hesitate to call Mironov a "traitor" whom "only Trotsky's intervention saved from being shot." Distorting facts that are easily ascertainable, Balakayev says that the man chiefly responsible for the victory over Wrangel's shock troops on the right bank of the Dnieper on October 11–14, 1920, was not the commander, Mironov, but his deputy, O. Gorodovikov, who in that battle allegedly saved Mironov "from death and shame." (*Volga*, 1973, No. 1, p. 83.)

GLOSSARY

This glossary includes both words which have been left in Russian at all times (e.g., *voisko*) and those which have usually been translated but occasionally, in special contexts, left in the original (e.g., *pai*). Needless to say, some of the meanings given here have become obsolete in the past half-century. This applies especially to the names of administrative-territorial units, etc.

ataman Chieftain of a host of Don Cossacks. (Corresponds to *hetman* among the Ukrainian—or Zaporogian—Cossacks.) Traditionally, the ataman was elected at a general assembly or *circle* (*q.v.*) and in time of peace had merely the function of presiding over the assembly, whereas in time of war he had absolute authority. His full title was *voiskovoi ataman* ("Ataman of the *Voisko*," *q.v.*), as distinguished from such later innovations as the "appointed ataman" (*nakaznoi ataman*), the "campaign ataman" (*pokhodnyi ataman*), etc.

circle (*krug*) Originally, a general assembly of Cossacks at which each one had a voice. But the latter-day Great Circle and Small Circle were elective governing bodies.

Cadet A member of the Constitutional Democratic Party.

"decossackization" (*raskazachivaniye*) The policy of dispossessing

and exterminating the Cossacks as an allegedly homogeneous reactionary element. Cf. "dekulakization" (*raskulachivaniye*). The
translation "dispossession" (of the Cossacks or kulaks) is frequently
employed as less clumsy; but it is clearly inadequate to describe
what was done to the Cossacks during the Civil War and to the kulaks
in the early 1930s.

desyatina A unit of land measure, equal to 2.7 acres.

district Usually (and in all proper names) this is a translation of *okrug*
—a primary subdivision of a *region* (*oblast*), *q.v.*

front 1. The usual meaning of "front" in English military usage.
2. An army group (or army) and its zone of operations; e.g., "the
staff of the Southern Caucasus front."

khutor A small Cossack village.

kommuna (pl., *kommuny*)* In Professor David Joravsky's definition:
   "The most completely collectivized form of agricultural enterprise.
   . . . Not to be confused with collective farm (*kolkhoz*), commune
   (*mir, obshchina*), or state farm (*sovkhoz*)."

krug See *circle.*

oblast See *region.*

okrug See *district.*

pai The land allotment of an individual Don Cossack.

pood Unit of weight, equal to about 36 lbs.

province Refers to a *guberniya*—a large administrative region directly subordinate to the central government.

raion (pl., *raiony*) A subdivision of a *district*, *q.v.*

region In most cases, this translates *oblast*, a region similar in size to
a *province* (*q.v.*) but under a special administration.

sazhen 2.134 meters.

stanitsa (pl., *stanitsy*) 1. A large Cossack village with its distinctive
Cossack socio-economic and administrative structure. 2. Such a village, plus the area under its jurisdiction and the tract of land belonging to it.

uyezd District (primary subdivision of a *province*, *q.v.*).

verst 3,500 feet.

* Plurals of Russian words have been anglicized except where indicated,
as here.

voisko (pl., *voiska*)   In standard Russian, (a nation's) army or armed forces. In strict Cossack usage, the (Cossack) population of a particular region; e.g., the Don Voisko. More loosely, a Cossack army.

volost   A small rural district. In the Don Region, a subdivision of a *stanitsa, q.v.*

yunker   A military cadet. (Not to be confused with Cadet.)

yurt   In Don Cossack usage: 1. a subdivision of a *stanitsa* (*q.v.*). 2. The land belonging to a small Cossack village, or *khutor.*

INDEX

261